VASCO BENDINI
OMBRE PRIME

Bruno Corà

La Galleria Nazionale, Rome
March 29 – June 19 2022

LA GALLERIA
NAZIONALE

FORMA

Dedicated to the memory
of Marcella Valentini Bendini

Rome, March 23 2022

An institutional greeting
As Vasco's partner for over forty years and Chair of the Libera Associazione-Archivio Vasco Bendini, I'm truly happy to be involved in this important anthological exhibition that seeks to commemorate the artist in his centenary year (1922-2022).

The exhibition narrative, at the curator's behest, unfolds through the decades, featuring significant works from the various periods of Bendini's creative process, which testify to his incessant, unrelenting and consistent experimentation throughout his long life.

The catalog pursues a broader and more comprehensive approach, encompassing valuable essays by Bruno Corà and Antonello Tolve, a poetic contribution by Irene Santori and a recollection by the artist SoHyun Bae.

Furthermore, as well as a handpicked selection of important authors of critical texts—including Arcangeli, Calvesi, D'Amico, Gualdoni and Villa, to name but a few—a number of Vasco Bendini's unpublished writings are feature in the catalog, so that the artist himself can speak in the first person, revealing his thoughts through the written word.

My special thanks go to Prof. Corà, who is the prestigious curator of the retrospective; to Irene Santori, Deputy Chair of the Libera Associazione-Archivio Vasco Bendini, who is particularly dear to me and has put a great deal of effort into this exhibition; to Dr Cristiana Collu, Director of the Galleria Nazionale d'Arte Moderna e Contemporanea in Rome, who has made it possible to organise this anthological exhibition.

Lastly, I would like to send a warm greeting to all those who will have the opportunity to visit the exhibition and also to those who will only be able to "see it" through the catalog.

Marcella Valentini Bendini
Former Chair of the Libera Associazione-Archivio Vasco Bendini, Rome

Perhaps Vasco Bendini's poetics, his precocious intuition as an artist and painter, is all in his 1946 *Autoritratto*.

The portrait retracts to make way for a paste (or mixture) of colour and a few lines. Precise yet precarious at the same time.

It marks the start of Bendini's movement, of his sculptural style, of form within painting, of form that holds the lines, albeit lines that vibrate and whose edges are not defined; indeed, they cast shadows when it is a question of sculpture.

Bringing the magical imprecision of life back to the canvas, outside any Cartesian relationship, yet inside every magmatic principle. His brushstrokes sink into the material as if it were primordial clay. Then, all the way through to the end, they question the enigma: that wonderment in front of creation, light and sky by day—by night the mystery is another and Bendini is less interested in investigating the dark side where the charm is not just one of magic or enchantment, but lurking fear. The exceptional aspect of his painting continues to be his ability to interpret analog movement, that which leaves a wake of matter behind it and marks a unique time, the time of transformation.

Cristiana Collu
Director of the Galleria Nazionale d'Arte Moderna e Contemporanea, Rome

VASCO BENDINI: SHADOWS, ILLUMINATIONS, OPENINGS ON REALITY OF AN ORACULAR PAINTING

Bruno Corà

ART, SIMPLE EVIDENCE

Now that the life, works and thought of Vasco Bendini—and also of his greatest exegetes—span an entire century, the time is ripe for a further reflection on his entire artistic career, hopefully the first of many more. Returning to consider, probe, view and focus this career with the attention it calls for and deserves is far from easy. It can indeed immediately be said that, among the artists that emerged in the second half of the twentieth century he is one of the most hermetic, problematic and, at the same time, lyrical to have orbited the firmament of Italian art. His was a solitary adventure, not without context, especially in terms of a possible belonging to or assiduous frequentation of a group or a trend. Except perhaps that more general inclination towards the sensitivity of the Informale—so packed with exponents that it scarcely counts—where he did leave valid traces that have been duly noted by the critics. Solitary, I would repeat, because his problematical poetics, his type of research and the manner of his experiences were individual and highly specific. And even because the readings of the scholars who addressed the different phases of his work and his linguistic pronouncements were so singular and diversified.

Malia dell'enigma (adolescenza), 2007, from the series *Malia dell'enigma*, oil on canvas, 180×200 cm, Galleria d'Arte Niccoli, Parma

An artist such as Bendini is commonly described as being aloof, withdrawn, thoughtful, or using other epithets related to human reserve. But, as for other character traits, this one too has to be immediately qualified by saying that, when he felt the circumstances to be right and favourable, he could show himself to be a fine, tendentially dialectic, conversationalist, arguing in the most original and decorative manner and arriving rapidly with conceptual synthesis at the heart of the matter with extreme simplicity.

I had the opportunity to meet and talk to Bendini on just one occasion of direct collaboration, and it left a strong impression on me, as happens when the presence before you emanates a particularly intense energy of psychic frequency. This was in 2008, little more than a handful of years before his last days, and I was able to appreciate the brilliance of his mind, not unlike the reverberation of the transparent colours of his works in the pentamorphic polyptych of the painting on canvas *Malia dell'enigma* [Bewitchment of the Enigma] (2007). This work was exhibited then, for the first time, at the Galleria d'Arte Niccoli in Parma, and is also displayed in this retrospective. Bendini resembled those large canvases of his that took upon themselves the umpteenth paradigmatic statement about the meaning of life and of "making art." As he himself described these images: "the beginning is impossible to evoke / impossible to repress / each work has its own fate / it's simply evident."[1]

This was the poetic frequency achieved and transmitted by the man and the artist. A *simple evidence* that no word can replace, but that the transparency of a nebulous state and chromatic humidity spread in rivulets over canvases traversed by emanations of light could indeed evidence. And in that simplicity they became images in Bendini's sensitive emanation of the vaporous, shadowy, nuanced and diaphanous forms of painting. They were the "flicker" of birth, the uncontaminated first perceptions, the enigma of youth, the balanced degree of sensitive maturity and, finally, the precipitation of all radiance, albeit in the ultimate vital splendour and silence of unqualifiable time. In accompanying that penultimate swan song of Bendini's, the line from T.S. Eliot that Edoardo Piersensini used as the incipit of his essay at the time of the Parma exhibition devoted to that cycle of works, is perfectly apt: "In my beginning is my end."

THE *OMBRE PRIME* EXHIBITION

Displayed at the entrance to the *Ombre prime* exhibition, organised to mark the centenary of the birth of Vasco Bendini, is the *Autoritratto*

1
Malia dell'enigma: Vasco Bendini (Parma: Galleria d'Arte Niccoli, 2008). Catalog of an exhibition of the same title, presented at the Galleria d'Arte Niccoli, Parma, 16 February-10 April 2008; essays by Bruno Corà and Edoardo Piersensini.

[Self-Portrait] (1946) from the Collezione Santori Lettieri. This is the greatest example among those produced by Bendini, where he adopts the plastic pose of the non-frontal versions but with a rotated profile such as to place his gaze in a sophisticated and divined centrality that gives the face a magnetism that can be observed in all great painting. The work continues to arouse an admirable solidity, emitting an intact presence or, rather, endowed with a forceful concentration that projects the artifice, offering fully to the observer the thoughtful and yet unknowable and serene quality that distinguishes him.

Autoritratto, 1946, from the series *I segni segreti*, oil on canvas, 54×43 cm, Collezione Santori Lettieri, Rome

The *Autoritratto* is placed at a distance from the other works on display, in view of its "classical" style, not devoid of an intense and silent reserve. Consequently, the precious *Autoritratto* acts as the trailblazer to Bendini's entire career and, above all, marks one of the cornerstones of all his painting. This is the recurrent theme of the face, enunciated in different ways in relation to the evolution of a reflection on identity, on the tangible existence of the face and the body, the intimate and physically real entity and constitution of matter itself, as deduced for some time now from the most advanced knowledge of modern science.

It is not exaggerated to define the trope of the *head* and the *face* as an authentic obsession for Bendini. And this is sacrosanct for an artist who does not paint to define or celebrate artistic genres—such as the portrait, the still life, the sacred, the epic, the picturesque etc.—but rather that supreme locus of the identity, the pondering on existence, on his own enigmatic human experience, on the Self and the Other as crucially pronounced in Rimbaud's matchless dictum "I is someone else" in the *Letters of the Seer* (1871). It is the face that brings to light the symptoms and signals of all that persists as unknown or extraneous in a human being, even though they are largely destined to remain inscrutable. And Bendini has interrogated the *head* and the *face* as morphologies that are ambiguous in their appearance and real substance. Twentieth-century painting had behind it the experiences of Divisionism, African sculpture, Cubism, Futurism and quantum physics. As a result, Bendini's acute and sensitive reflection no longer allowed his unquiet soul to address the representation of the forms, sites and matter of these subjects of head and face in a way that was obsolete and trammelled by a cognitive baggage devoid of any real scientific foundation.

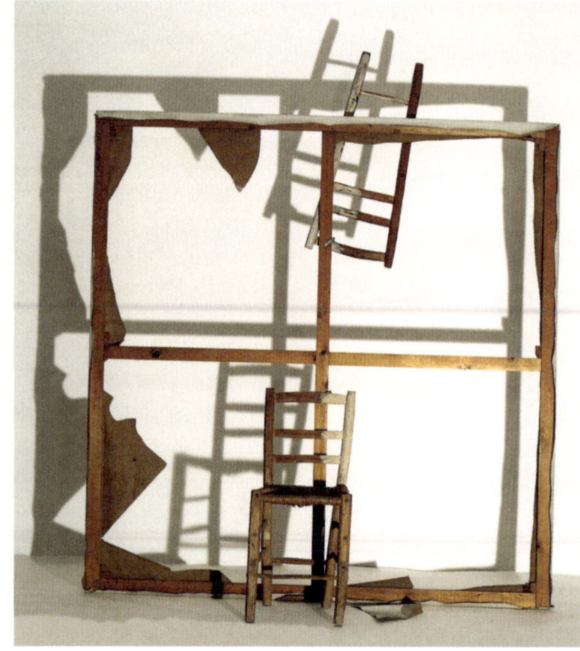

Ombre prime, 1966, from the series *Senso operante*, frame, cut canvas, clamps, chair and seatback (spotlight), 230×200×50 cm, Frittelli Arte Contemporanea, Florence

Starting from this series of *heads* and *faces*, the exhibition traces Bendini's artistic career through works symbolising his most important poetic phases from the 1950s on, and over the span of about seventy years, in a dense synthesis dictated by the space available. In the construction of the critical framework, it was decided to divide into two extensive areas a production that is anything but linear in view of the poetics expressed and the changes in the linguistic elaborations introduced.

The work *Ombre prime* [First Shadows] (1966) was identified as a hinge that at once connects and distinguishes these two areas. This particular work represents the creative phase marked by Bendini's increasingly evident intention to question not only his own complex *Weltanschauung*, but also the condition and role of the observer of his works and of art more generally. Displayed in the rooms preceding the *Ombre prime* are several selected works dating backwards from 1966 to the *Autoritratto.* Conversely, the display of the creations subsequent to *Ombre prime* incorporates works that are particularly significant within the vast repertory that culminates in the group of large paintings that are poetically interconnected and titled *Malia dell'enigma*, together with several other paintings produced a few years before Bendini's death in 2015.

2
E. Piersensini, *Vasco Bendini: fra il nulla e l'infinito* (Rome: Ulisse Editore, 2006).

Looking again at all the works in the exhibition, and considering the seminal and detailed comprehensive study already carried out at the beginning of 2000s,[2] it is clear that Bendini was a significant exponent of Italian painting in the period stretching from after the second World War up to about a decade ago. His presence and participation in the most important public events conceived to review and certify Italian artistic creation—the Venice Biennale, the Quadriennale of Rome and others—confirm his importance as a protagonist. Furthermore, with a very few exceptions, the leading interpreters of Italian art history and criticism have addressed his work on various occasions over the years, offering acute and fundamental readings of it. The idea here is to offer in the pages that follow a critical anthology, albeit selective, documenting the attention devoted to Bendini's work. The principal tensions, the most assiduous concerns and also the undeniable originality of this work has, therefore, already been brought to light.
The idea that it is the art market which actually decrees the fame and honours due to an artist is one that is alien to me. On the contrary, I believe that the inventions introduced by the linguistic qualities of the works are what ought to be evaluated by collectors, museums and academic institutions. Nevertheless, we have to ask ourselves why the work of Vasco Bendini continues to be appreciated by a smaller public than that gravitating around the works of Vedova, Accardi, Dorazio, Uncini, Turcato, Castellani and numerous other painters of his generation. Although this is hard to explain, there has to be a reason and it needs to be identified.

COMPLEXITY OF THE WORK AND RELATION WITH THE OBSERVER

As I see it, a possible answer to the question I have raised here—specifically on the occasion of an exhibition held in what is the academically most prestigious gallery in Italy, that in itself confirms Bendini's worth—lies precisely in the role of the spectator before the work of art and the greater or lesser capacity to extract its most profound contents. It is indeed a well-known fact that a work of art can present diverse and multiple degrees of complexity. From as far back as the time of his *Autoritratto*, Bendini was already pondering and reading about the major issues in physics and biology, the dimensions of space-time, the study of the psyche and other domains, with a view to endowing his own art with such knowledge and cognisance. In the atomic age, his conscience as an artist could not ignore the highest levels of speculative thought, convinced as he was of its centrality in artistic practice too.
Bendini read the peerless analyses made by Johan Huizinga in *In the Shadow of Tomorrow* (1938) and by Jacques Monod in *Chance and Necessity* (1970), and was interested in quantum physics and Heisenberg's uncertainty principle, as well as in the theories of Freud and Jung. From an early stage, these and other contributions to his reflections on his own anthropological condition and on reality itself struck him as inevitable cognitive foundations in the process of his artistic creation and in relation to the formation of the linguistic constructions rendered visible in his painting. All these elements that nourished his demanding and scrupulous identity were metabolised through a sensitivity capable of deriving from them signs, qualified pictorial matter, and images. However, we have to ask ourselves to what extent these were fully able to reach the observer's sensitivity, awareness, and mind and, ultimately, how equipped the observer was to appreciate the work. The work that is, proverbially, aimed at everyone but that, at the same time, clearly demands from each observer a degree of engagement for its appreciation and enjoyment, since it is visual language and not banal communication.

Bendini's work has an objective complexity that may perhaps have represented a difficulty not only for certain observers but even for those with a professional interest in circulating it within the art market.
Whatever the reasons for his slow affirmation among the greater public, Bendini must have become aware of the communicative aspect of his work in the crucial cultural climate of the second half of the 1960s, inducing him to devote himself intensely, and in several operational episodes, to his relation with alterity.
This major linguistic and theoretical-conceptual shift in the production of the work is evident in various experiences starting from 1966, and including *Ombre prime*. It was unquestionably and primarily aimed at the observer, and at the observer's relation with the mode of meaning of his art and, at the same time, even at himself.

THE RELATIONAL AND INTERACTIVE IMPORT OF THE WORK

The works produced in the years between 1966 and 1969 clearly display a novelty of pictorial and plastic experiences, in some cases even engaging the artist's own body in demonstrative actions. They also appear bent on assuming an explicitly pedagogical character and on engaging the observer. It has been observed and written that those works from the second half of the 1960s had

> "no aesthetic value: in their presence they are not ends to be proposed to the spectators but means, instruments to be supplied to a public which, in this way, becomes an actor and partly, perhaps, creator of the work (or at least of the aesthetic experience deriving from it). Following this reading, works such as *Come è* [As It Is] (1966) or *Cabina solare* [Solar Cabin] (1967), to give just two examples, take on the quality of devices, of premises conceived to bring about particular consequences and experiences that vary from one spectator to another (or rather, one actor to another). In these works, the result varies along with the variation in the data of the problem—namely, the spectators with their experiences and their actions, all different [...]. The function of the work is to furnish constant experimental conditions for the different experiences of the spectators."[3]

3
Ibid., p. 153.

As well as *Come è* and *Cabina solare*, this group of works should also include the already mentioned *Ombre prime* and *La ruota* [The Wheel] (1967), *Una delle duemila parole* [One of Two Thousand Words] (1968), *Mille e una notte* [A Thousand and One Nights] (1968), *La tavolozza* [The Palette] (1966), *Il mio spazio* [My Space] (1966), *La Sorgente* [The Source] (1969), *Per una essudazione totale* [For a Total Exudation] (1967), *Finzione 1* [Pretence 1] (1966) and others, including the action *Io. E io ora*, [I. And I Now] (1969).
This moment in time and these experiences have often been discussed in view of their contemporaneity with those of the early militant Arte Povera artists such as Pistoletto, Calzolari, Pascali and others. Regarding this phase, it is illuminating to note what Bendini himself said about it:

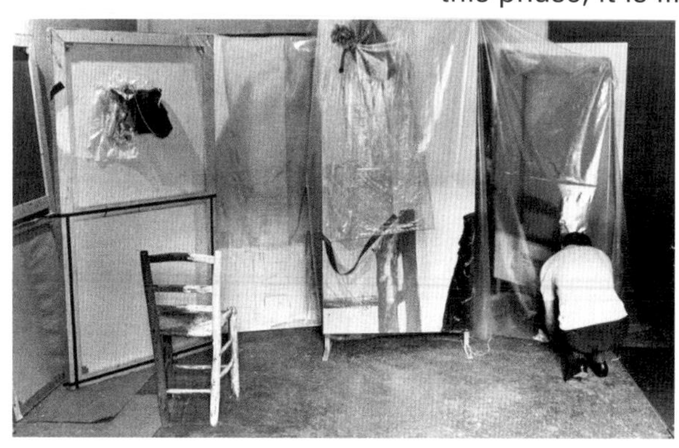
Vasco Bendini in Palazzo Bentivoglio setting up the installation *Finzione 1*, 1966

> "[...] by 1966, I realised that my hereditary baggage would lead me to new acquisitions, but the only way to be sure of continuity was to be ready for further developments. My active imagination would thus reach and express its own life, guided by an internal logic. And I was by then ready for this next step. From the 'relentless extroversion of a persistent and obsessive introversion' I passed on to a perception of the other, considered objectively. I began to explore neutral and public physical space. I analysed how the world acted on me and on others, and how others act in the world. It was a question of grasping the point of synchronisation and managing to visualise the field of harmony existing between myself and others. I then imagined

offering the other-than-me some tools, complete with instructions for use. Tools that would be set in motion by the direct action of the spectator. These intentions of mine were accompanied by a reflection of Merleau-Ponty 'No sooner has my gaze fallen upon a living body in the process of acting than the objects surrounding it immediately take on a new layer of significance: they are no longer simply what I myself could make of them, they are what this other pattern of behaviour is about to make of them.' It is indeed another person who is using my objects and treating the objects I experimented with in a different way, though similar to mine. Thus, my own body finds a sort of extension of itself and its intentions in the other body. We become like two minds which have found a common, though indirect, way of communicating. Two types of behaviour are triggered and mesh with each other. Solitude and communication thus become aspects of a single phenomenon. It was from these thoughts that, in the early months of 1966, my first three behavioural works were born: *Come è*, *Finzione 1* and *Il mio spazio*."[4]

4
V. Bendini, "Cerchio supremo," in *Creativa*, year II, no. 8, May-June 1986, republished in *Vasco Bendini. Opere 1950-2006*, (Florence: Spaziotempo; Siena: Carlo Cambi, 2007), p. 83. Catalog of an exhibition of the same title, presented at Frittelli Arte Contemporanea, Florence, 10 February-31 March 2007.

These statements of Bendini's were actually formulated twenty years after the events of this period. Nevertheless, they clearly convey the urgings that led to the creation of this group of works declaredly aimed at processes of relation between the artist and the spectator of the work. As such, they are closer to experiences of a gestaltic nature, related to self-knowledge and interaction, and in my opinion different from those of Arte Povera, which were differently conceived.

Rather, for me the most interesting fact that emerges is the strong ethical component present in every moment of Bendini's work, both when the *cogito* related to the work is entirely personal and introspective, and when it affects the spectator. This provides a framework for exploring Bendini's behaviour that will allow us to make further investigations and considerations on his work.

FROM 1946 TO 1966

Now the analysis of this exhibition can return to examine the two large operational areas mentioned above: the first related to the years 1946 to 1966 and the second to the years from 1970 up to 2013.

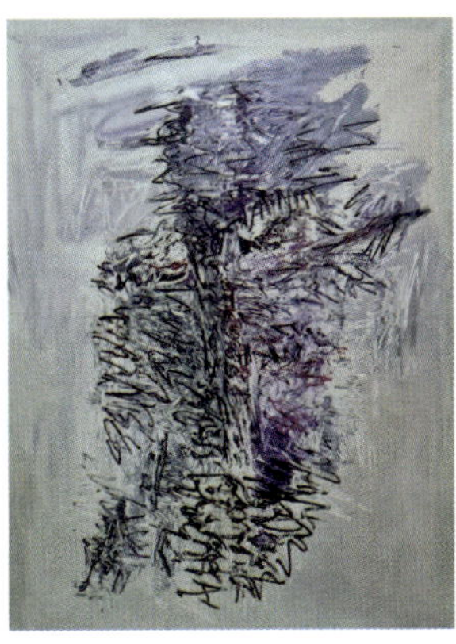

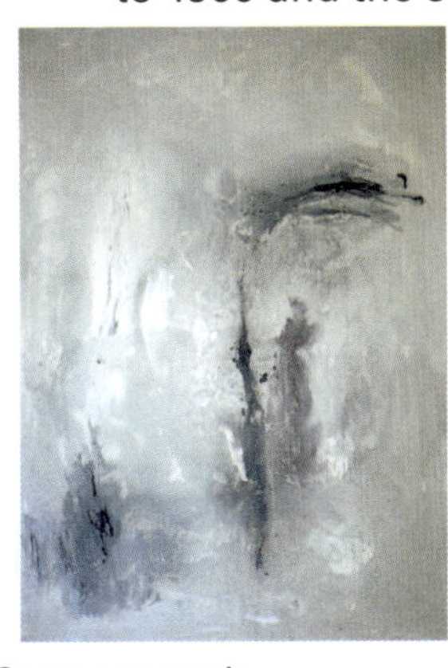

Testa, 1962, from the series *Gesto e materia*, oil on canvas, 200×150 cm, Collezione Tonelli, Terni
Testa, 1958, from the series *Gesto e Materia*, acrylic tempera on canvas, 140×100 cm, private collection, Rome

The first area includes the *Testa* [Head] and *Volto* [Face] subjects belonging to the series that Bendini called *Segni segreti* [Secret Signs]. A considerable number of these are on show in the exhibition, mostly dating to the 1950s, but also others, such as the *Testa* (200x150 cm) of 1962 from the Tonelli collection. The versions of the *Testa* on canvas-backed paper from 1950, 1951, 1952 and the *Autoritratto* of 1953, as well as the *Testa* (1956) and the *Testa* (1958), are all acrylic temperas, unlike the large *Testa* (1962), which is an oil on canvas. The acrylic temperas are characterised by an accentuated essentiality in the rendering of the head through black signs traced with evident rapidity. Instead, the oil on canvas *Testa* and *S.T.* (1960) are the result of pictorial signs aimed at producing thickenings, layered coats, gestures traced in zig-zags like broken segments and extensive superficial knife-work.

It is an acknowledged fact that Bendini's early painting looked to that of the *Volti* of Virgilio Guidi, his teacher at the Accademia di Belle Arti of Bologna (as was Giorgio Morandi). Instead, in these just-evoked works he has already consumed much of the figurative quality of that lesson, and the signs make it clear that Bendini is now also feeding on other notions that are not just pictorial but also aesthetic and

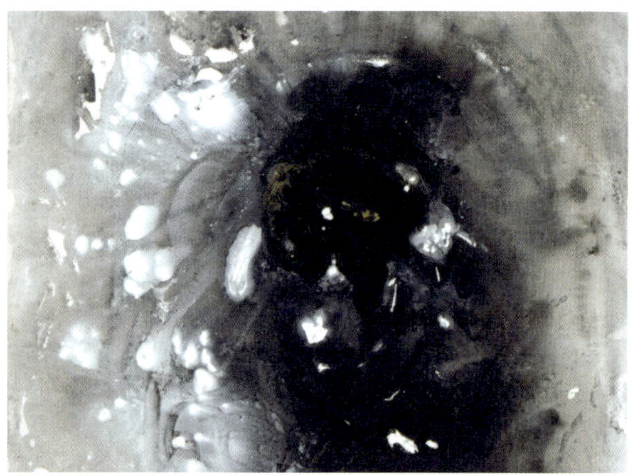

Reliquie nere, 1958, from the series *Gesto e materia*, acrylic tempera on canvas, 140×100 cm, GNAM, Rome (detail)

scientific, aimed at suggesting other considerations about physical matter.

For a good stretch of road, in those years and also later, Bendini's painting was under the constant critical scrutiny of Francesco Arcangeli, who even included his work among the "last naturalists", primarily comprising his better-known colleagues Morlotti, Moreni, Mandelli, Romiti and Vacchi. Nevertheless, Bendini swiftly freed himself of this critical assimilation, turning his action towards an atmospheric painting that appeared to come first from Turner and then from Constable, but in any case, ethereal and vaporous. In the mid-1950s his painting became less of sign and more of matter, giving rise to a whole series of paintings grouped under the heading *Gesto e materia* [Gesture and Matter] that included *Reliquie nere* [Black Relics] (1958) from the Galleria Nazionale d'Arte Moderna e Contemporanea of Rome; the *Testa azzurra* [Blue Head] (1956) and *1 agosto* [1st August] (1958). Prior to these results, it is illuminating to read Bendini's own notes on these periods:

"1950-1953 [...]. Matter has lost its solidity and substantiality. The notion of substance, in the sense of a permanent entity with shifting states is no longer applicable in the real world [...]. For the philosopher the crucial point in modern theory is the disappearance of matter as 'thing.' It has been replaced by emanations from a location [...], my works graze the abstract. 'They seem to emerge artlessly from a fresh, tender area in which the forms rough themselves out, dissolve and recompose in a world on the verge, or perhaps something that is in gestation.' Creation becomes a process of 'emanation.' 1956-58 – 'For modern man, everything is internal and everything is external' [...]. Chance is intercepted, conserved and reproduced by the mechanism of invariance and transformed into 'order, rule, necessity.'"[5]

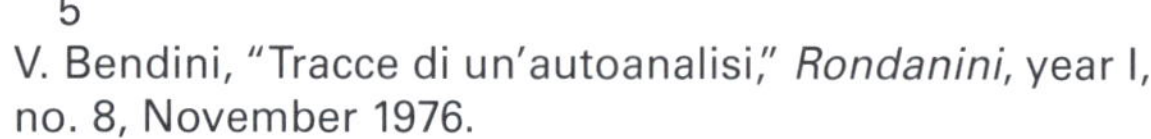

5
V. Bendini, "Tracce di un'autoanalisi," *Rondanini*, year I, no. 8, November 1976.

In the 1960s, along with the works of this period already mentioned, the multimaterial canvases present in the Rome show are similarly striking for their incisiveness: *Due minuti* [Two Minutes] (24 March 1966), from the Museo di Arte Moderna e Contemporanea del Castello di Masnago in Varese and *Il ricordo è questo* [Memory is This] (1969-70) from the Valentini Bendini archive. These do not feature the relational objective that *Come è* and *Finzione 1* are endowed with. Rather, in terms of their materiality, the pictorial elaboration and the spatial effect—also resulting from collage—the two canvases are closer to certain New Dada works than to the nascent Italian Arte Povera. *Ombre prime* itself, very close to the approaches of Rauschenberg, cannot be attributed a Povera sensitivity, since a crucial role is played by the intangibility of the shadow and the suggestion that it can be opportunely perceived through the illumination of the work.

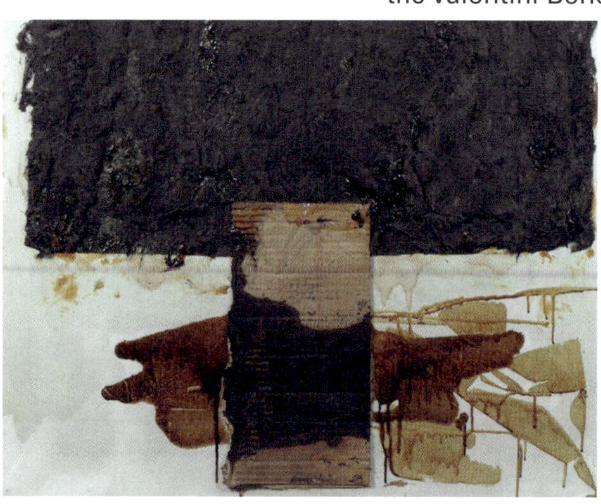

Il ricordo è questo, 1969-70, from the series *Senso operante* polimateric on canvas, 116×89 cm, private collection, Rome (detail)

Finally, we cannot forget that in 1964 Bendini displayed his work in a solo show at the 32nd Venice Biennale, coinciding with a massive presence of American artists destined to take the European and international artistic scene by storm with New Dada and Pop Art, and with the Leone d'Oro being awarded to Robert Rauschenberg. Just to be clear, Bendini was in no way influenced by the Texan artist, but in the *Zeitgeist* of both there was an unbridled Dada and Duchampian *esprit* of objectual primacy. It took the shows and articles produced by Argan, Arcangeli and Calvesi in those years to recognise Bendini's originality and credit him with it.

THE CYCLES FROM 1970 ON

We now look at the vast area of experiences that followed the turning point of those years of work (1966-1969) that Bendini devoted to a relational contact with the spectator and the environment. This includes cycles such as the new paintings of the *Gesto e materia* series represented here by *S.T.* (1970, based on newspaper, resin, glue, tea and coffee on canvas, 100×80 cm), the oil paintings on aluminium of the *Alchimia dell'immagine* [Alchemy of the Image] series presented by Emilio Villa at the L'Attico gallery in Rome in 1980, represented by two versions of the *Memorie* [Memories] (1980), as well as the large works from the series *Il ciclo delle parvenze* [The Cycle of the Appearances] (1988), *Segni come sogni* [Signs as Dreams] (1989) and *Ipotesi d'attesa*, [Hypothesis of Waiting] (1990), all oils on canvas. The exhibition ends with the five large canvases in oil and acrylic tempera of the *Malia dell'enigma*, surrounded by the oils on canvas of the *L'immagine accolta* [The Welcomed Image] (2007-2010) series and a further "frame" of oils on canvas (all measuring 110×90 cm, but of different dates) mostly coeval with the larger polyptych. Together with the latter, they reconfirm the spatial-cosmological painting of the artist who—according to Calvesi, one of his greatest exegetes—has always been "among the protagonists of the true Italian Informale."[6]

6
M. Calvesi, "Nel segno della continuità," in *Vasco Bendini*, ed. Giorgio Cortenova, (Milan: Mazzotta, 1989), 11. Catalog of an exhibition of the same title, presented at Palazzo Forti, Verona, December 1989.

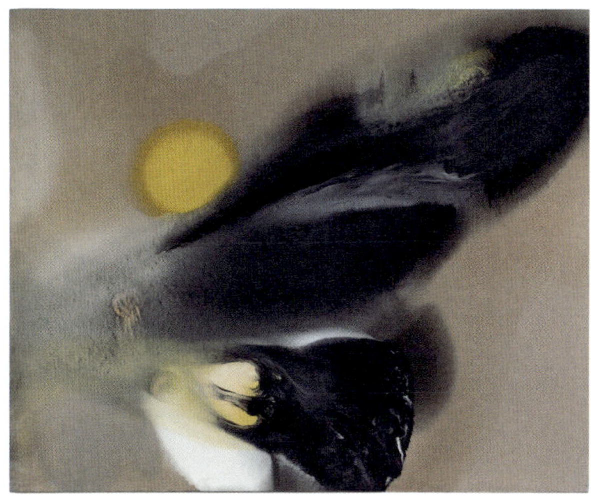

22-23 febbraio 2011, from the series *L'immagine accolta*, oil on canvas, 110×90 cm, Collezione Francescopiero Calzolari, Bologna

While other exhibitions and celebrations open elsewhere in Italy and abroad to mark this centenary of Vasco Bendini with new contributions from scholars of different qualities, it is quite astounding how much critical attention his life and work has attracted—even more since his death—and how, paradoxically and despite being encircled by a sensitive mythography, Bendini continues to appear a "secret" artist. Bendini's experience as an artist proves to be authentically "new" in that he did not separate the questioning of his own existential and biological condition from the means which he had early on decided were to be employed for a visualisation of himself in the world and in time, namely painting, drawing and his own body. At the same time, he did not neglect or separate the action of cognitive enquiry and enunciation of what the language of painting should be, of what its constituent elements and referents are, and of how to decipher the real and the relation with men and things. With all this and more Bendini faced up to a single, challenging venture, subject moreover to an incessant movement and transformation of the sensitive data of which his painting has become the mirror and seismograph.
He is one of those people who will go down in history as a Sisyphus of the art of our times.

June 2022

WORKS

Series I SEGNI SEGRETI

Autoritratto, 1946, oil on cavas, 54×43 cm, Collezione Santori Lettieri, Rome

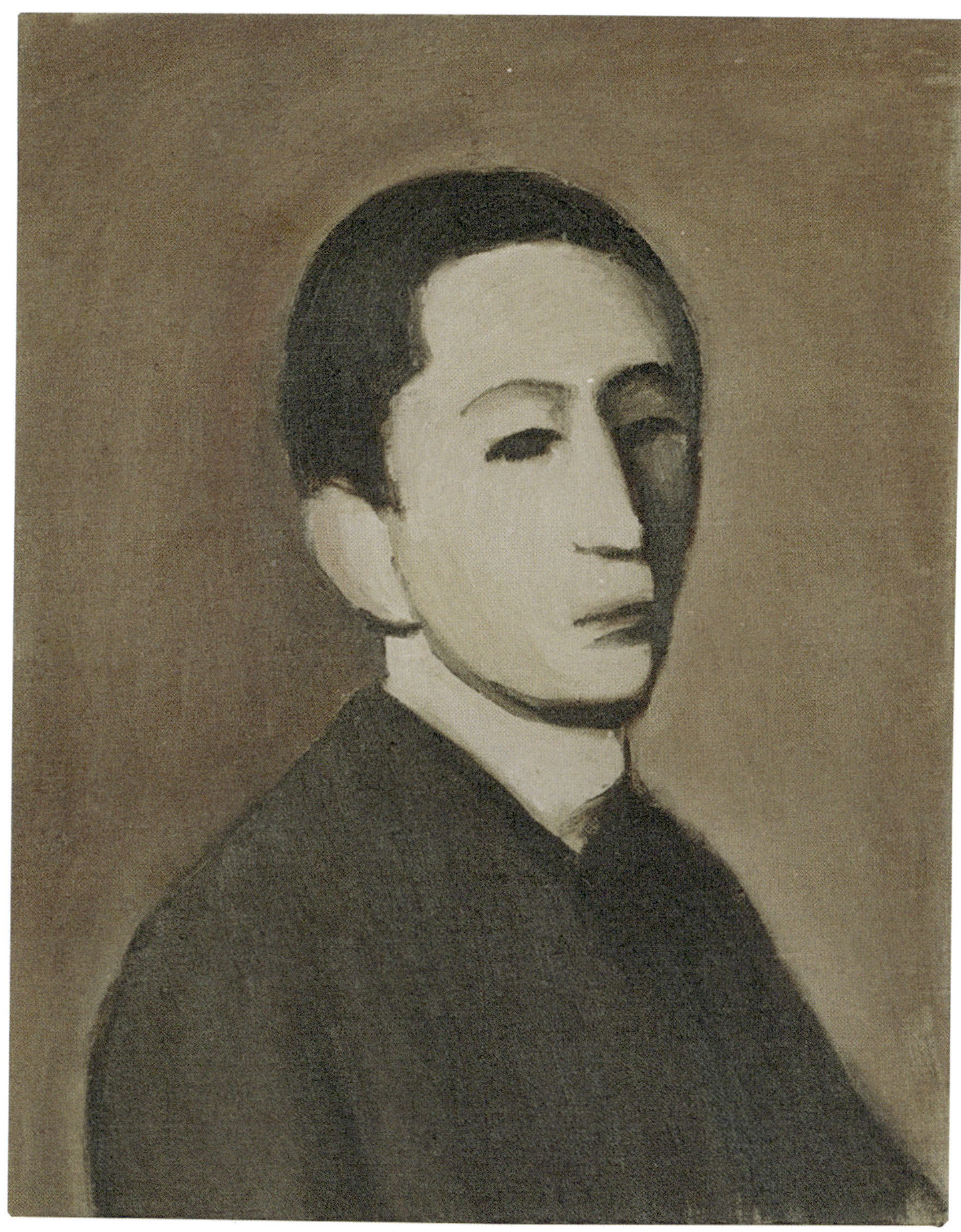

Testa, 1950, acrylic tempera on canvas, 70×50,5 cm, private collection, Rome

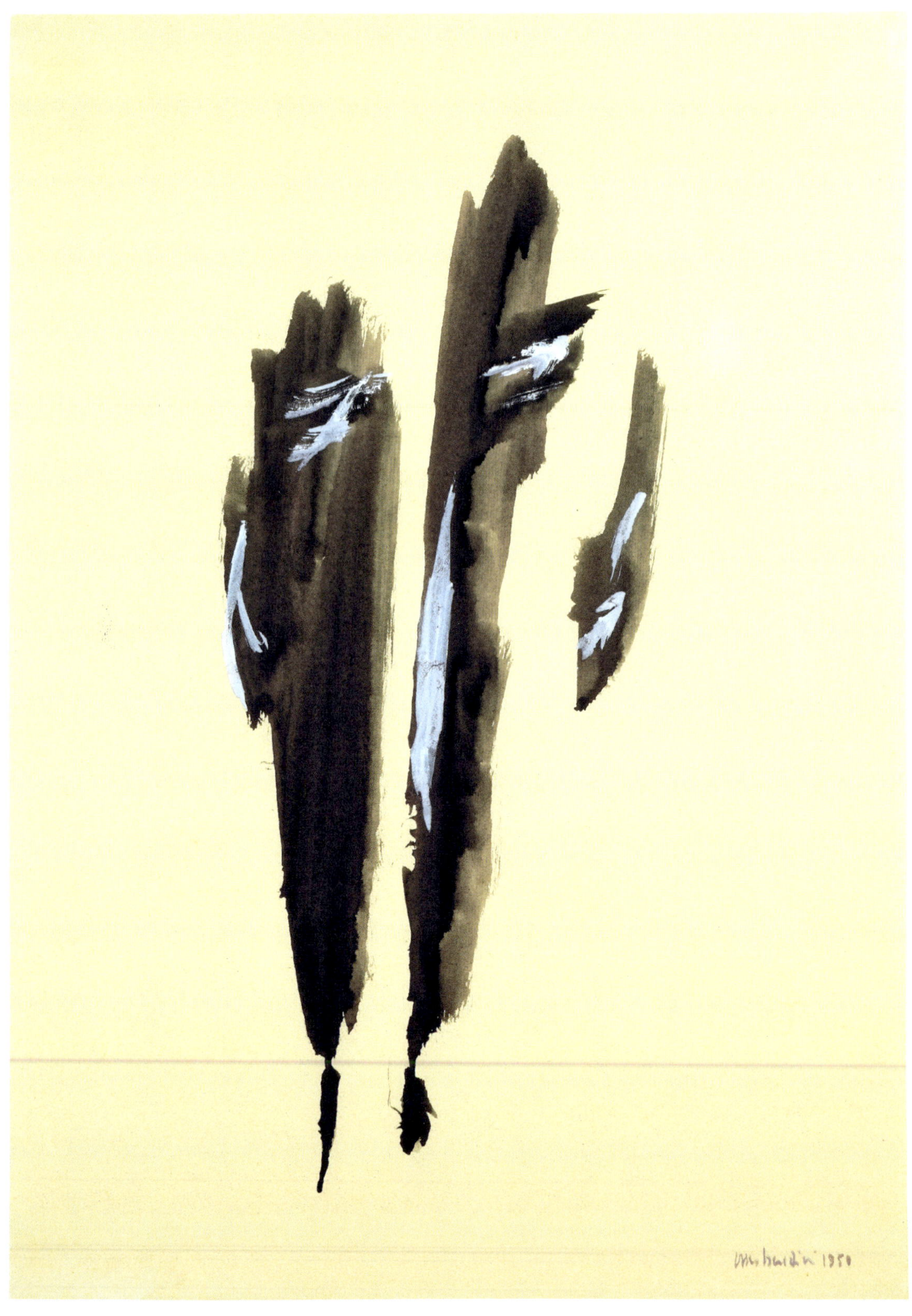

Testa, 1951, acrylic tempera on canvas paper, 72,5×50 cm, private collection, Rome

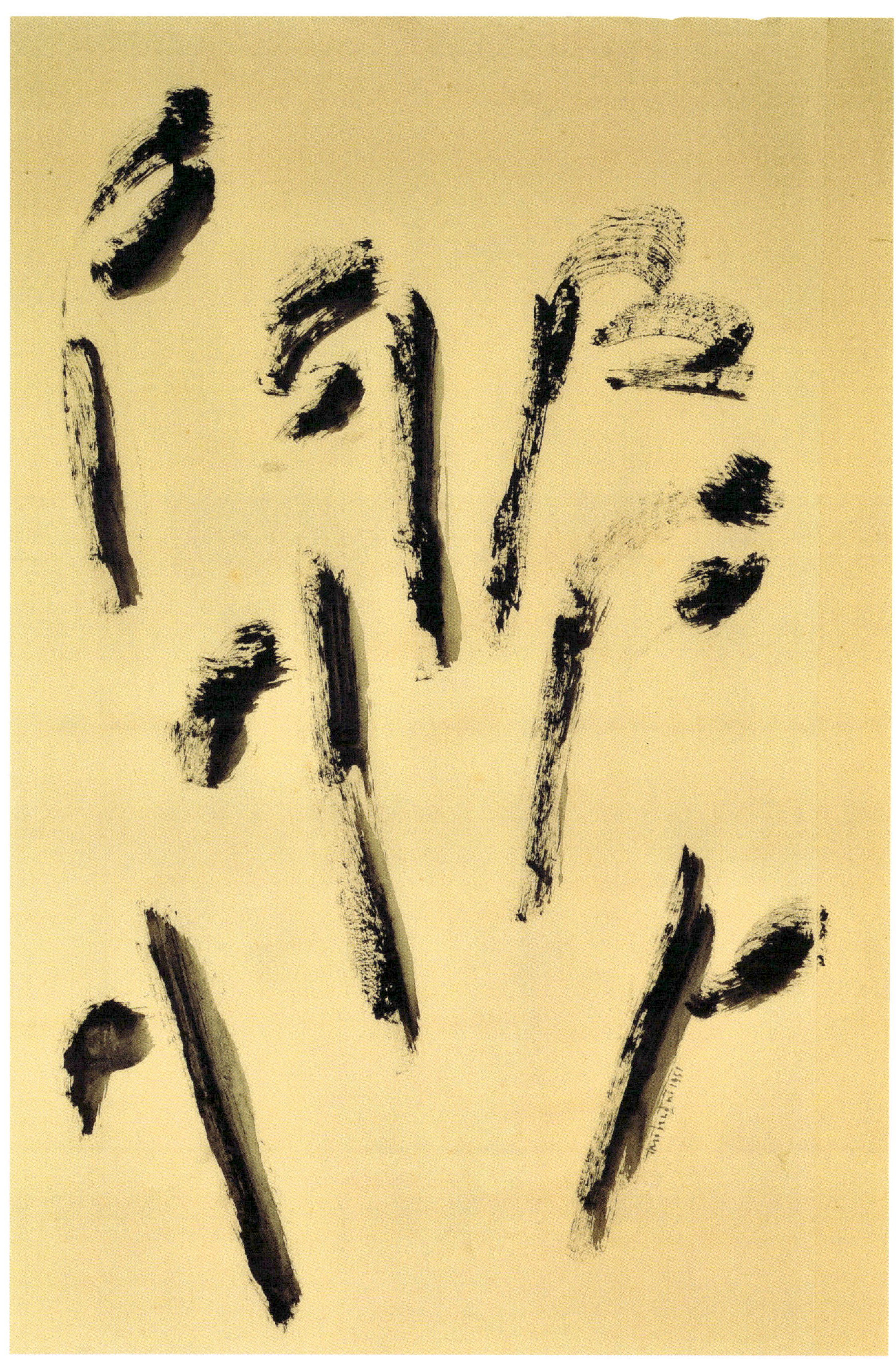

Testa, 1952, acrylic tempera on canvas paper, 78,5×39,5 cm, Collezione Santori Lettieri, Rome

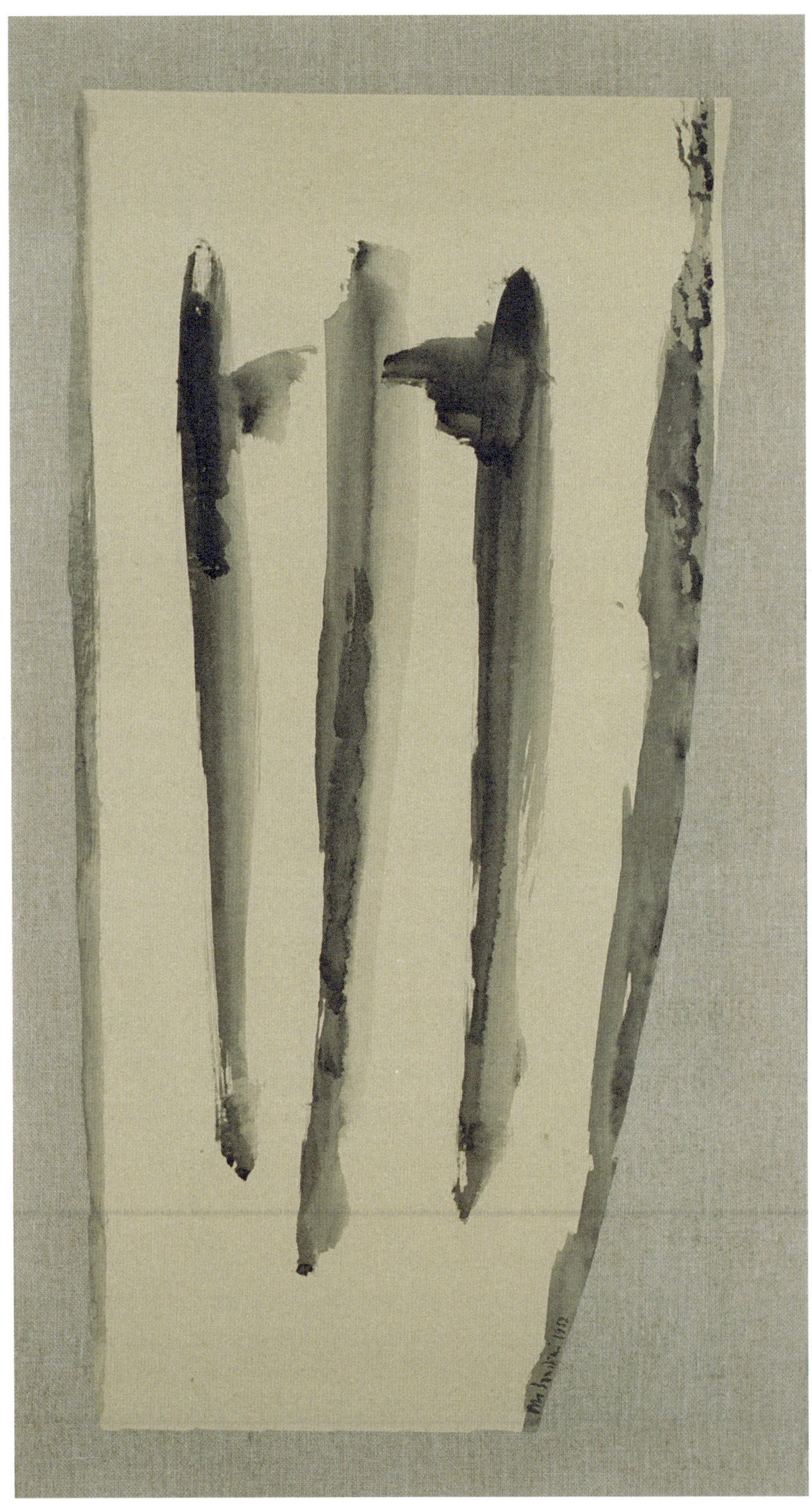

Autoritratto, 1953, acrylic tempera on canvas paper, 76×55 cm, Collezione Francescopiero Calzolari, Bologna

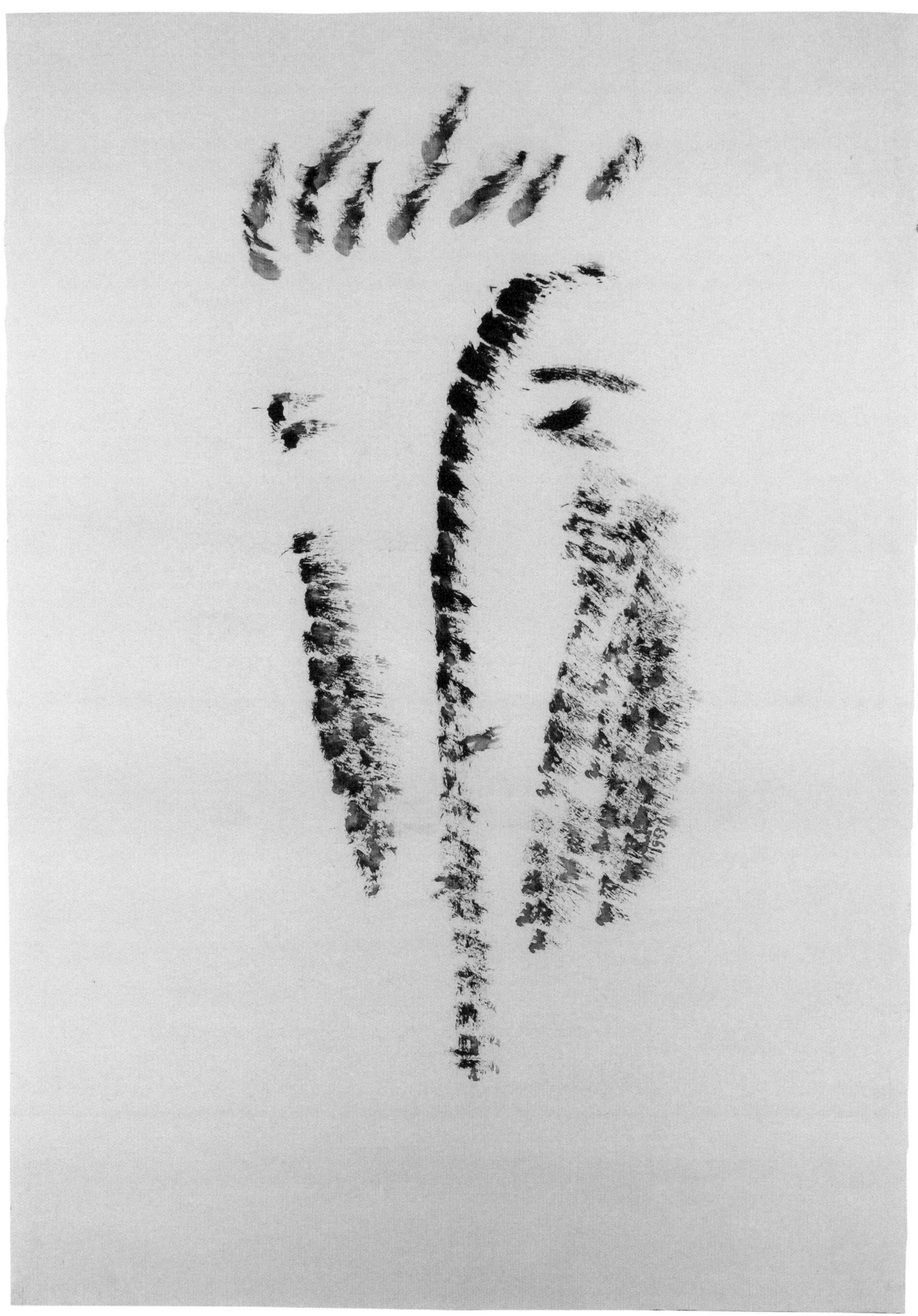

Series GESTO E MATERIA

Testa, 1956, acrylic tempera on canvas paper, 84,5×108 cm, private collection, Rome

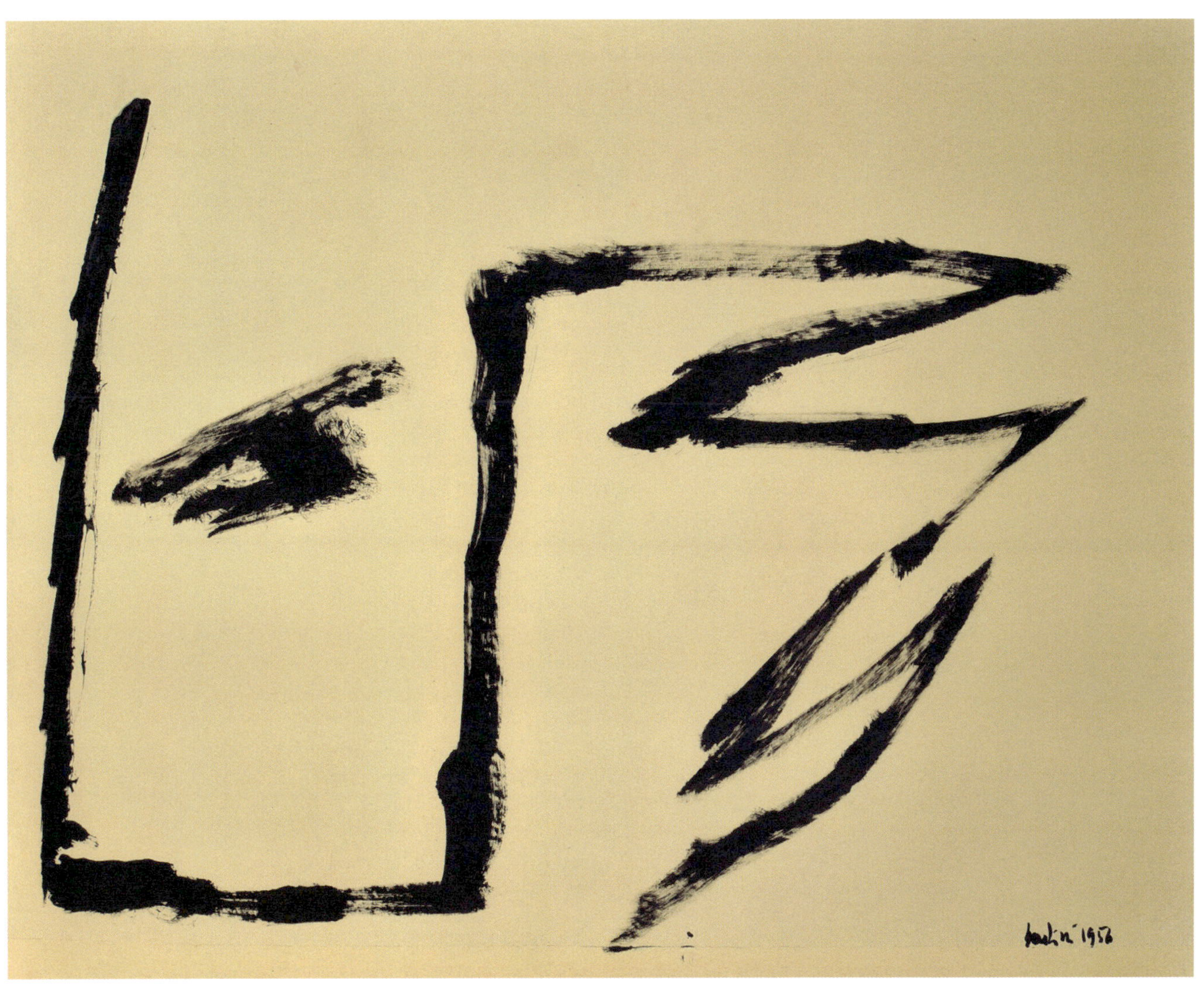

Testa, 1958, acrylic tempera on canvas, 140×100 cm, private collection, Rome

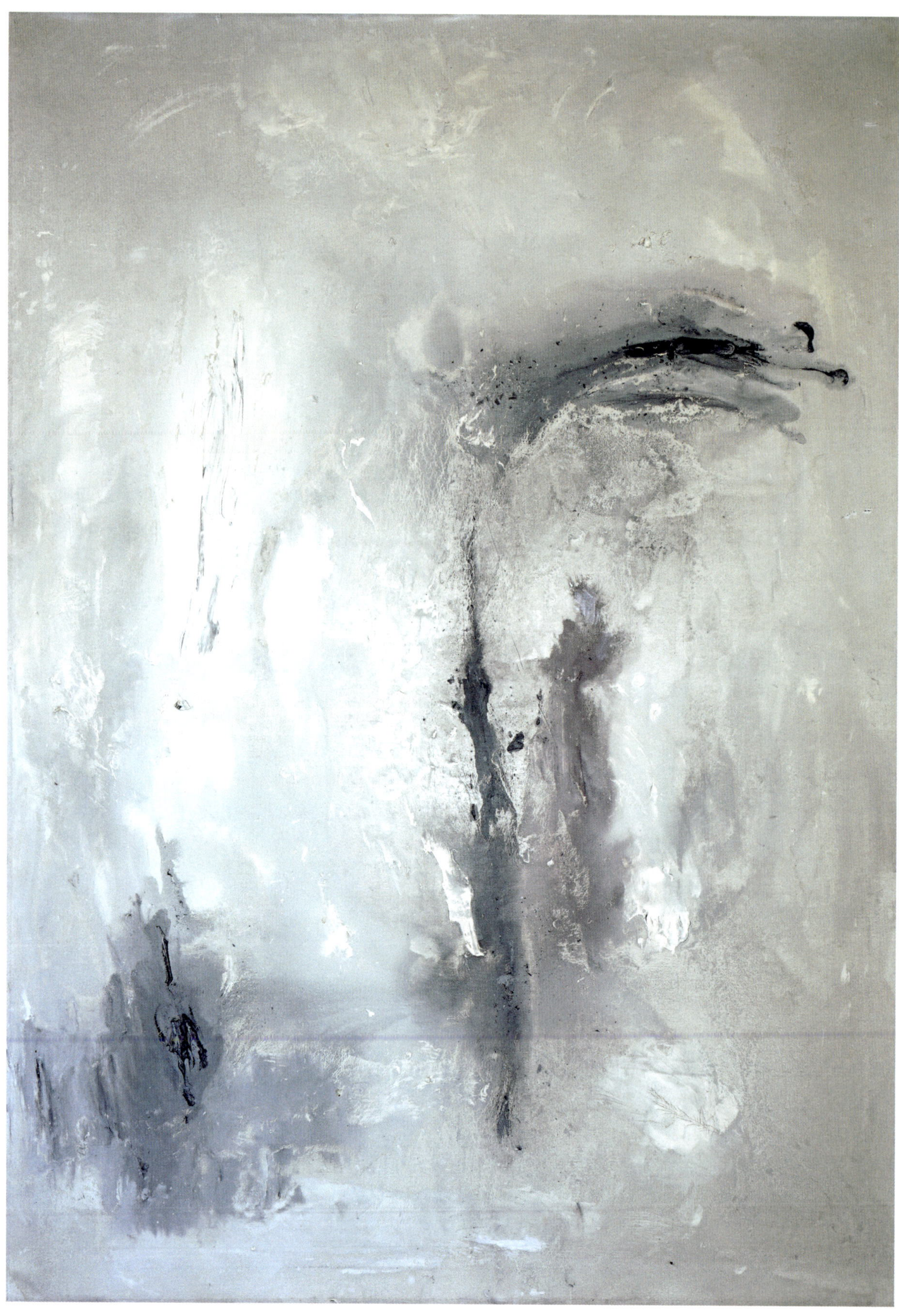

Reliquie nere, 1958, acrylic tempera on canvas, 140×100 cm, Galleria Nazionale d'Arte Moderna e Contemporanea, Rome

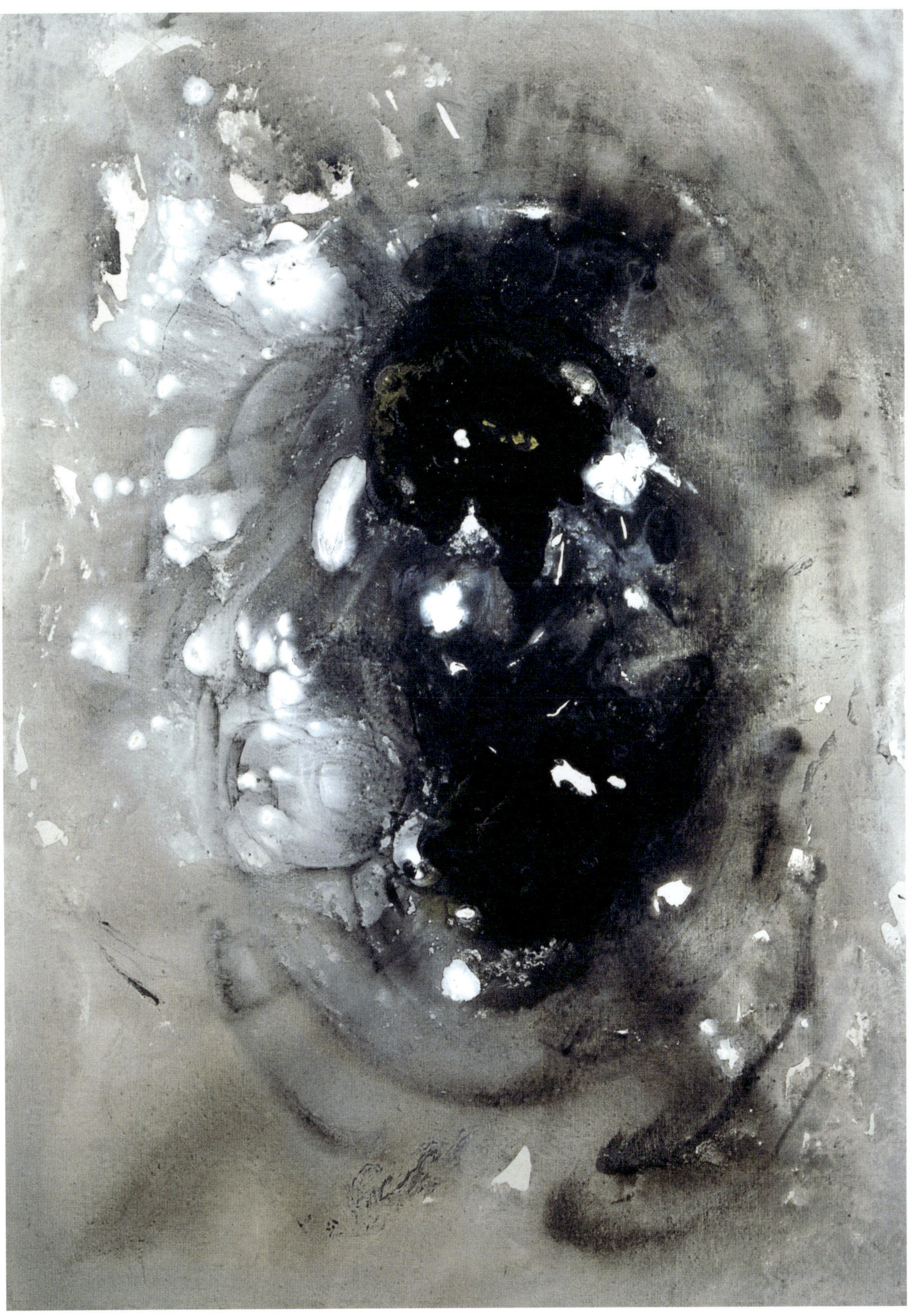

S.T., 1960, oil on canvas, 200×130 cm, Collezione Tonelli, Terni

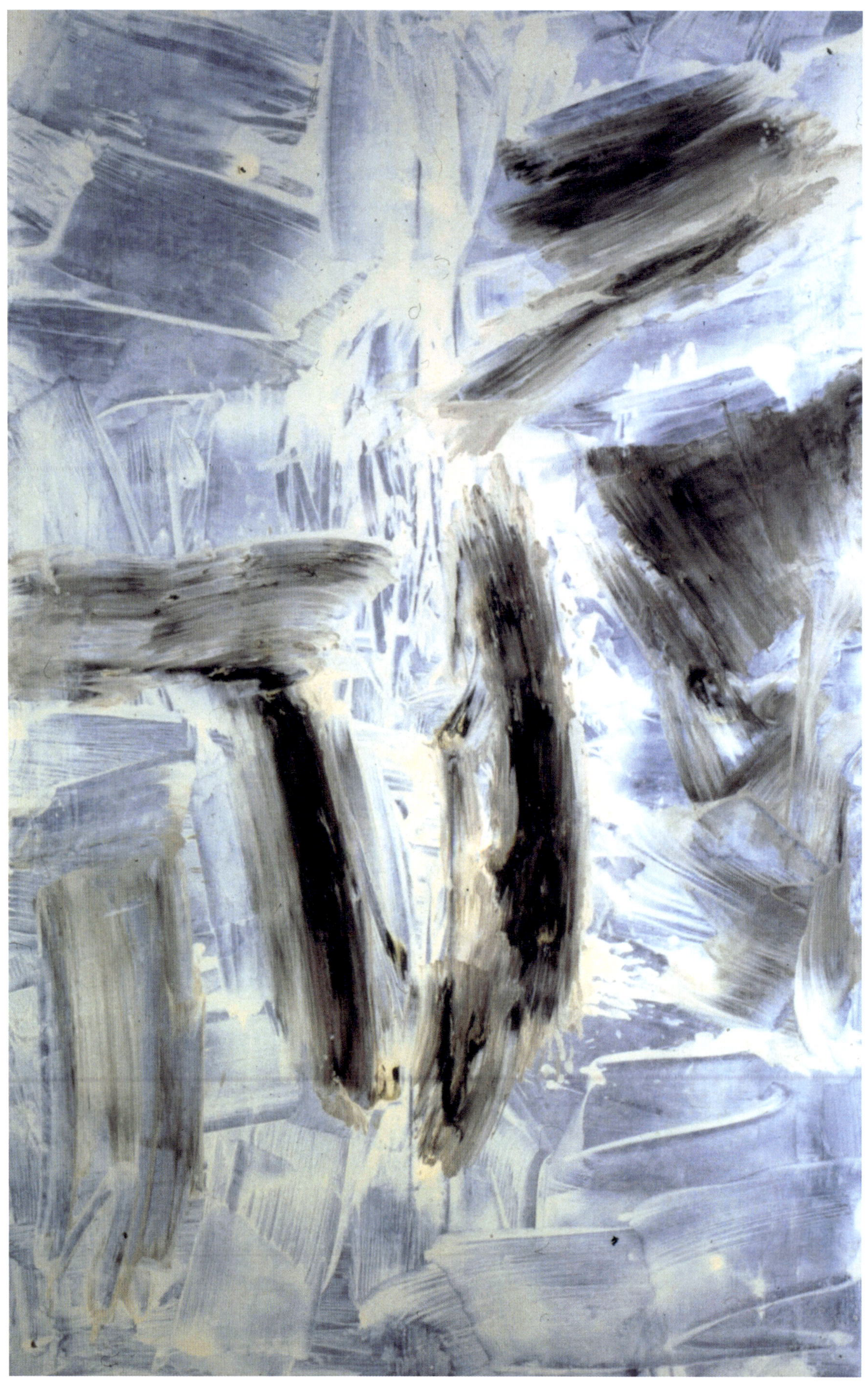

Testa, 1962, oil on canvas, 200×150 cm, Collezione Tonelli, Terni

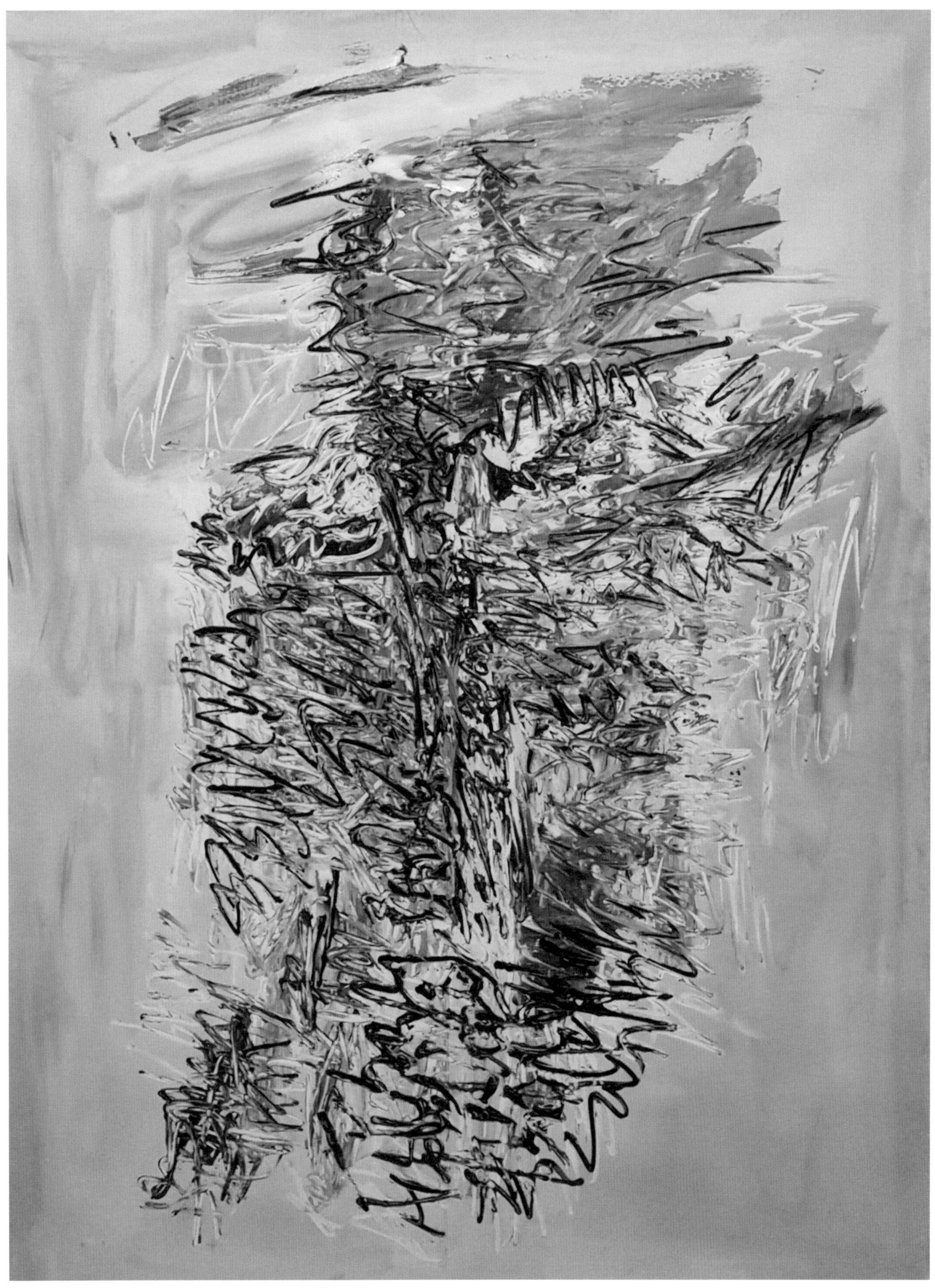

S.T., 1970, newspaper, resin, glue, tea and cofee on canvas, 100×80 cm, private collection, Rome

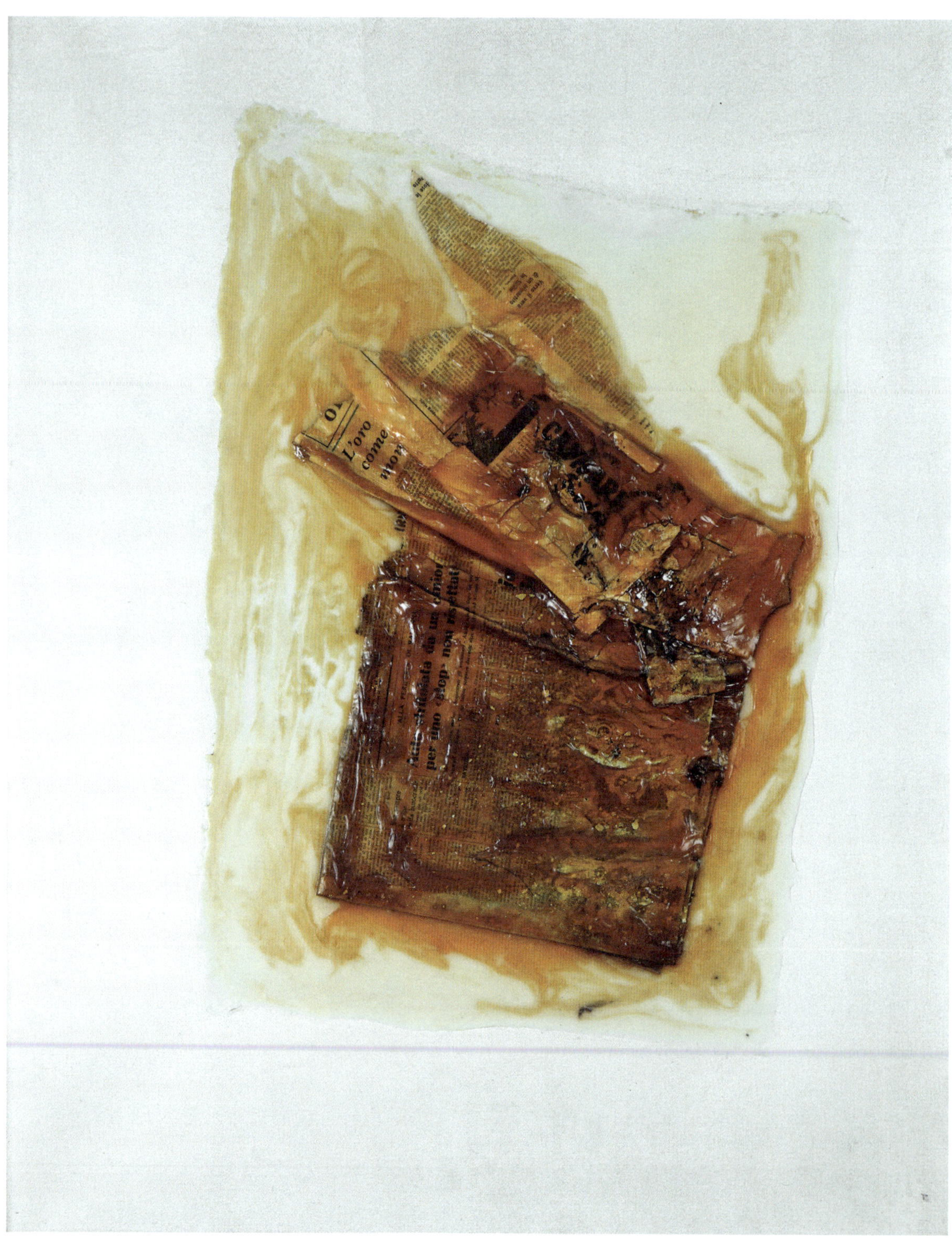

La soglia dell'eros, 1974, alluminium plate, wadding, dried flower petals, oil and colored powders on canvas, 160×140 cm, private collection, Rome

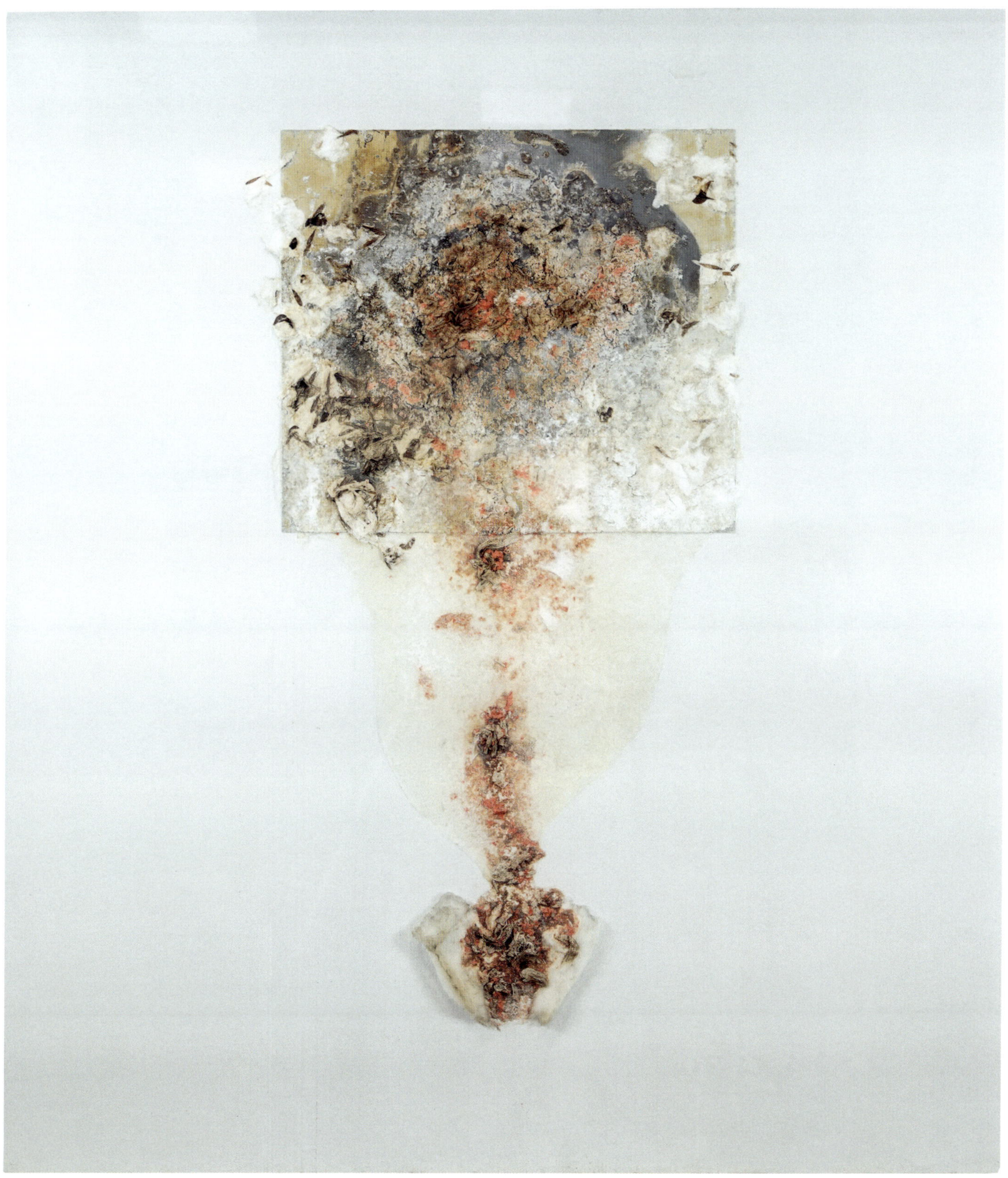

Series IPOTESI ULTIME

S.T., 1963, oil on canvas, 130×97 cm, private collection, Parma

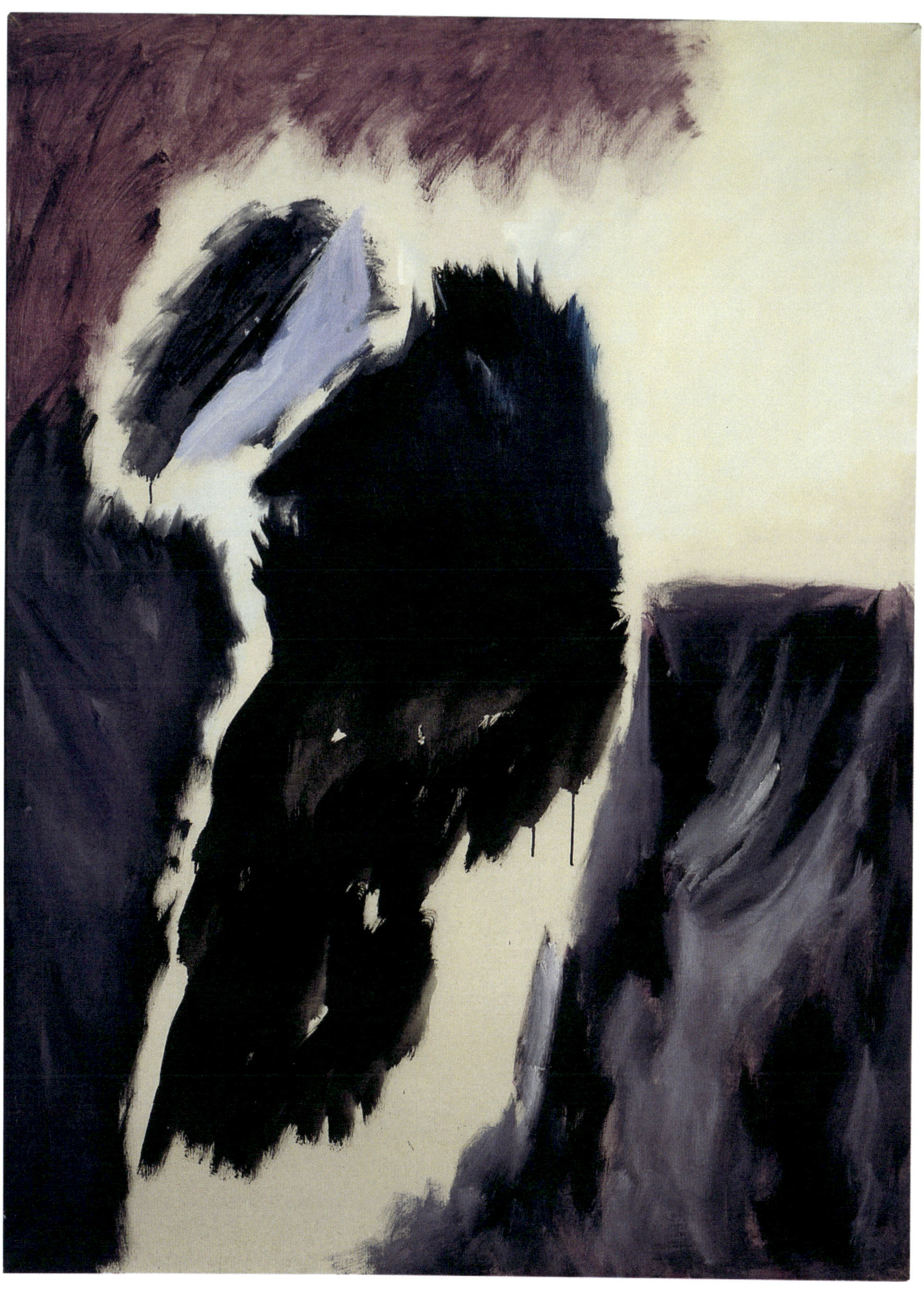

Series SENSO OPERANTE

Ombre prime, 1966, frame, cut canvas, clamps, chair and seatback (spotlight), 230×200×50 cm, Frittelli Arte Contemporanea, Florence

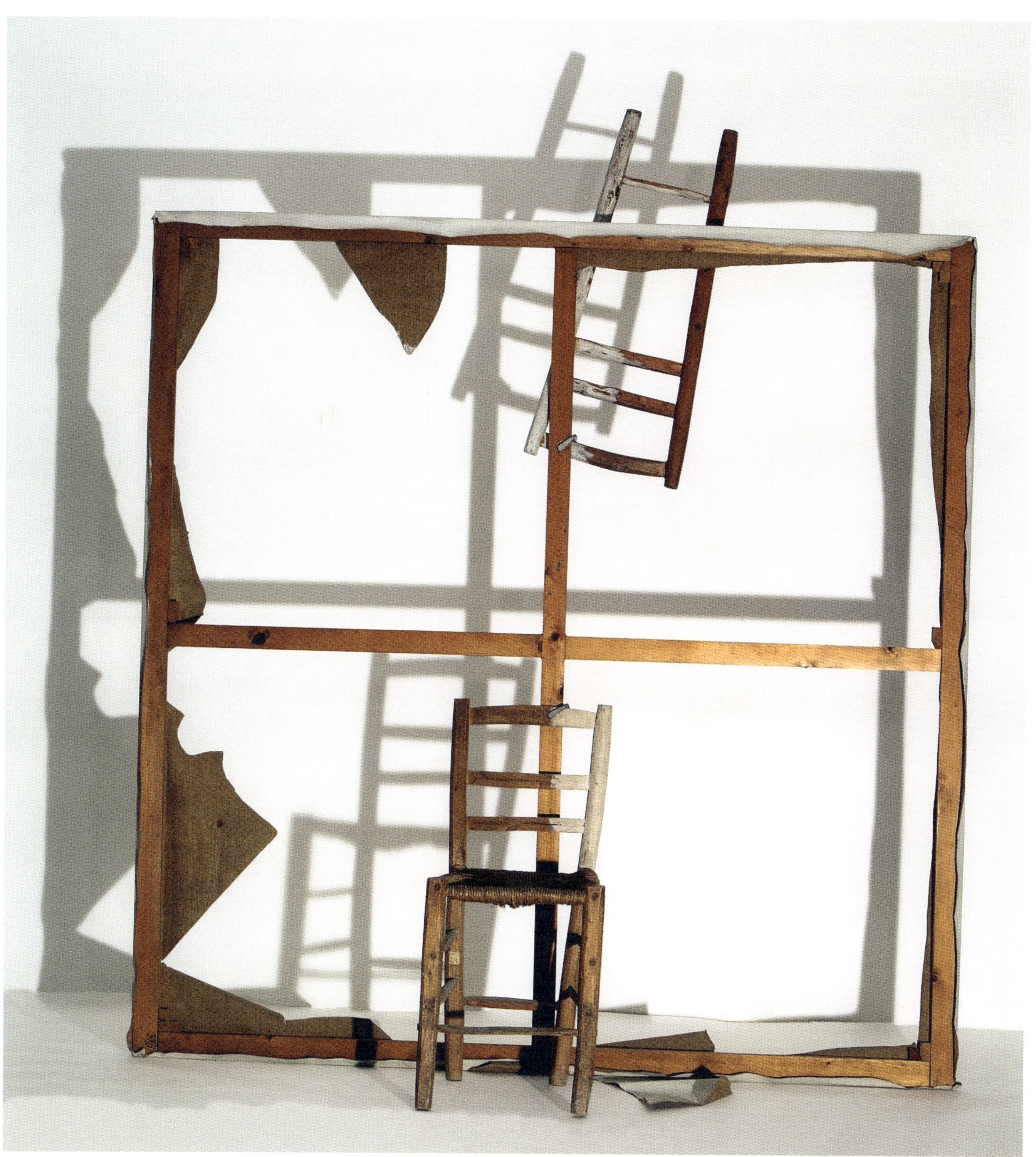

Due minuti, 1966, polimateric on canvas, 190×190 cm, Museo d'Arte Moderna e Contemporanea, Varese

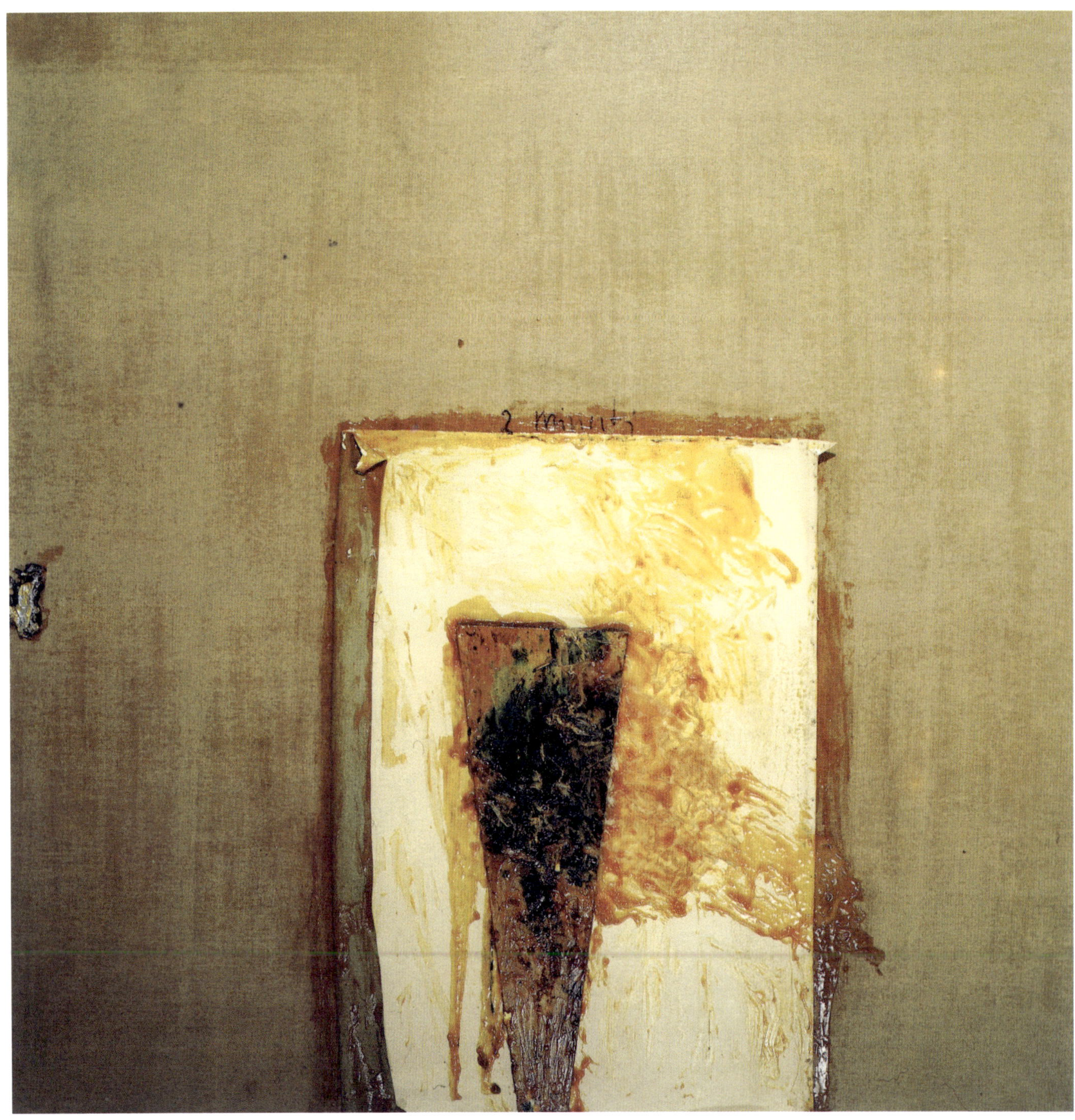

Una delle duemila parole, 1968, trunk, red neon, 25×90×27 cm, private collection, Rome

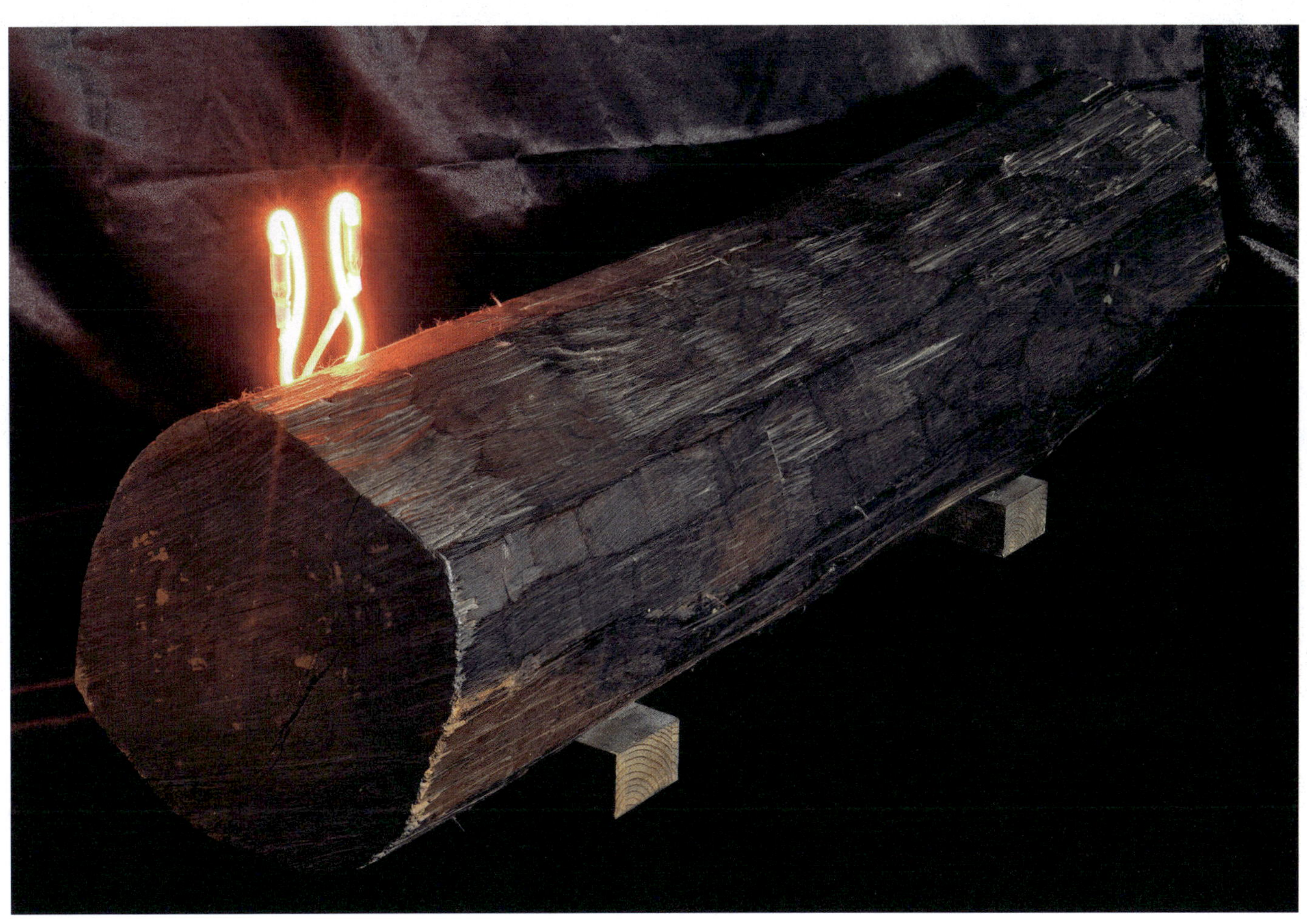

Mille e una notte, 1968, white neon and burnt wax candles inside a cristal box, with transformator, 34,5×34,5×4 cm (box), 12 cm diameter (white light neon), private collection, Rome

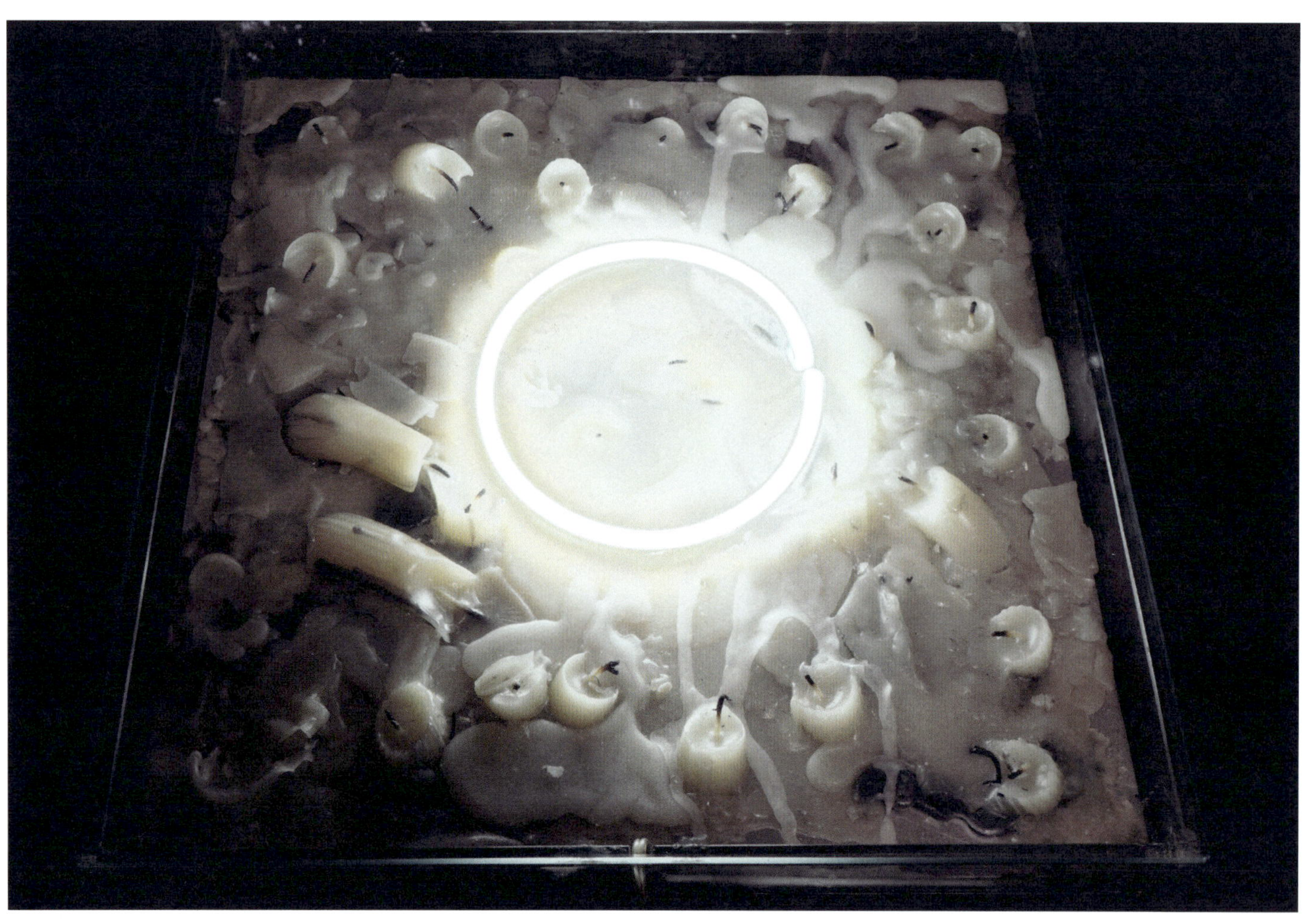

Il ricordo è questo, 1969-70, polimateric on canvas, 116×89 cm, private collection, Rome

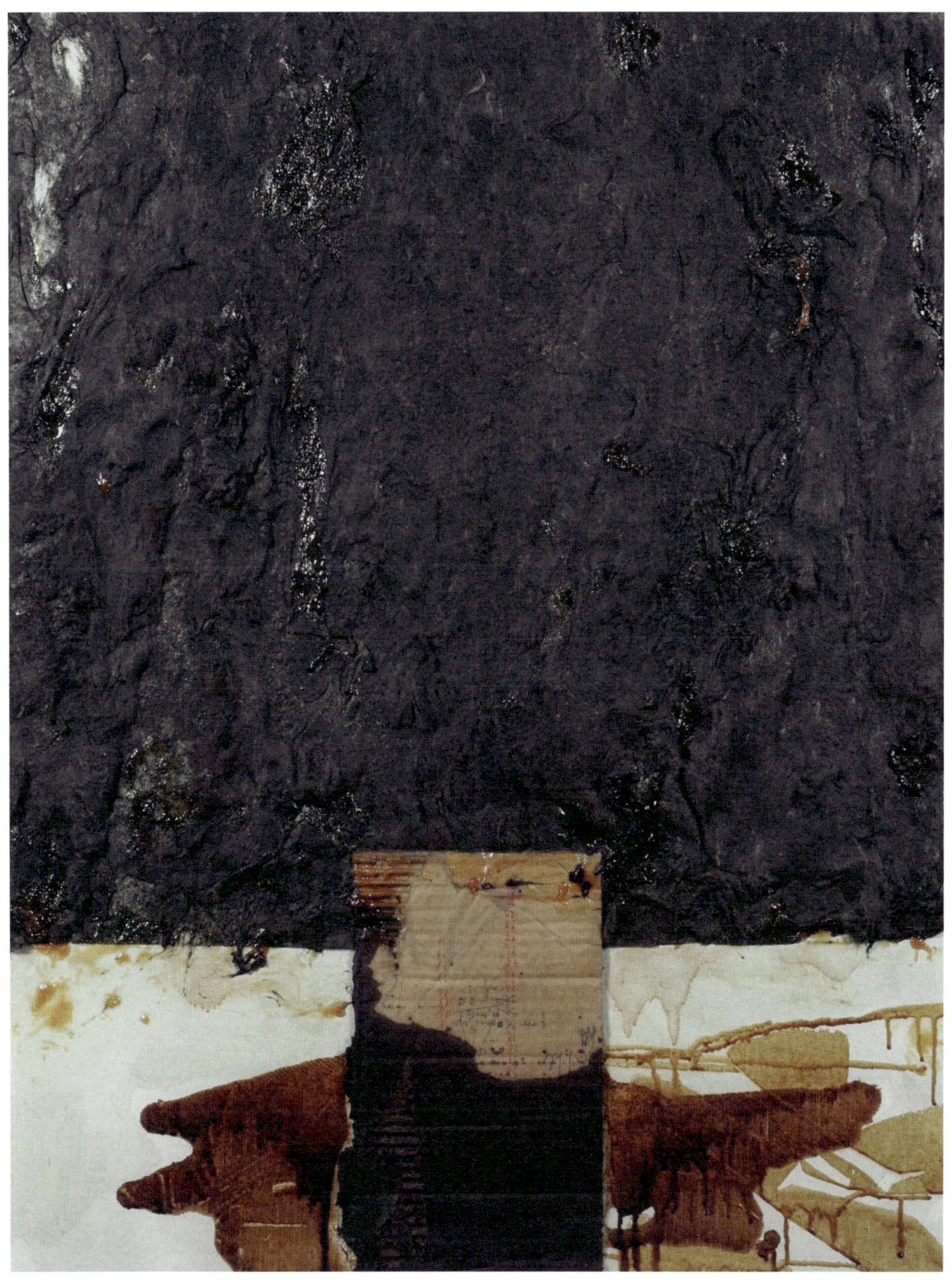

Series MEMORIE

S.T., 1980, oil on alluminium plate, 66×55 cm, private collection, Rome

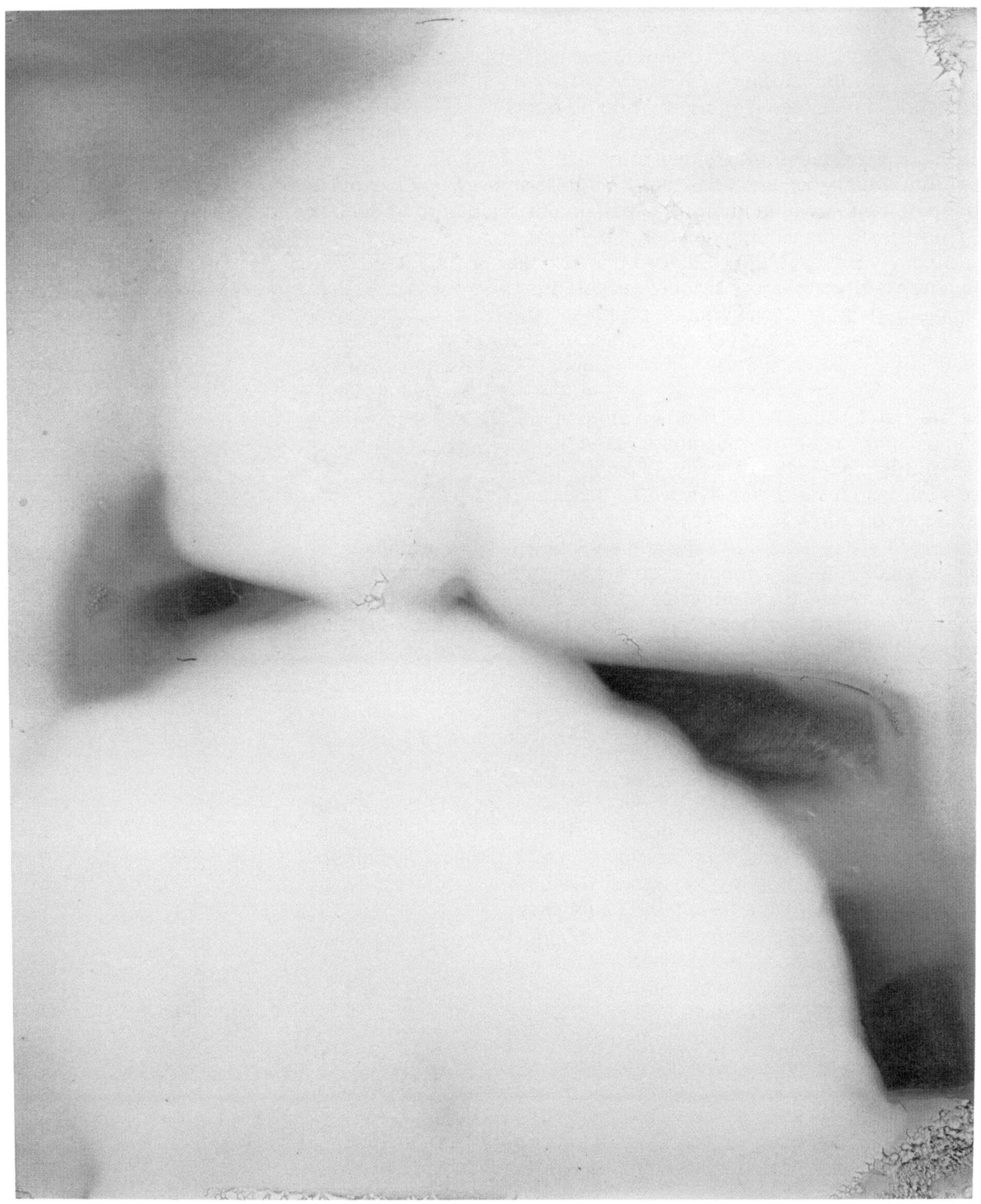

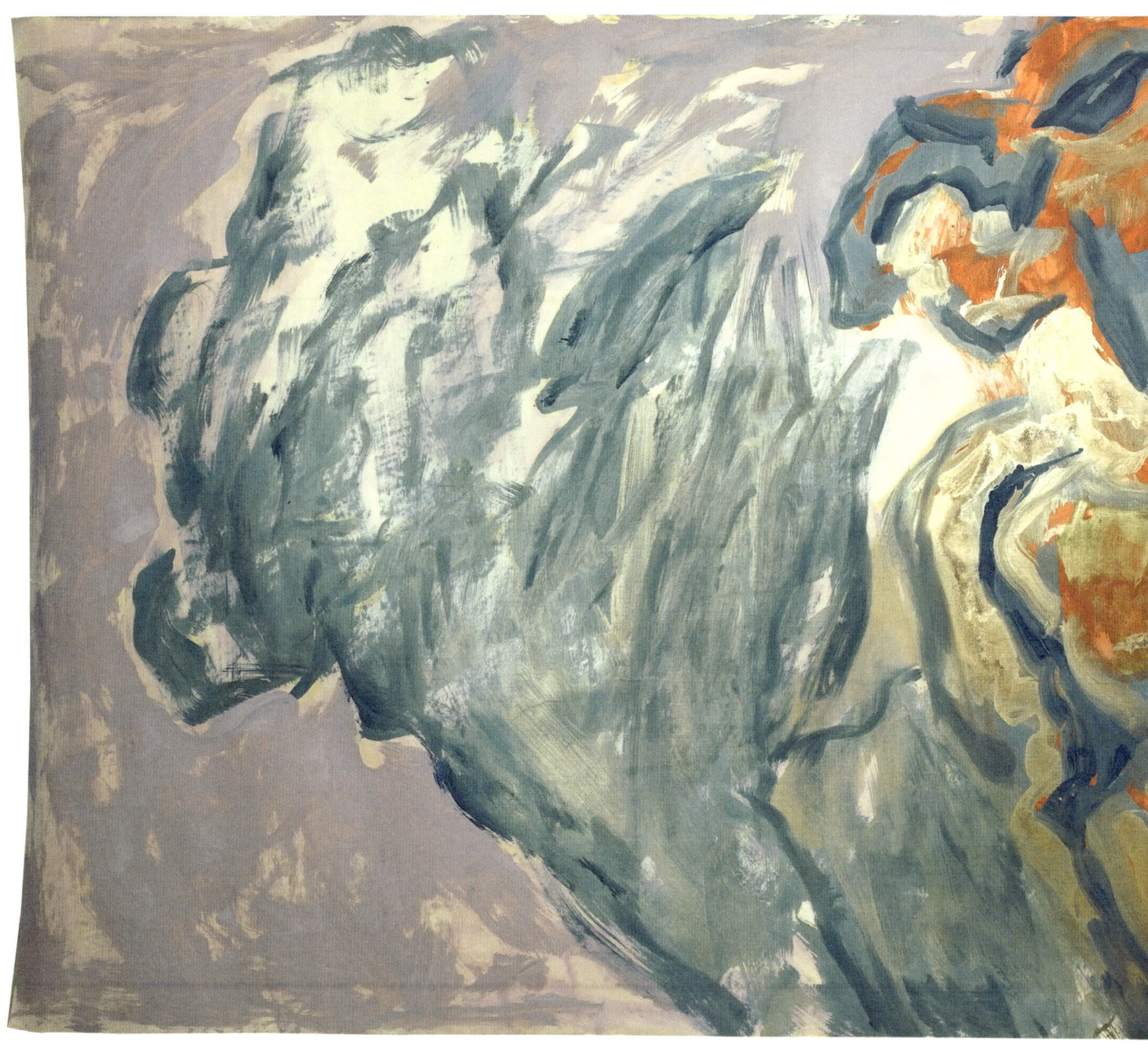

S.T., 1988, oil on canvas paper, 150×390 cm, private collection, Rome

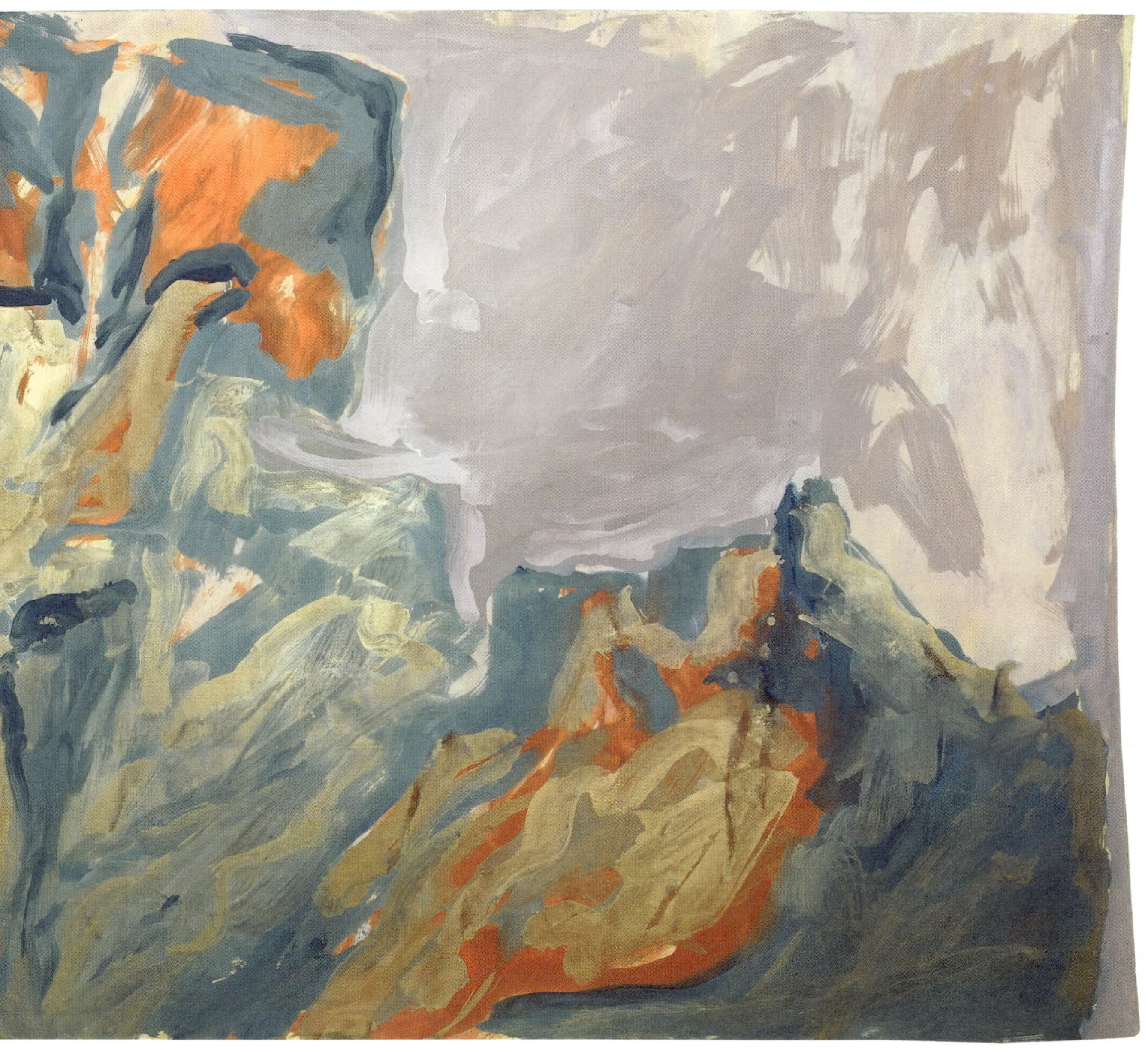

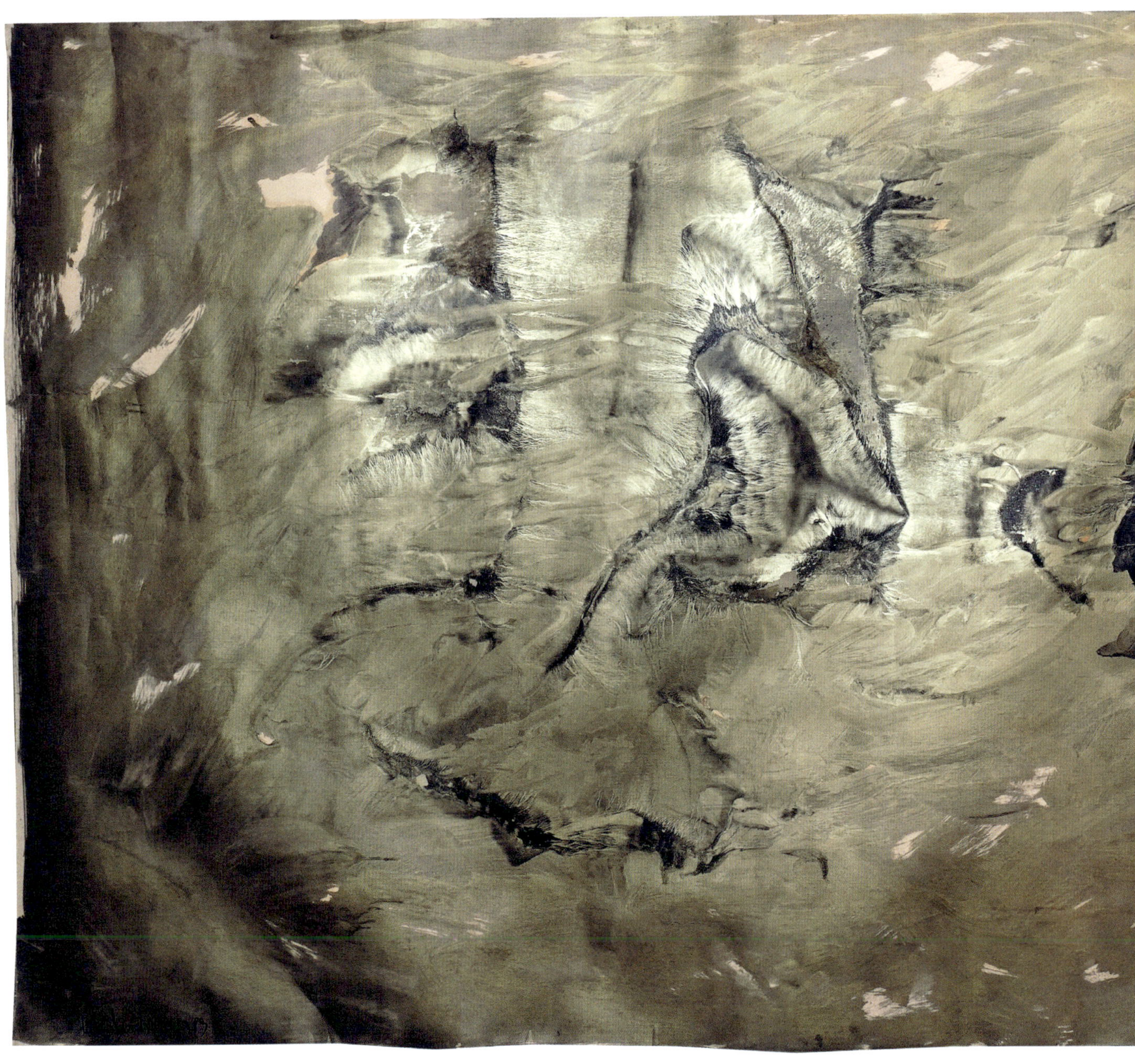

S.T., 1989, oil and gold powders on canvas paper, 150×382 cm, private collection, Rome

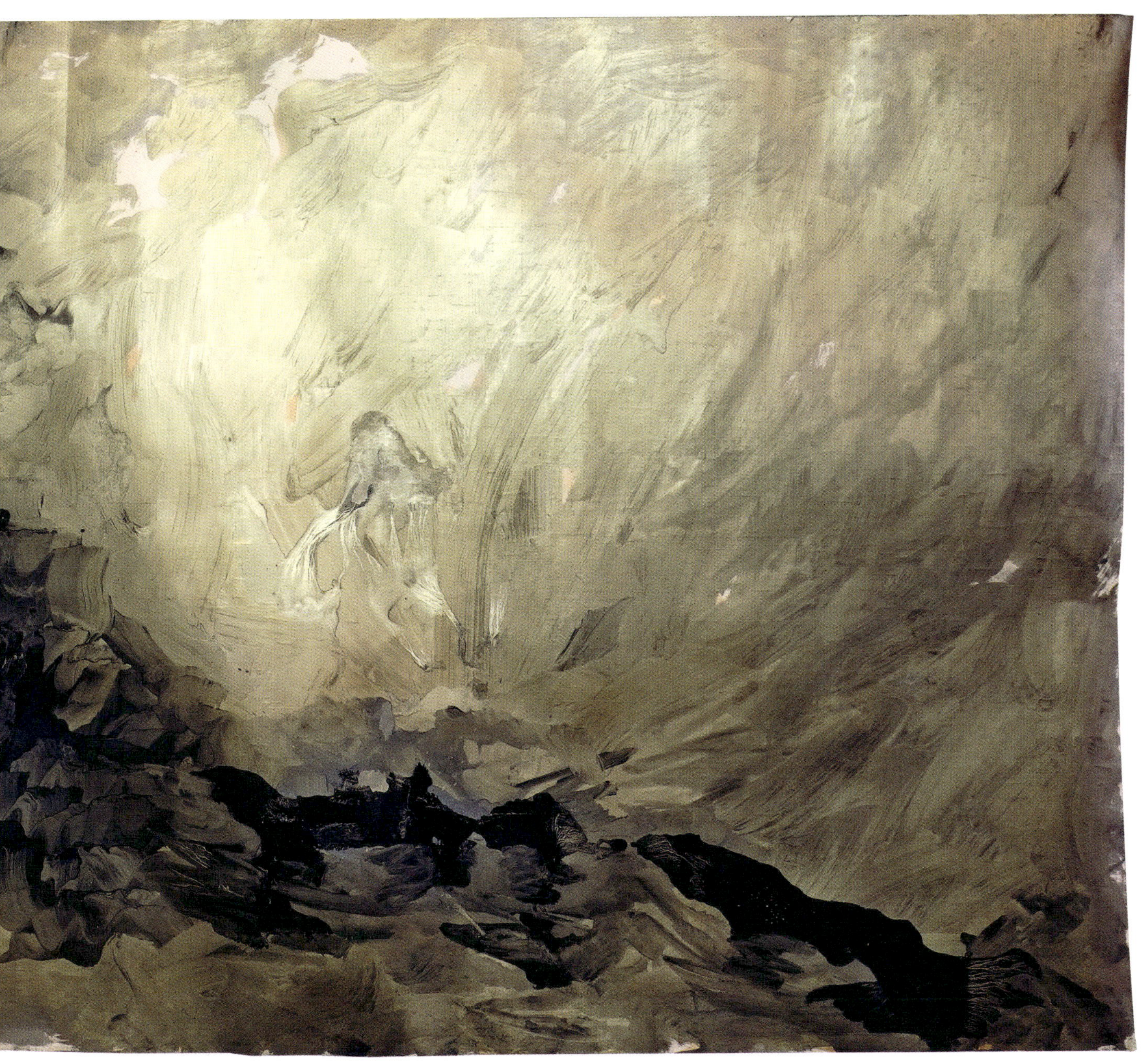

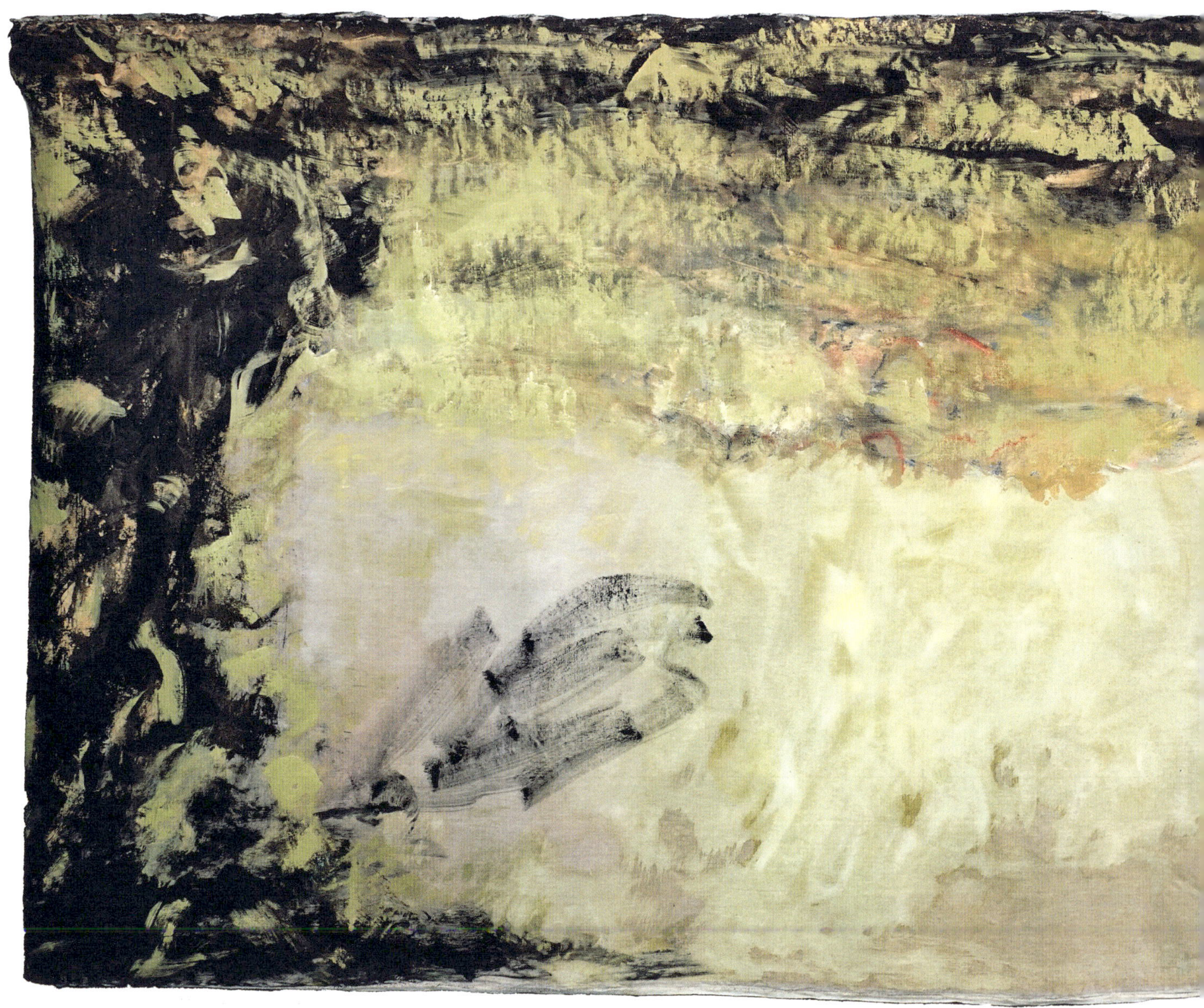

S.T., 1990, oil on canvas paper, 150×560 cm, private collection, Rome

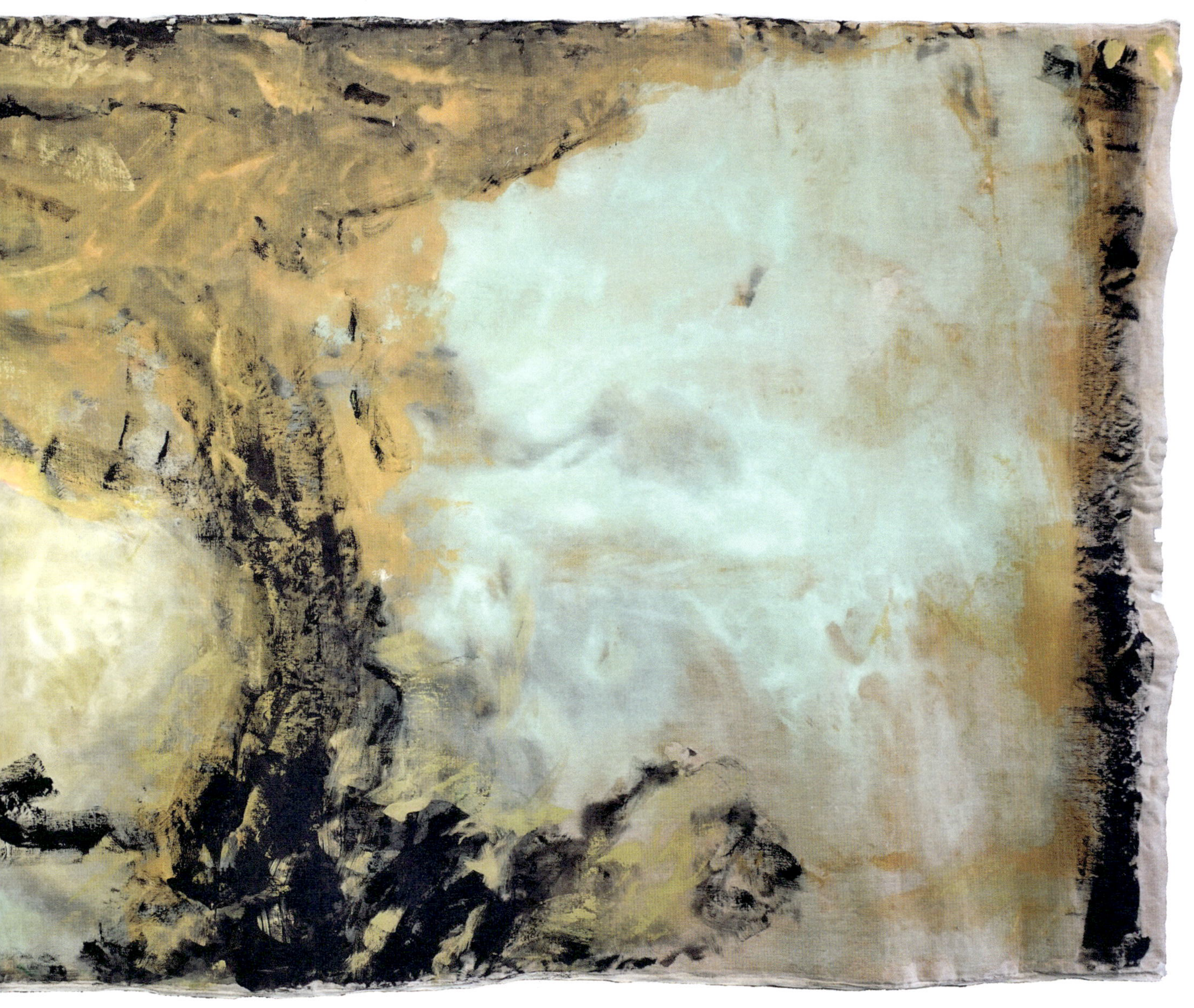

Series INQUIETI SILENZI

S.T., 1991, acrylic tempera on canvas, 200×190 cm, private collection, Rome

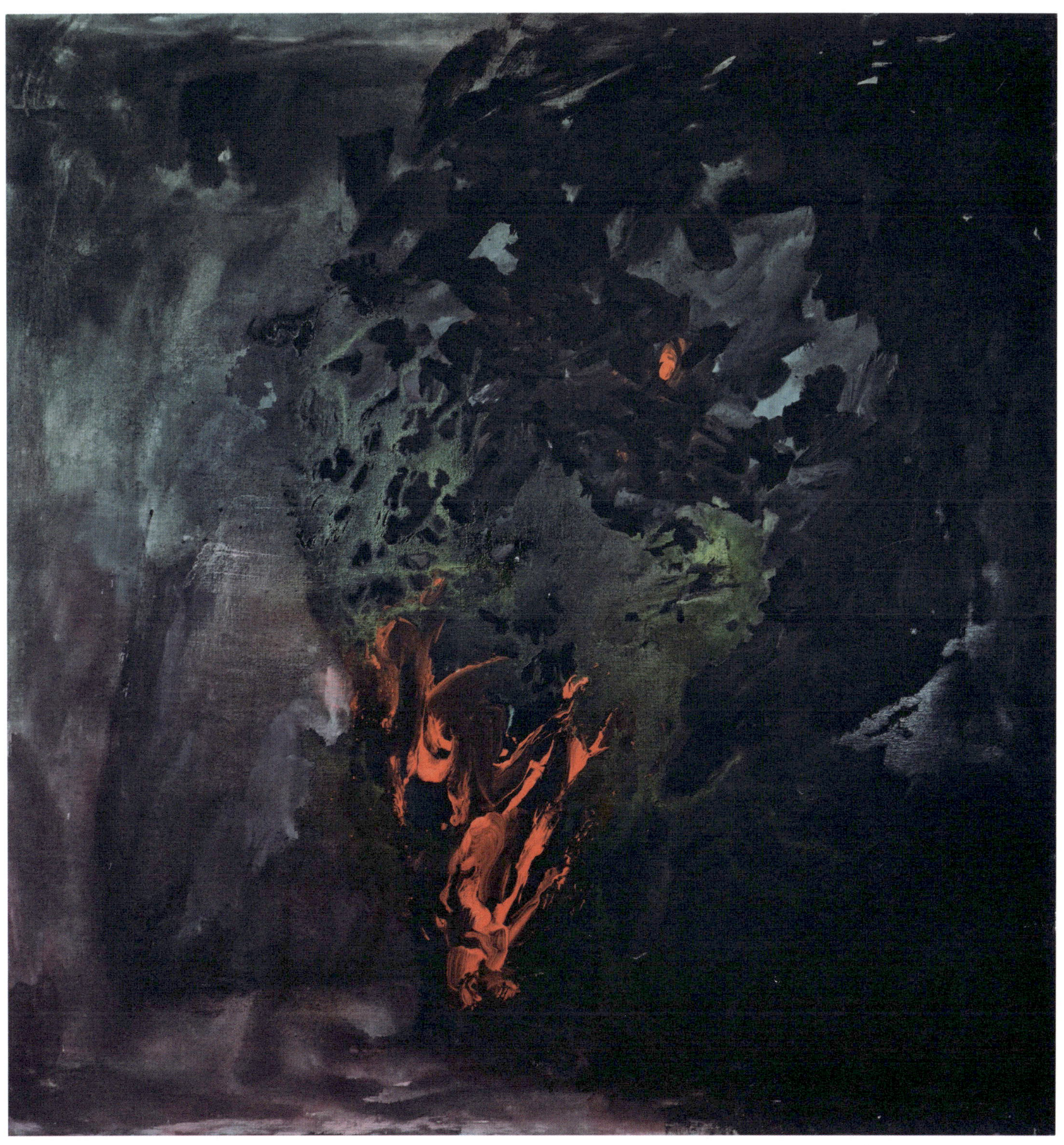

Autoritratto 2, 1995, acrylic tempera on canvas, 200×195 cm, Collezione Delogu, Rome

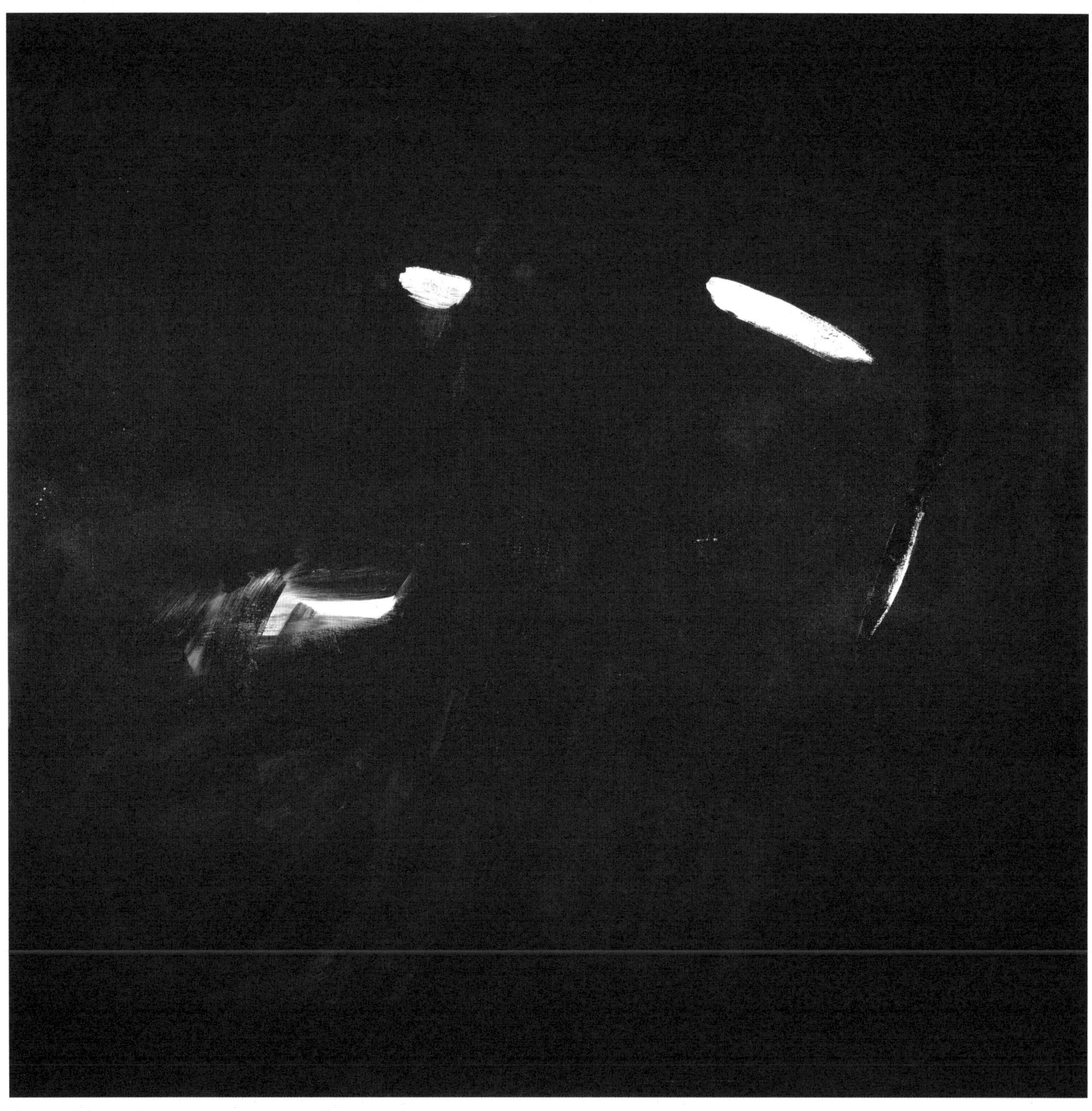

Series L'MMAGINE ACCOLTA

Autoritratto, 2000, acrylic tempera on Fabriano paper, 28×20,7 cm, private collection, Rome

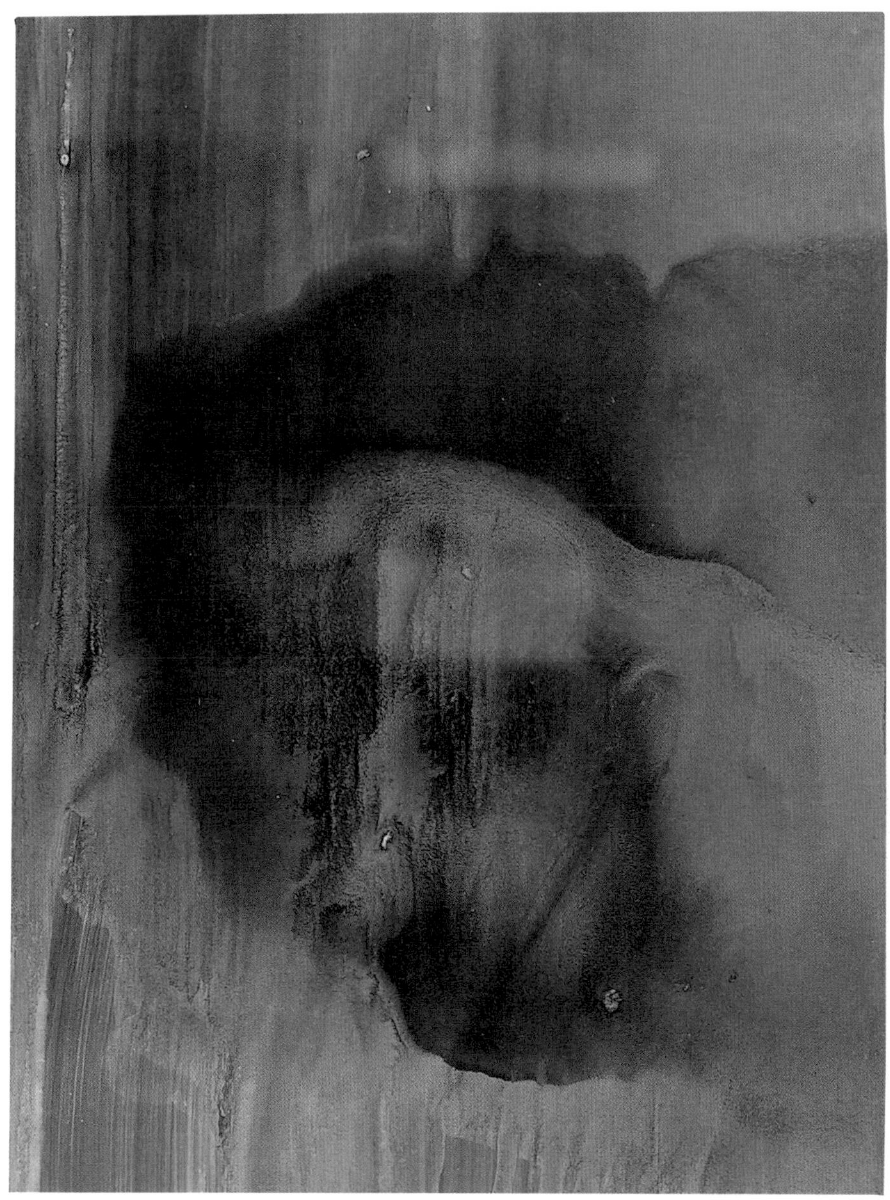

S.T., 2007, oil on canvas, 90×90 cm, private collection, Rome

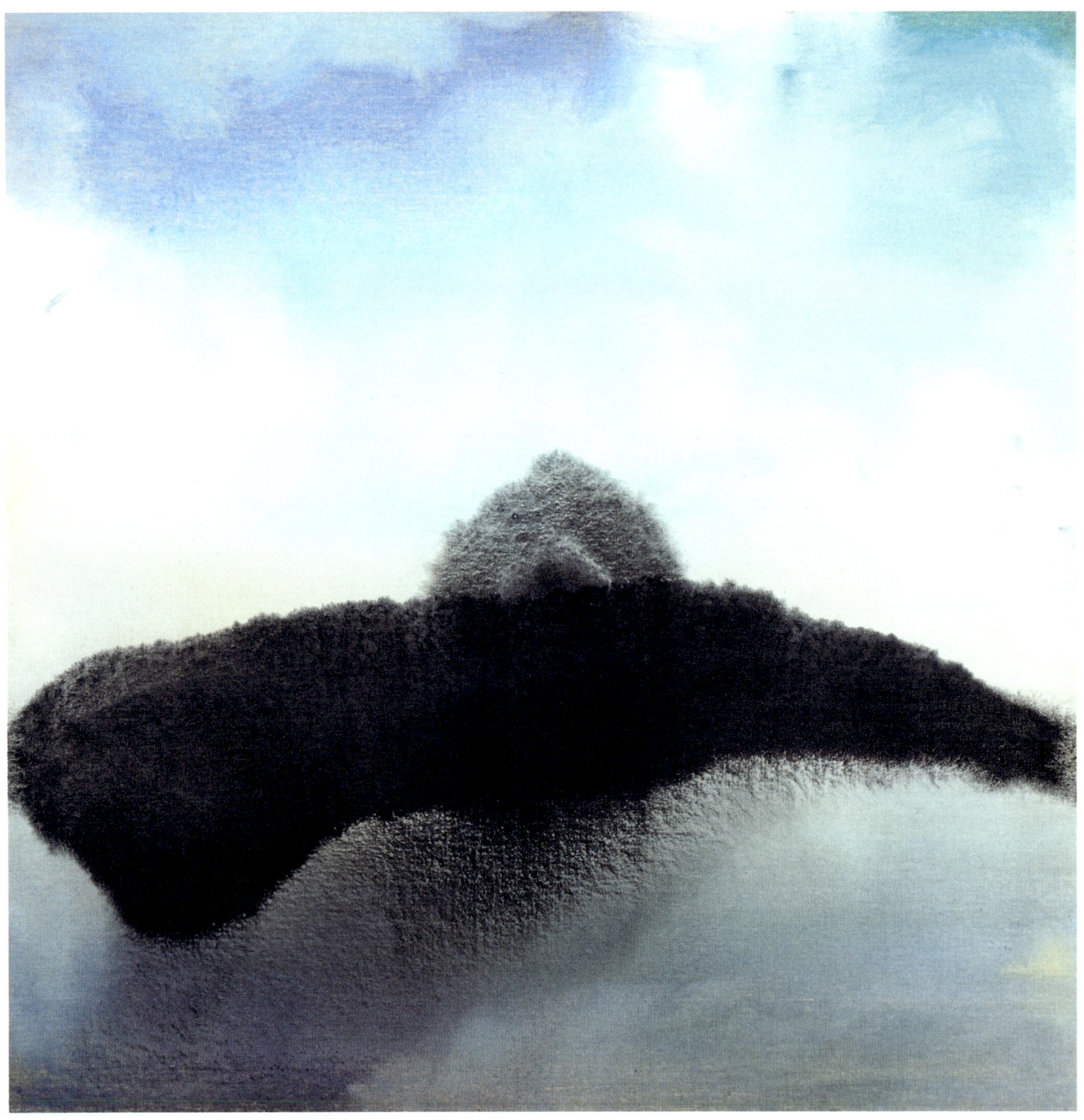

30 aprile 2008, oil on canvas, 110×90 cm, private collection, Rome

13 giugno 2008, oil on canvas, 110×90 cm, private collection, Rome

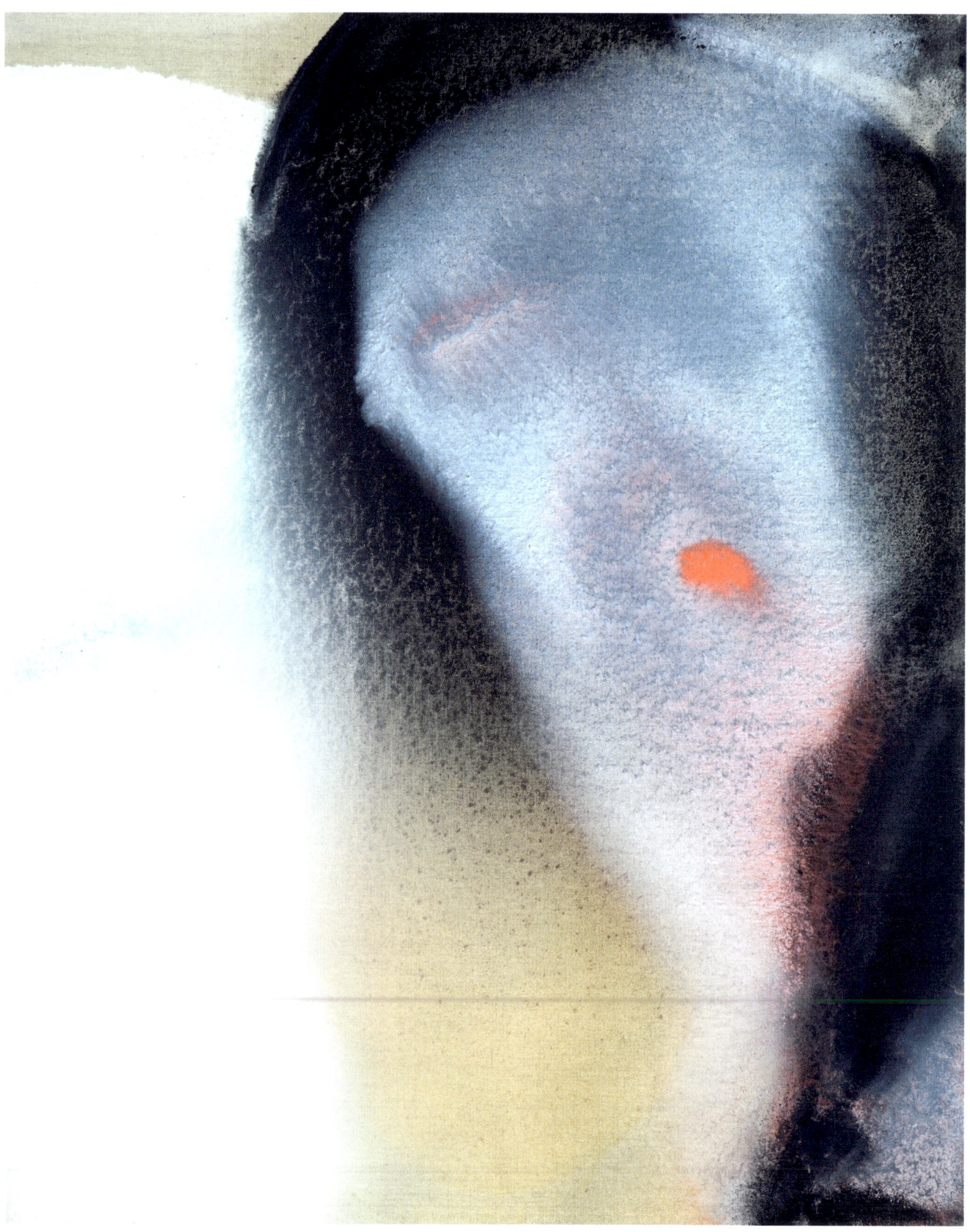

30 ottobre 2008, oil on canvas, 110×90 cm, private collection, Rome

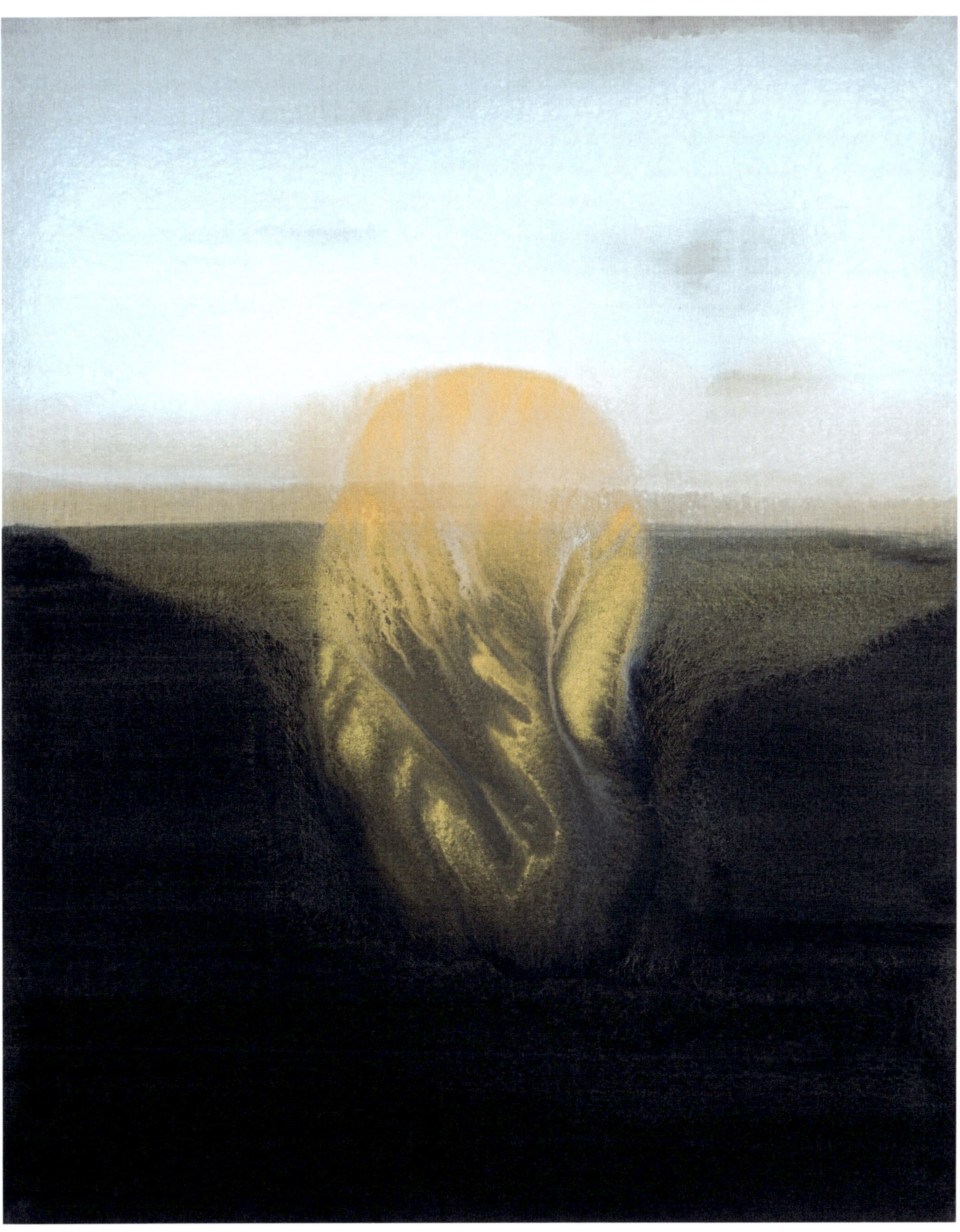

S.T., 2010, oil on canvas, 110×90 cm, private collection, Rome

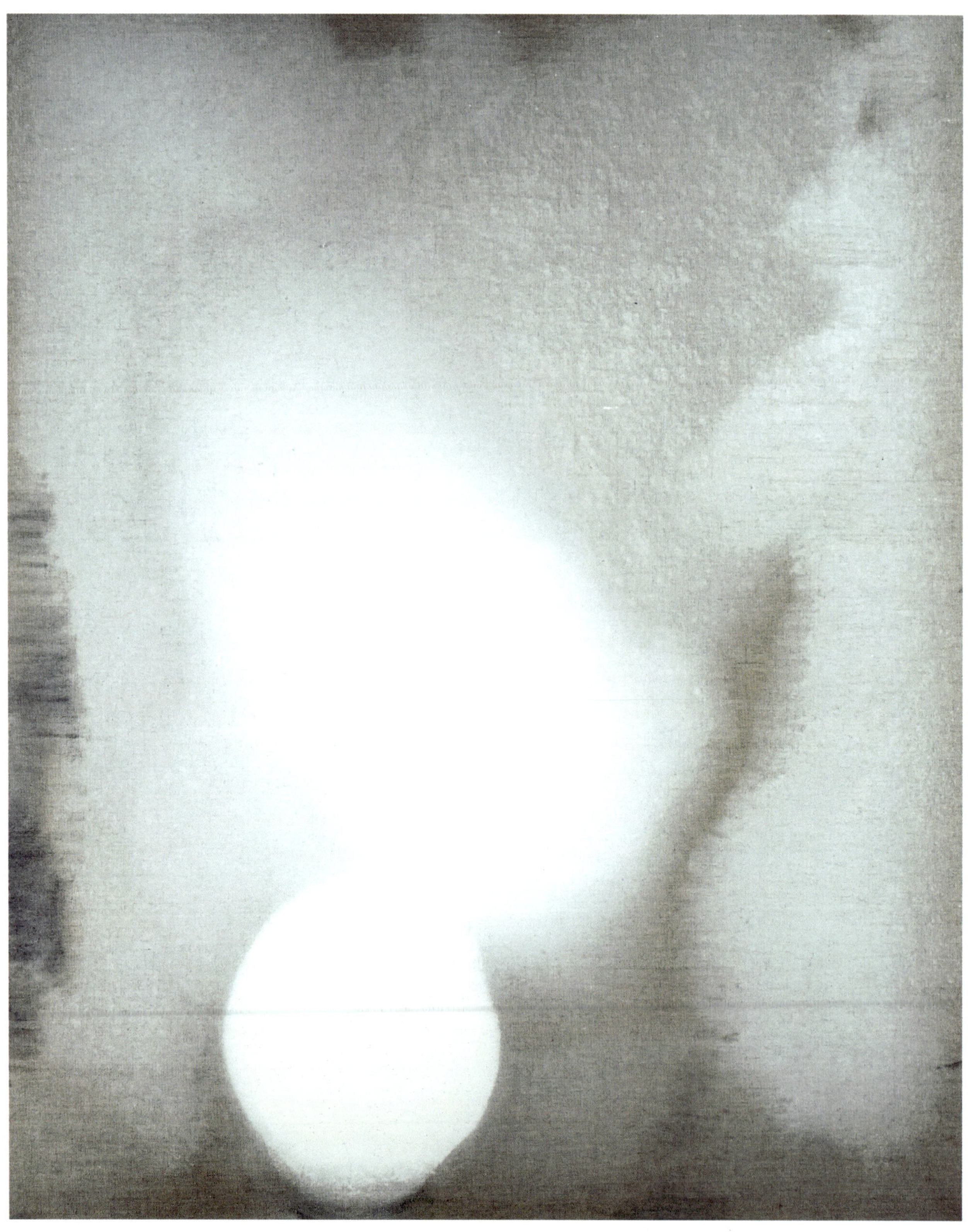

22-23 febbraio 2011, oil on canvas, 90×110 cm, Collezione Francescopiero Calzolari, Bologna

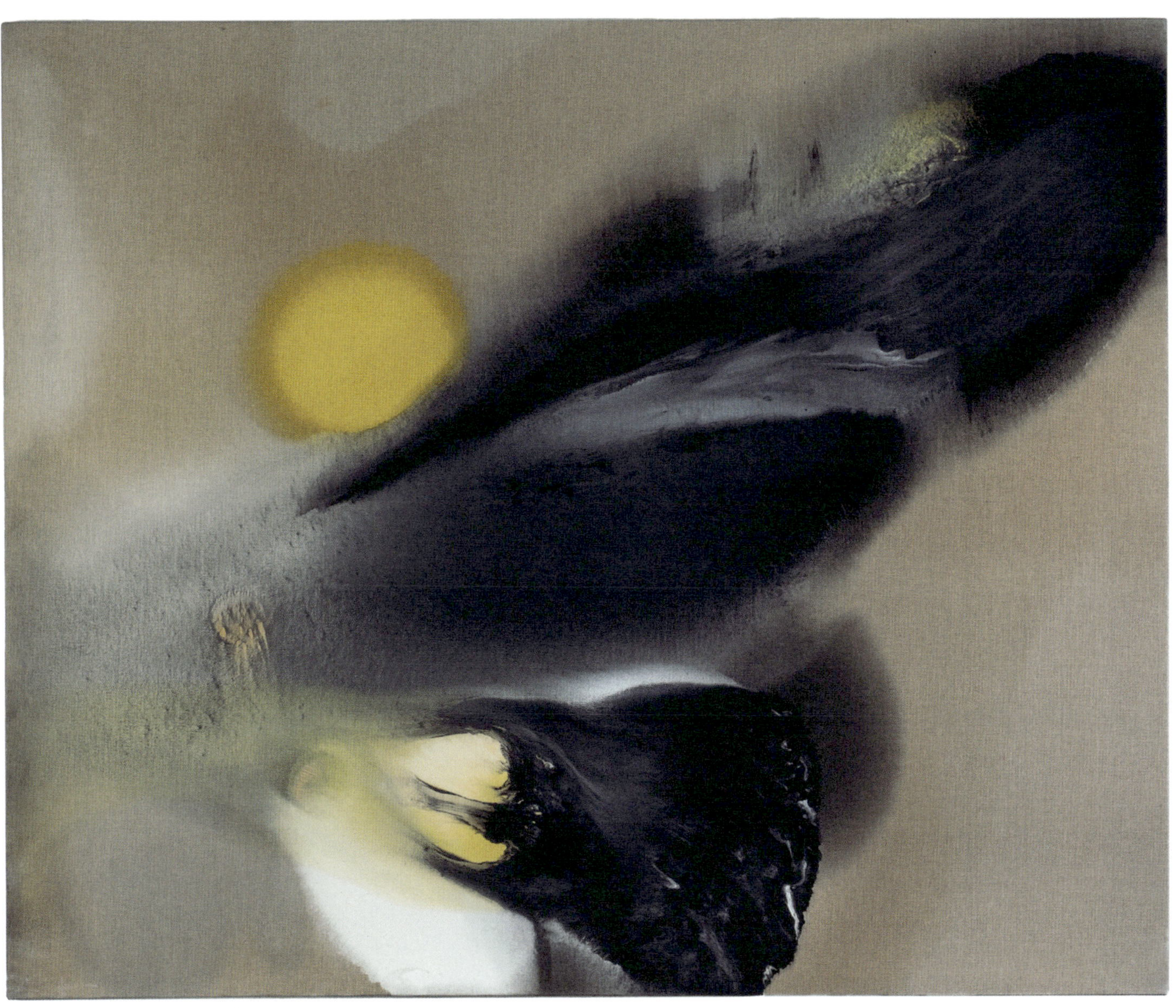

11 giugno 2011, oil on canvas, 110×90 cm, Collezione Francescopiero Calzolari, Bologna

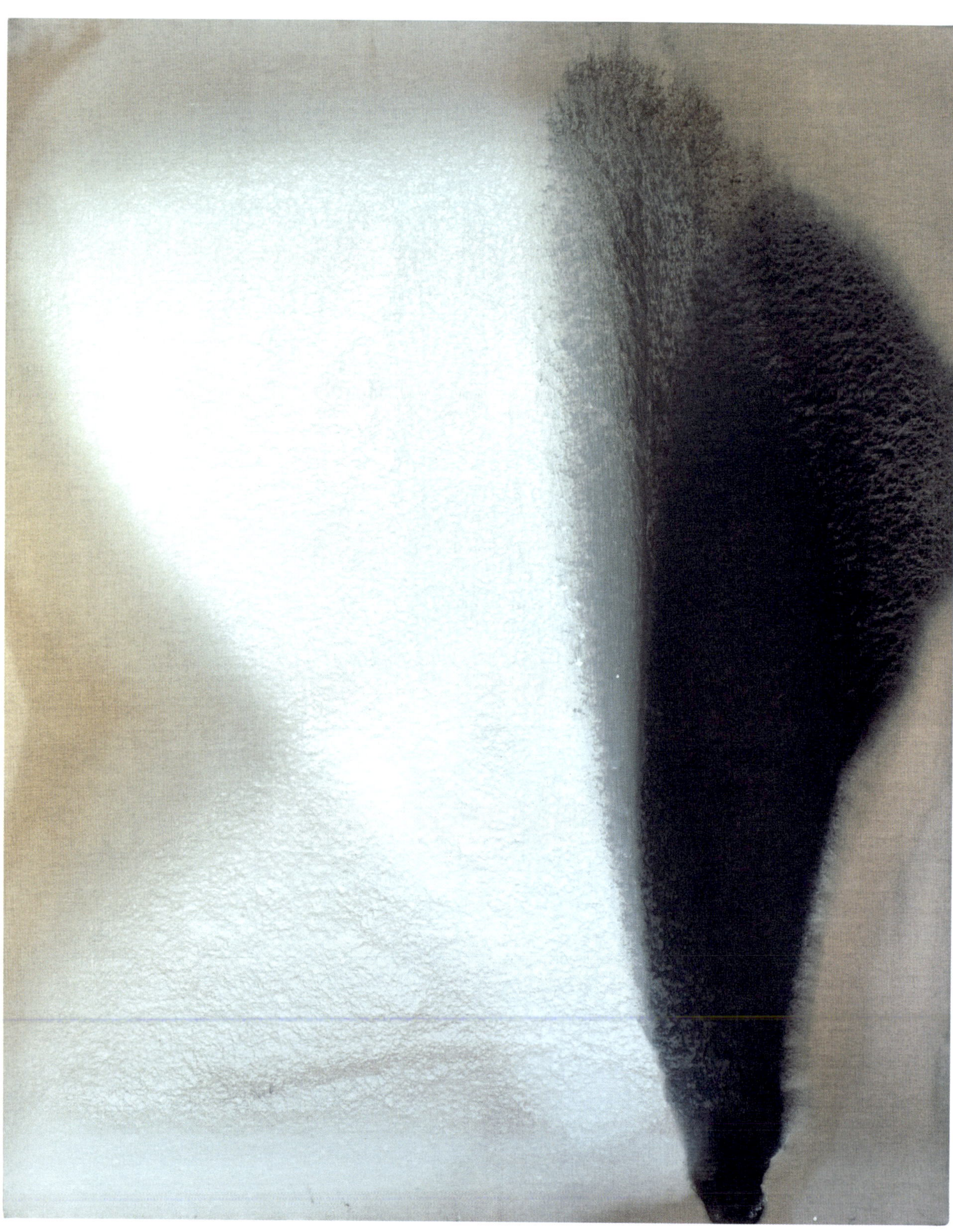

12 giugno 2011, oil on canvas, 110×90 cm, Collezione Francescopiero Calzolari, Bologna

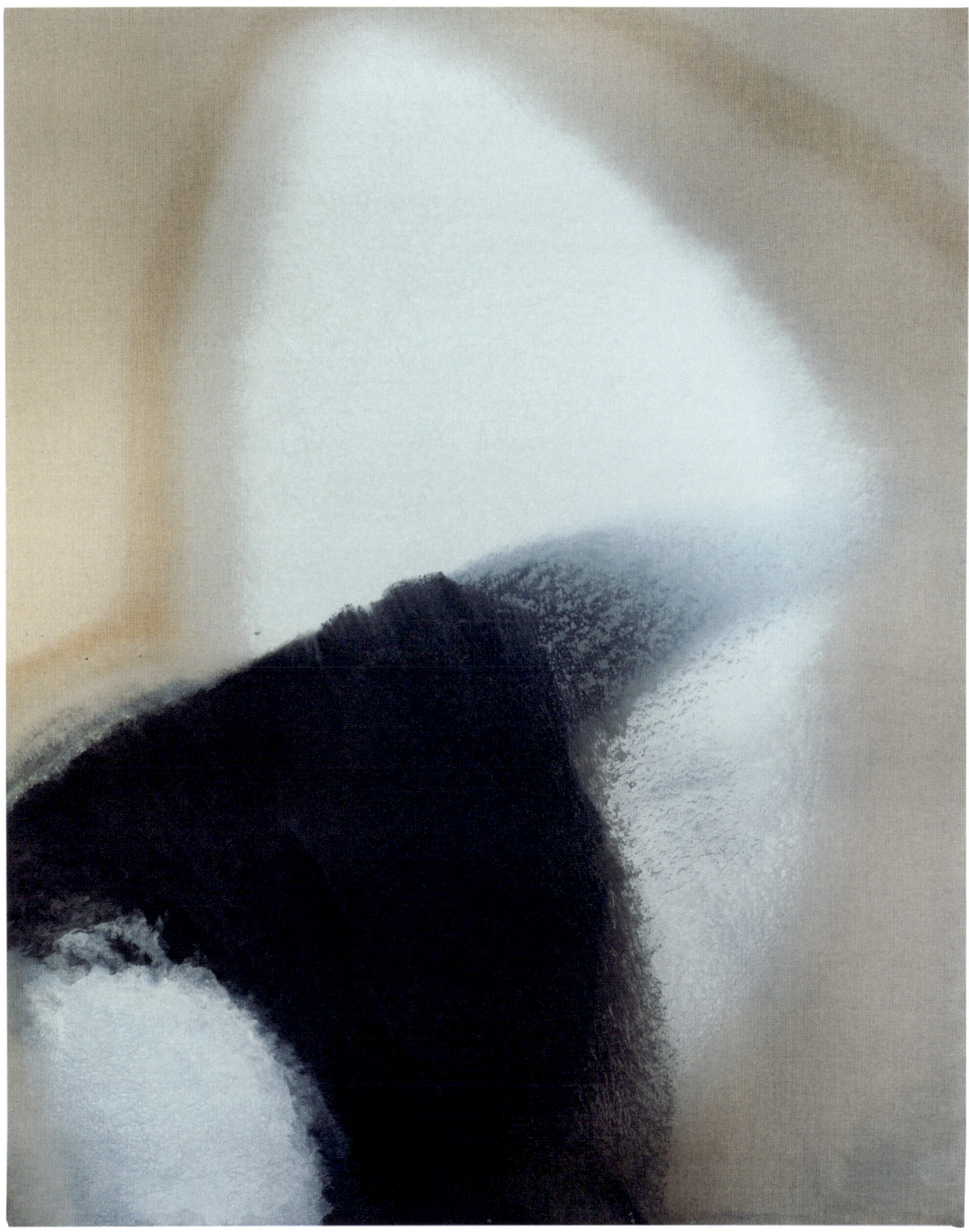

Angelo, 2012, oil on canvas, 110×90 cm, private collection, Rome

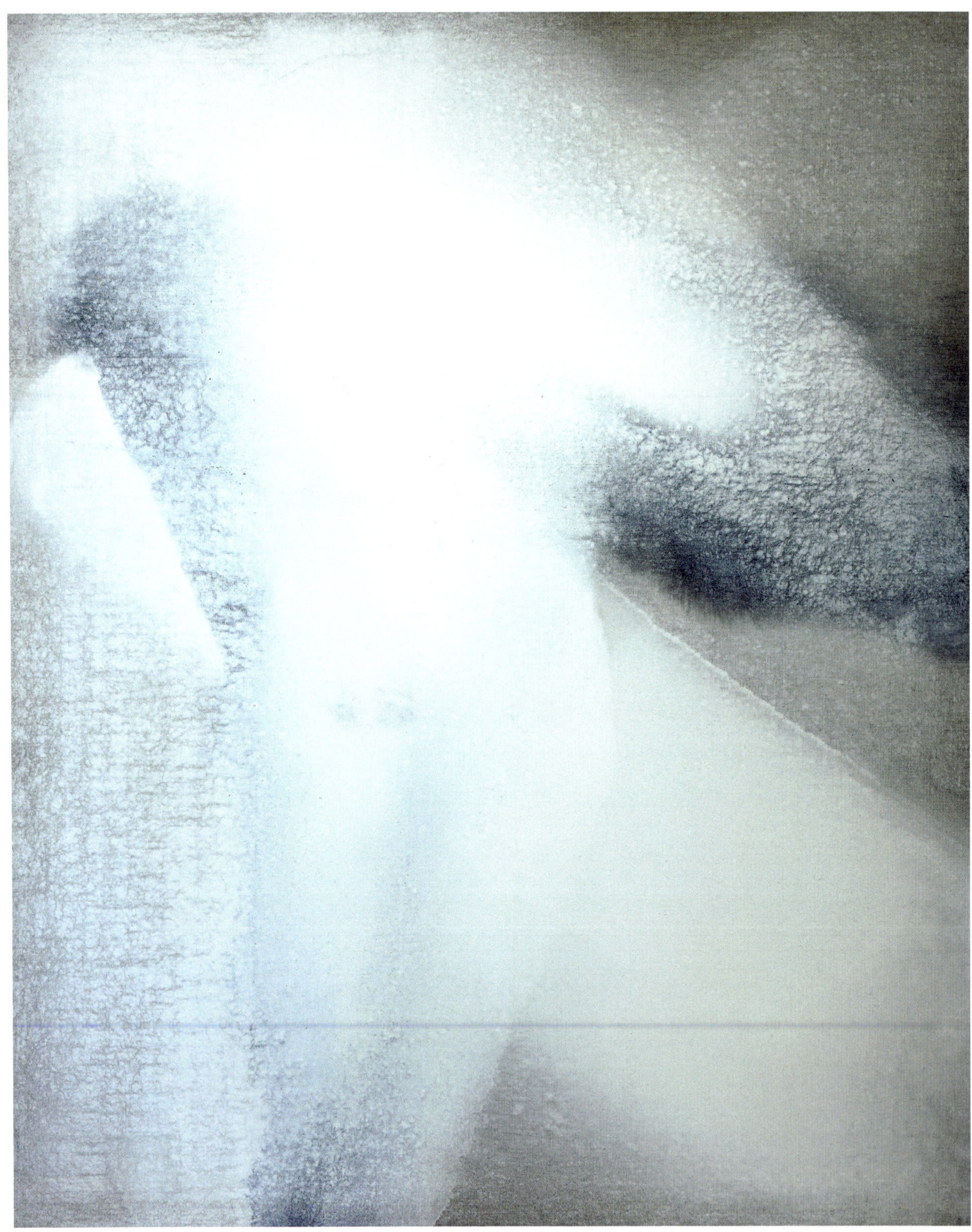

Series ALCHIMIA DELL'IMMAGINE

14 agosto 2004, oil on alluminium plate, 66×55 cm, private collection, Rome

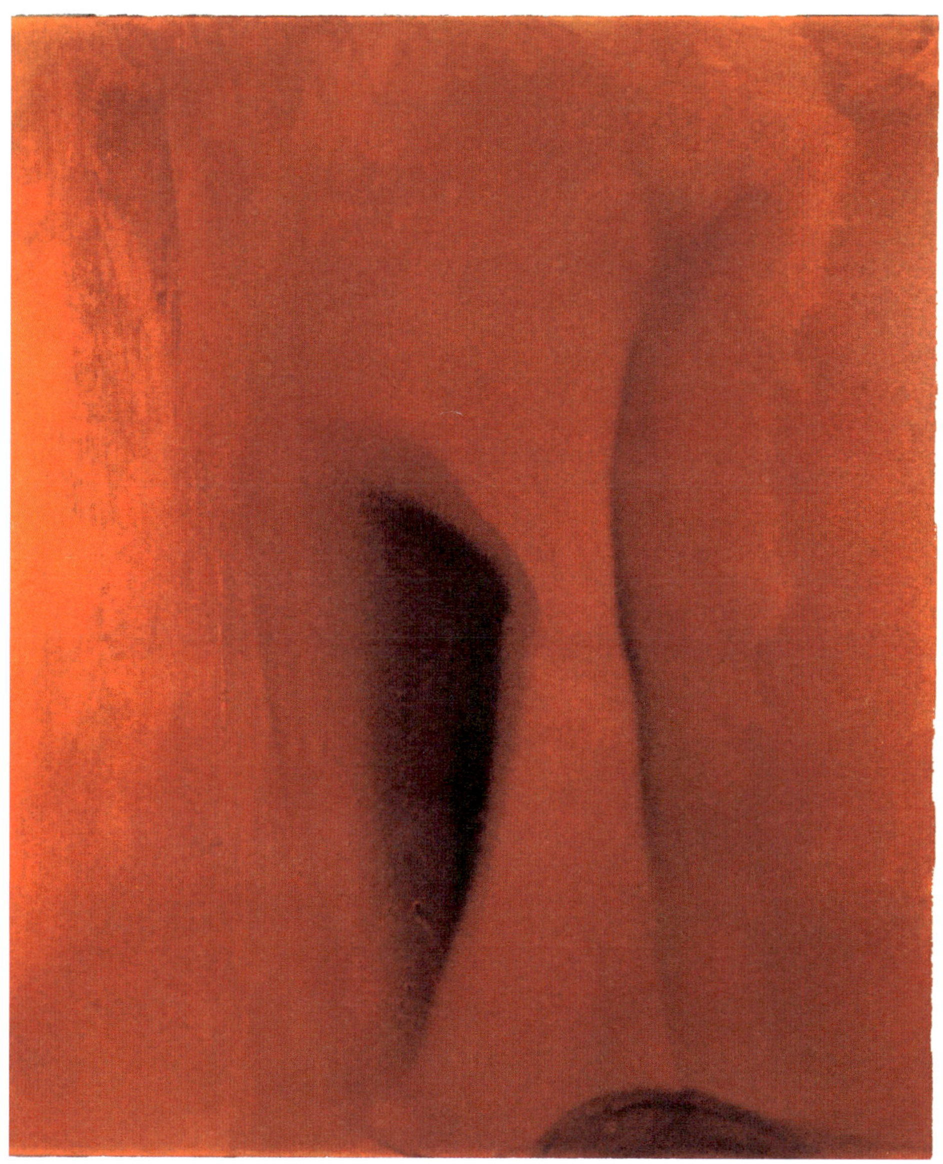

Series MALIA DELL'ENIGMA

Oscuro fremito (nascita), 2007, oil and tempera on canvas, 200×180 cm, private collection, Parma

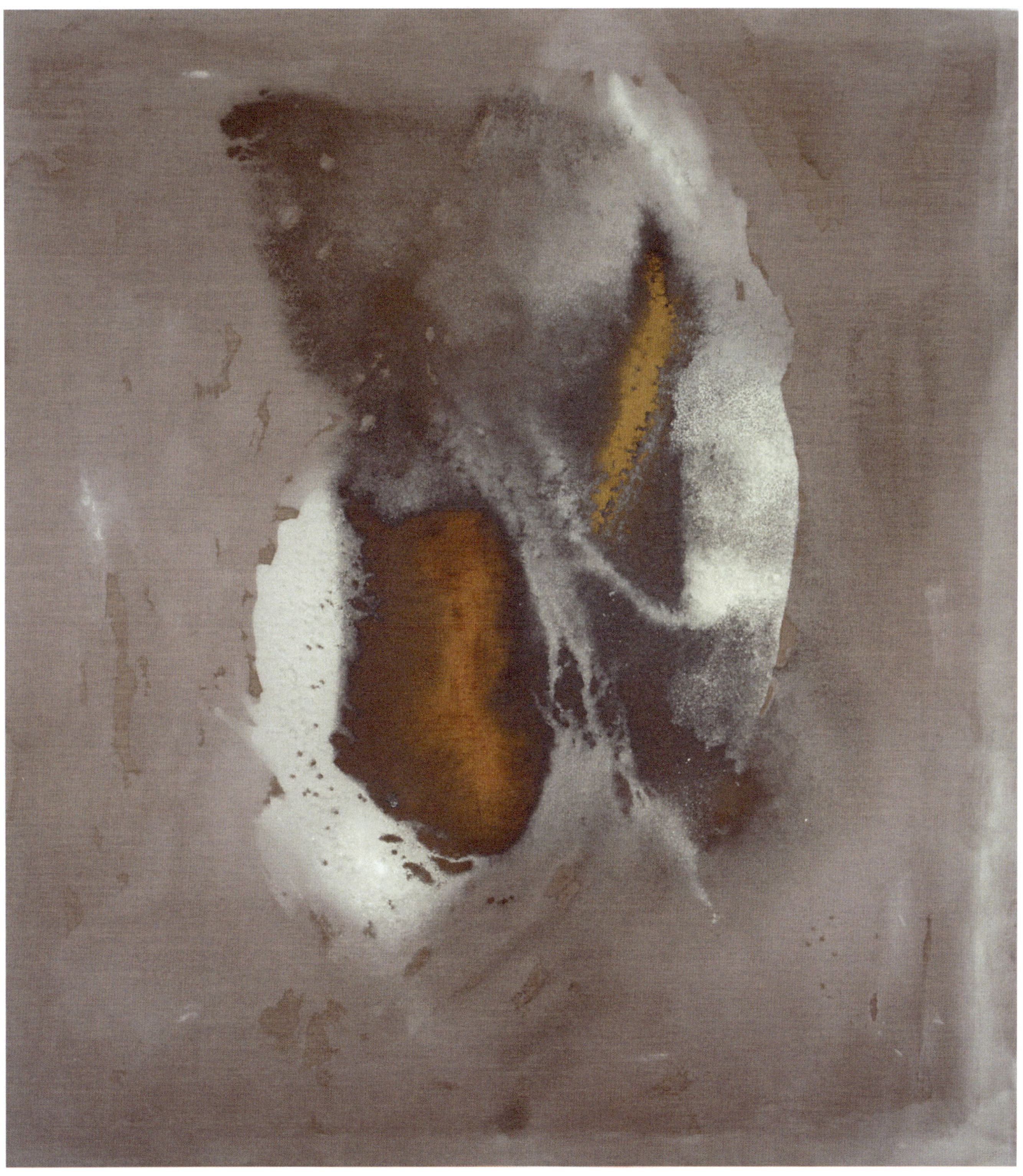

Bellezze dell'incontaminato (infanzia), 2007, acrylic tempera on canvas, 200×180 cm, private collection, Parma

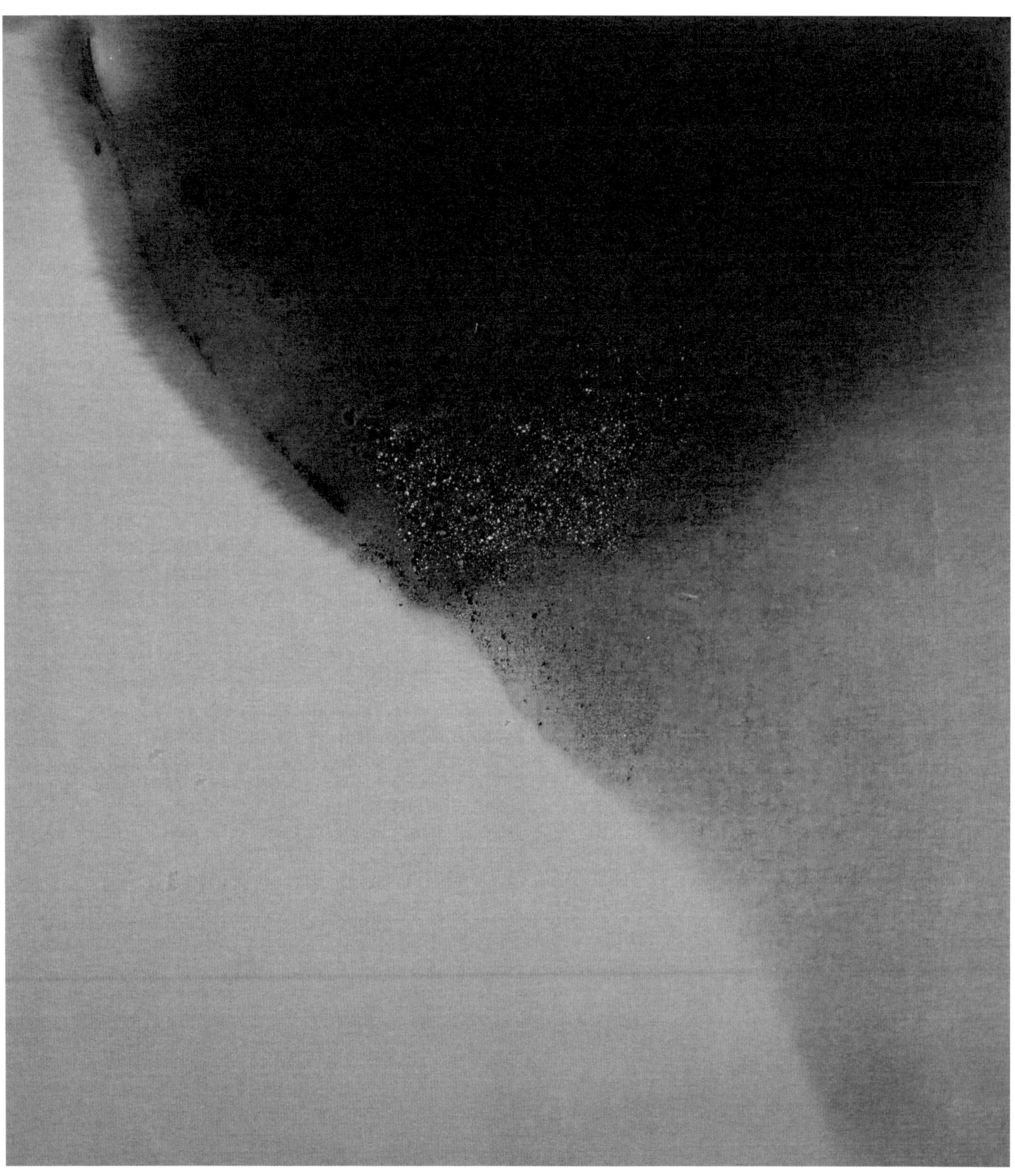

Malia dell'enigma (adolescenza), 2007, oil on canvas, 180×200 cm, private collection, Parma

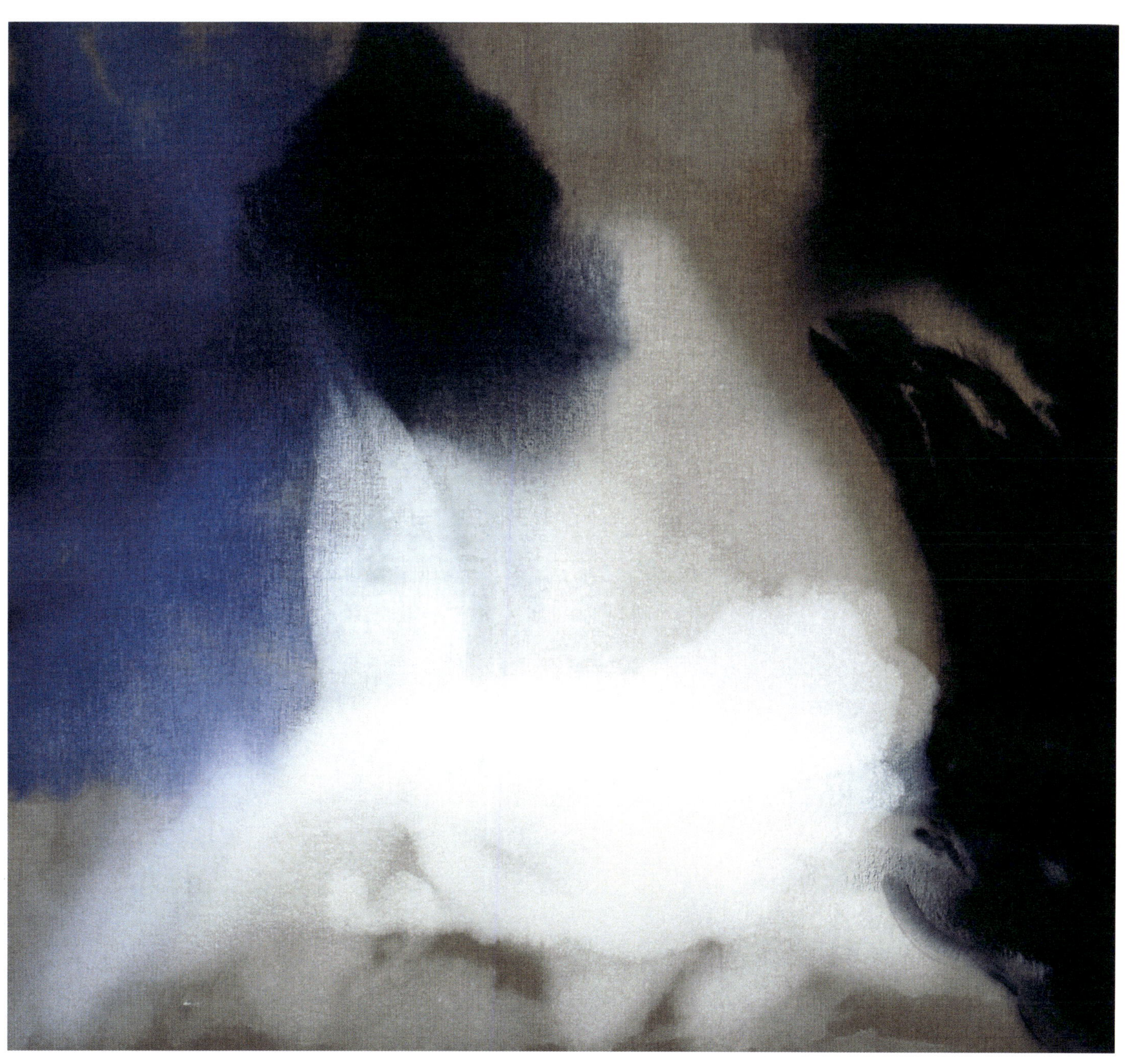

Fra il nulla e l'infinito (maturità), 2007, oil on canvas, 180×200 cm, private collection, Parma

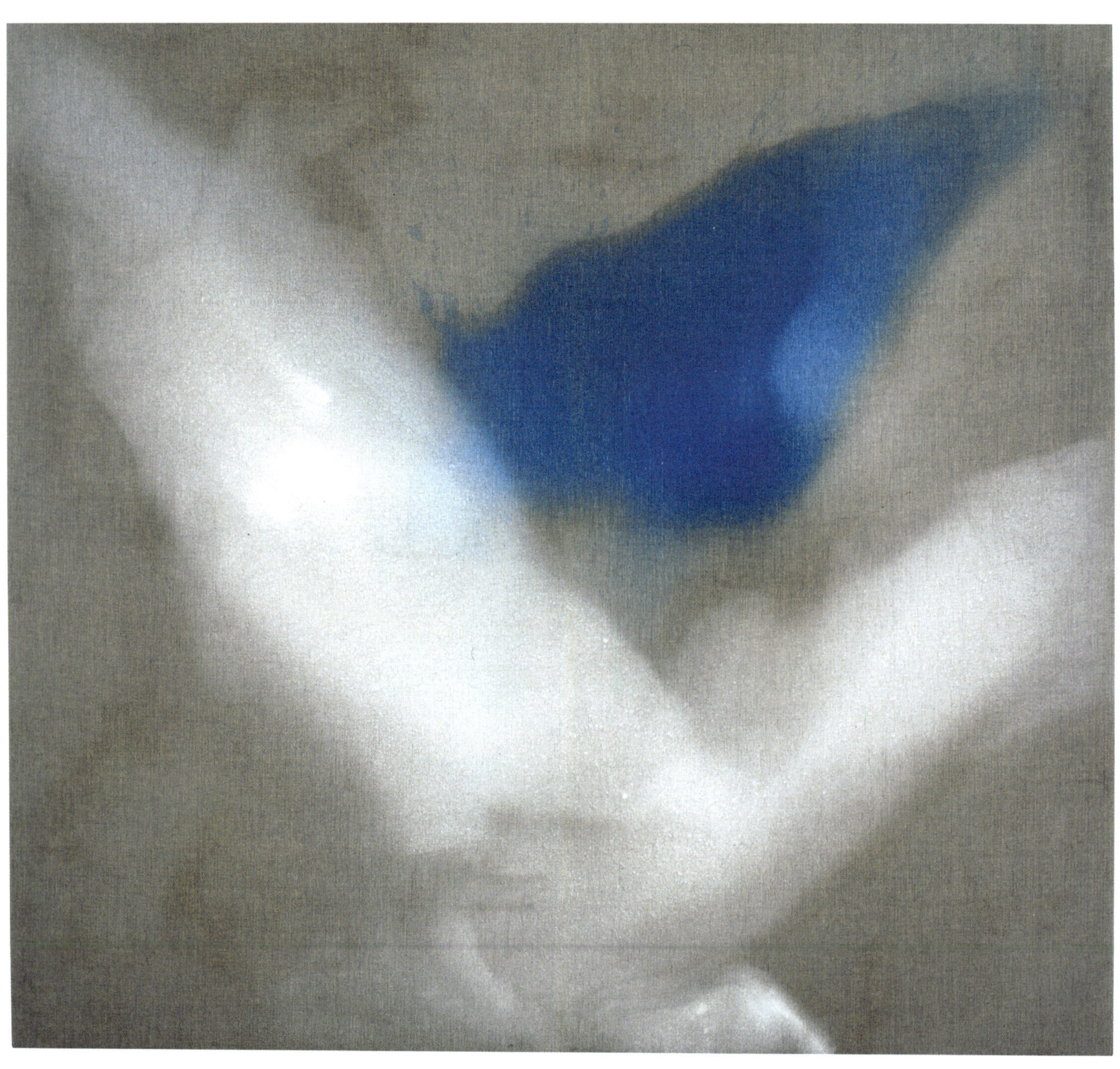

In attesa dell'ultima eclisse (vecchiaia), 2007, oil on canvas, 200×180 cm, private collection, Parma

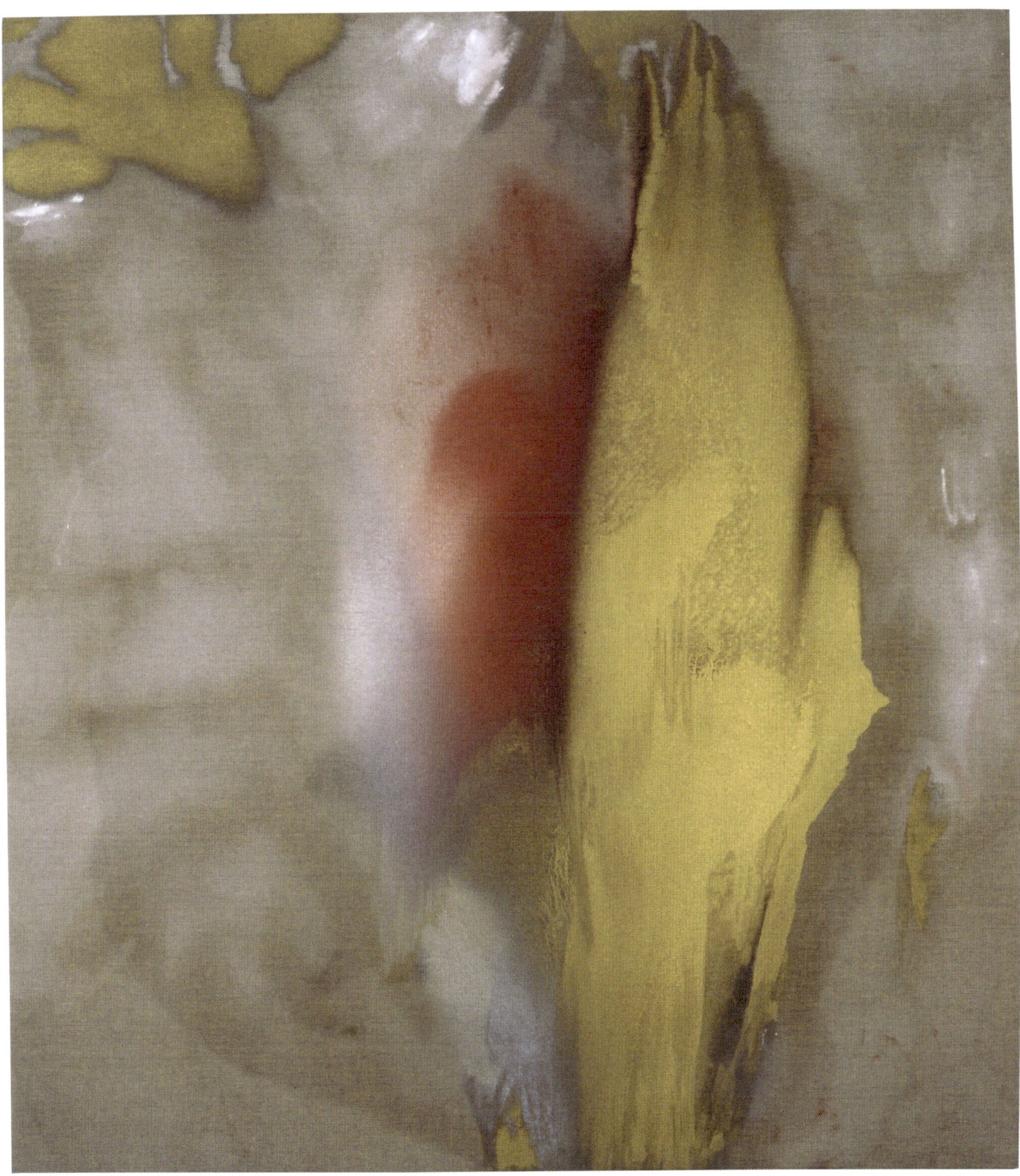

MEMORY OF THE FUTURE

Antonello Tolve

Memory as a place, as a building, as a sequence of columns, cornices, porticoes. The body inside the mind, as if we were moving around in there, going from one place to the next, and the sound of our footsteps as we walk, moving from one place to the next.
Paul Auster

Vasco Bendini's artistic path pivots on a dual investigative practice, favouring here the surface and the super-historical quality of mindfully metabolised masters, and there the energetic extroversion of the work into the world of life, almost seeking in its globality a sort of dialectical unity between aspects and elements perhaps at first sight conflicting. It is also a path marked by powerful intuitions, ferocious second thoughts and analyses that make constant recourse to a reality deconstructed on the keynote of reflection.

An initial period was linked to figures such as Virgilio Guidi, who was one of Bendini's teachers at the Accademia di Belle Arti di Bologna where he trained and was also able to contemplate stylistic leanings such as the twentieth-century atmospheres of Mario Sironi and Morandi's discreet crepuscularism. This was followed by an immediate addressing of the pictorial tools that channelled the thought along felicitously gestural paths connected to the strands of a vital and lively informality still in the full flush of its strenuous emergence as an international movement.

The teachings of Morandi and Guidi are evident in the "metaphysical rarefaction"[1] of youthful works such as *Colline* [Hills] (1942), *Alberi e case nella sera* [Trees and Houses in the Evening] (1942), *Dalla finestra* [From the Window] (1945), *Ritratto di ragazza* [Portrait of a Girl] (1945), *Sera* [Evening] (1946), *Villa Aldini* (1946), *Self-Portrait* (1946) or *Testa* [Head] (1947). As Italo Cinti commented at the time of the two-man show with Vigo Samorini: "Bendini is already possessed of a conspicuous autonomy vis-à-vis the real on which he clearly meditates in the greatest earnest, again in the footsteps of Guidi, a master to many, and in the wake of certain Giottoesque themes."[2] Such figures were never forgotten, but rather always remodelled–rethought, transformed–in line with an exquisitely personal sense of time. As early as 1950, these were followed by certain pioneering works where the marked abstract swerve and the adoption of an energetic gestural expression led the artist to arrive naturally in the prairies of the Informale. This was conceived as the site of a narration that does not lose sight of the figurative, but rather stylises bodies or faces using swift and reckless strokes, capricious thrusts and spins, leaps and darts engendered by what Silvio Giannelli brilliantly defined "automatic fantasy"[3]. While apparently akin to the swift, flying brushstroke of Franz Kline and other New Yorkers, albeit decidedly more cultured–Calvesi recalls that "1950 was a year of study, conducted mainly on Masaccio or, in freer exercises, on Matisse and Picasso"[4]–more serene, and aimed at the evocation of a face or a landscape, the works produced by Bendini from 1951 on are chromatic flayings of an "elementary expressionism"[5] that leaves the narrative task to just a few colours. Like vibrating splinters of colour, where a frothy and at times labyrinthine light points up the desire to proceed towards the dematerialisation, evanescence and spiritualisation of the image,[6] the works of the early 50s are indefinite, fast and fleeting forms, charged with cultural forces–for Bendini "culture seems to be a restless source of research, bordering on the abstract"[7]–which "even when they graze the abstract *seem to emerge artlessly from a fresh, tender area in which the forms rough themselves out, dissolve and recompose.*"

Bendini was mindful of Dorfles' sharp reprimands ("at the Bergamini I recall three young men: Bendini, Monducci, Feriani, whose praises I cannot sing but at most mention their names because their art is

1
M. Calvesi, "Nove casi della giovane pittura italiana", in *Commentari. Rivista di critica e storia dell'arte*, a. X, fasc. I, De Luca, Rome, January-March 1959, p. 48.

2
I. Cinti, *Pittori Vasco Bendini e Vigo Samorini*, catalog of the exhibition (Bologna, Palazzo Re Enzo, 30 May-8 June 1946), Bologna 1946.

3
S. Giannelli, "Bendini", in *Il Mattino dell'Italia Centrale*, 16 June 1953, p. 3.

4
M. Calvesi, Ibid., p. 48.

5
S. Giannelli, Ibid., p. 3.

6
On the idea of spiritualisation of the image see the short article by A. Bonsi, "Mostre d'arte", in *Il Giornale d'Italia*, 10 June 1953, p. 2.

7
S. Giannelli, Ibid., p. 3.

too enmeshed in outdated and obsolete ways, or too close to that of artists who are themselves already of little interest");[8] of the encouragements of Mario Radice ("it is highly likely that they can rapidly improve");[9] of the curt rebuke of Leonardo Borgese (products, trials and exercises that avoid the pictorial anacoluthon but "show a devout obedience to Guidi's luminous academy").[10] Then, at a double solo exhibition with Luciano Ferriani at the Galleria Bergamini in Milan, Virgilio Guidi introduced him, speaking of *a youth whose young painting aspires* "to be a function of time",[11] and Bendini himself focused in a short note on *the idea of a new reality*, conceived as a "powerful imaginative (and I don't mean fantastic) and rational seduction".[12] And so, the artist radically changed the tack of his research to a line that waived all didactic illustration or indication of the subject to enter the Gotha of the Informale as a star among stars.[13] Works such as *Inverno mediterraneo* [Mediterranean Winter] (1947-1948), *L'orto di Getsemani* [The Garden of Gethsemane] (1948) or *Siepe contro un muro* [Hedge against a Wall] (1948) now made way for massive psychographical agitations deposited on the canvas to create "reverberations of a long-nurtured meditation, proposing not conclusions or proven points but the pauses of silence that fall from it onto the moist layer of the senses."[14]

So, with the *Diluvi* [Floods] of 1951, which Arcangeli defined as "whirlwinds that I can barely recall, vexed black spirals that collapse in avalanche upon themselves",[15] Bendini launched a new programmatic challenge to art. Defined by Eugenio Riccomini as "definitely a most singular episode and hard to overlook",[16] this opened up to coeval European experiences, quickly latching onto the international muses and generating surprising rarefactions of form and shifts from a strictly representative atmosphere to an interior emotion–a lucidity of imprecision–made up of swift gestures, sudden swerves and radical derelictions of the figurative. Although in 1954 Arcangeli had placed him in the fold of a *late naturalism* that Turcato had defined as a pathetic Romantic compromise,[17] Bendini had by then scattered the clues of a poetics that was consolidated in a "decidedly material character",[18] more autonomous and extraordinarily original compared to the dominant artistic climate. In effect, after a brief period of closeness to the idea launched by Arcangeli, Bendini turned to a mental rhythm: the narrative level made way for an abrasion of the form and *the sign of abstract nature merged with the traces of a reality evoked by memory*. "With the decanting of naturalism into the Informale, the image returns to the surface central and coordinated in its nucleus of light, following a vibration that becomes entirely inner to the matter and from extensive becomes intensive, from atmospheric introspective" to the point of thickening "against the transparency of the ground" where "clots and blobs" play, pursuing tangles of vibrant signs.[19]

Bendini thus entered the vast horizon of European thought and, as Calvesi so perspicaciously observed, we should recall that this entry into the Informale was of the artist's own making, not "an acquisition from outside, but an ancient, connatural and solitary departure, a complex and personal root."[20] After this the artist was finally able to liberate and extend his own pictorial temperament, by now fully mature and open to the *Bezirke* of the Informale, albeit without following trends or keeping pace with the times, but rather to unravel *strand by strand a dense eddy subtly rippled by lights and shadows*. "Images that are not dreamt but rather dramatically investigated, as if it were always and only the imprint of his own face or his own soul that was to be recognised in that delicate chaos of impasto."[21]

8
G. Dorfles, "Pittura a Milano", in *Europeo*, 15 October 1947, p. 26.

9
M. Radice, "Mostre d'arte", in *L'Italia*, 12 October 1947, p. 7.

10
L. Borgese, "Mostre d'arte", in *Corriere della Sera*, 26 October 1947, p. 9.

11
V. Guidi, in *Vasco Bendini / Luciano Ferriani*, catalog of the exhibition (Galleria Bergamini, Milan, 26 February-10 March 1949), Tipografia S.A.B, Bologna 1949.

12
Ibid.

13
On this variegated and complex season of painting see A. Zevi, "L'informale italiano: continuità o rottura?", in *Peripezie del dopoguerra nell'arte italiana*, Einaudi, Turin 2005, pp. 93-130.

14
M. Calvesi, Ibid., p. 48.

15
F. Arcangeli, in *Vasco Bendini*, catalog of the exhibition (Milan, Galleria del Milione, January 1958); now also in F. Arcangeli, *Dal Romanticismo all'Informale*, Einaudi, Turin 1977, p. 506.

16
E. Riccomini, "Vasco Bendini", in *La Città. Rivista bimestrale di lettere e arti*, no. 4-5, October 1964, p. 65.

17
See A. Basaldella, in L. Venturi, *Pittori italiani d'oggi*, De Luca, Rome 1956, pp. 93-94.

18
R. Pasini, "L'ultimo naturalismo e la situazione a Bologna negli anni Cinquanta", in L. Caramel (ed.), *Arte in Italia. 1945-1960*, Vita e Pensiero, Milan 1994, p. 192.

19
M. Calvesi, Ibid., p. 50.

20
Ibid., p. 49.

21
Ibid., p. 50.

22
R. Barilli, in *Bendini*, catalog of the exhibition (Rome, L'Attico, February 1961); now also in R. Barilli, *Informale Oggetto Contemporaneo. Volume primo. La ricerca artistica negli anni '50 e '60 (1Z979)*, Feltrinelli, Milan 2006, p. 202.

While over the course of the 50s the palette became delicate and the face gradually defleshed, at the beginning of the 60s Bendini's poetics became more intense, displaying what Renato Barilli in 1961 called an "inexhaustible variation"[22] and demonstrating the power of a reflection that not only shuns all labels but also renders visible the urgency of the future, to the point of intuiting new paths and making him a precursor of discourses and routes, modes and trends.

Presented by Calvesi in room 36 at the 32nd Venice Biennale, Bendini sought to map out a clear itinerary conceived to rupture the Informale coagulum that he now felt to be too limiting. Alongside *Esperienza prima* [First Experience] of 1961, the *Segni segreti* [Secret Signs] of 1962 and the various *Ipotesi ultime* [Ultimate Hypotheses] of 1963 –the works on display started from 1956 and Calvesi stressed the resurfacing of memorial elements, of a "mysticism of silence" of "musical lacerations" and "a vague, distanced face, marked halfway by a long, sloping groove or by a hemispheric passage of light"[23]–the artist was very keen to display his most recent research that radically shifted the needle of the compass to what there could be for him after the *Informale*. In works such as *Ester*, *Oggi* [Today] or *Men-Made Paradise* (rejected by the 32nd Venice Biennale) the mind of the artist rides and overrides his time to sneak a look at a new creative opening, and close scrutiny shows the strong connections these works display between the dregs of the Informale, Pop and visual poetry. As Riccomini rightly stressed, "Bendini is one of the artists most ready to catch on the wing the shifting moods of the international muses."[24] He was indeed ready to give life to new adventures of form and matter that would bring him–through *Senso operante* [Operating Faculty] and *Sentimento come storia* [Feeling as History] executed approximately starting from 1965–to an extraordinary new breakthrough in his work.

23
M. Calvesi, *Vasco Bendini*, in catalog of the 32nd Biennale Internazionale d'Arte, (Venice, 20 June-18 October 1964), p. 101.

24
E. Riccomini, Ibid., p. 64.

The developments of this period might be seen as a reply to the linguistic surges brought into play by the New Dada, but on closer analysis Bendini was actually following a personal, creatively auxological, route that allowed him to pioneeringly push beyond the boundaries of painting: we should not forget that the work *Tre soggetti* [Three Subjects] dates to 1964. So, in the mid-60s Bendini ruptured the fixity of the painting, unseating representation to shift the axis to presentation: the gesture and crinkle of the painting become alternative behaviour,[25] relocation to a broader field that shatters the canvas to open up to the real space, amidst tangible objects, where the observer is no longer merely contemplative, but activated, transformed into a catalyst and witness of the event. It was indeed precisely in 1966, at the time of an unforgettable show at the Studio Bentivoglio in Bologna, that the sense of research and experimentation led him towards spaces that appear to welcome thought and presence: that go beyond painting and willingly address the framework of reality, with all the physicality of objects (silent, impenetrable, once again metaphysical and familiar) and of spectators, conceived as actors functional to setting the work in motion.

25
See at least A. Bonito Oliva, *Il territorio magico. Comportamenti alternativi nell'arte*, Centro Di, Florence 1971; new edition S. Chiodi (ed.), Le Lettere, Florence 2009.

So, at the crossroads between Via delle Moline and Via delle Belle Arti, Bendini launched his new research, "along with the younger Pier Paolo Calzolari, his pupil, and Nino Ovan, who had moved from Friuli to Venice to study art, soon to be joined by Maurizio Mazzoli and Bruno Pasqualini."[26] This not only offered the observers what Argan called "a tool", "also giving them the instructions for use", making the "direct and personal intervention of the observer indispensable,"[27] but also mapped out primary routes that showed and demonstrated an attentive shift from the face of painting to that of reality. Indeed if–as astutely noted by Renato Barilli–all those paintings made by Bendini over a good ten years always and obsessively represented a contracted or a dilated face, starting from *Cos'è* [What it is] (1966)

26
P. Fameli, "Fatti dello Studio Bentivoglio", in *Intrecci d'arte*, no. 4, 2015, p. 74.

27
G. C. Argan, in *Vasco Bendini*, catalog of the exhibition (Rome, Galleria Senior, Palazzo Taverna, November-December 1968) Istituto Grafico Tiberino, Rome 1968.

the measure and yardstick is the real body, the pitiless *topia*, the face with all its lineaments and its mutability.

The mixed techniques that Bendini adopted in this period are taken to a stage where things are conceived as objects, bodies, imprints, real matter, tongues of light and drools of colour. They register not only the climate of the time but also the artist's lucid analysis of the artistic and aesthetic dynamics of his own pulsating present.

The experiences of the years 1966-1968[28] are all connected with a fundamental question, accompanied by a reflection of Maurice Merleau-Ponty: Bendini wants to grasp "the point of synchronisation" of the interaction and aims to "visualise the field of harmony existing between myself and others." "No sooner has my gaze fallen upon a living body in the process of acting than the objects surrounding it immediately take on a new layer of significance: they are no longer simply what I myself could make of them, they are what this other pattern of behaviour is about to make of them. " Therefore, the artist finds *in the body of the other* almost "an extension of itself and its intentions", "like two minds that have found a common, though indirect, way of communicating."[29]

Bendini was ahead of the aesthetic climate of his time in being a precursor of experiences connected with space and with the object, in exactly the same way that Toti Scialoja distinctly anticipated the work of Jasper Johns and Robert Rauschenberg, or Giuseppe Uncini who, with his *Terre*, his *Cementarmati*, *Ferrocementi*, *Strutture spazio* and *Mattoni* kept the following generations in check. From 1966 Bendini proposed a linguistic geography that radically shifted the axis to "practices of exploration and aesthetic re-elaboration of the environment, performative actions and conceptual redefinitions of reality"[30].

Works such as *Cestino* [Basket], *Ciotola* [Bowl], *Icone* [Icon], *Urna votiva* [Votive Urn], *Ombre prime* [First Shadows], *A memoria di gesso* [In Memory of Plaster], *Polvere e plastica* [Dust and Plastic], *La tavolozza* [The Palette], *Due metri cubi di silenzio* [Two Square Metres of Silence], *Cassa d'ignoto* [Coffin of an Unknown Person], *Come è* [As It Is], *Quattro soggetti* [Four Subjects] and *La scatola U* [The U Box] of 1966 are outright relational devices which, along with *Cabina solare* [Solar Cabin], *Ruota*, [Wheel], *A Johnson*, *PAD* and *Per una essudazione totale* [For a Total Exudation] dating to the following year–*Contenitori* [Containers], *Resina di cielo* [Resin from Heaven] and *Una delle duemila parole* [One of the Two Thousand Words] are from 1968, while *La sorgente* [The Source] dates to 1969–authentically represent seminal projects "of a new opening towards the *environment*, like those that the young Calzolari was to test in his wake. The object, icon of the consumer society, the society of having, was by now a limit to be overcome though the retaliation of being: the need to establish a stronger contact with the world, a more direct relation with the environment, and hence to test the relational dimension is increasingly noticeable. This is the direction of the works displayed by Bendini in September 1967 at the Studio Bentivoglio, some of which had already been shown in Venice in 1966. For instance, *Come è* and *Senso operante* engage the individual visitor, invited to enter what Scardovi defined as 'toilettes of the ego', consisting of chairs placed in front of bare frames with a microphone ready to record the voices and sounds, with the aim of fostering moments of reflection on the existential question, becoming aware of oneself and triggering an apperceptive process. Maurizio Calvesi saw this clearly, claiming that such works 'produce a parenthesis in the flow of our experience and our perceptive activity, forcing it to fall back on the only object that is always excluded: ourselves'"[31].

Exactly when Michelangelo Pistoletto was creating his newspaper *Sphere*, the over-neglected Ugo Marano was organising his iron sculptures (1966-1967) and Pino Pascali was proposing his December *Nuove sculture* at the L'Attico gallery (1966), Vasco Bendini was charting a new path in Bologna. While on the one hand this anticipated the Milanese and Roman experiences–Eliseo Mattiacci's *Tubo* [Tube] dates to 1967–on the other it

28
On this precise moment of his artistic activity, see *Vasco Bendini. 1966-1967*, G. Simongini (ed.), catalog of the exhibition (Rome, Macro Museo d'Arte Contemporanea, 28 February-5 May 2013) Quodlibet, Macerata 2013.

29
V. Bendini, "Cerchio supremo" (1986), in *Vasco Bendini. Opere 1950-2006*, catalog of the exhibition (Florence, Galleria Frittelli Arte Contemporanea, 10 February-31 March 2007) Centro d'Arte Spaziotempo, Florence / Carlo Cambi Editore, Siena 2007, p. 83

30
P. Fameli, Ibid., p. 74.

31
Ibid., p. 78.

pointed the way for the young Bologna artists: "the older artist has to be given the merit for having played in advance all along the line from conceptualism to behaviourism, since already in 1966 he had conceived and produced" contextual and highly connective works, some of them left only in the larval stage as generic notes. One instance is *Altalena a due* [Swing for Two], "safim edgeboards for the steel framework of an open room 4x4x3, two swings in the centre, synchronisation of the oscillation of the swings via metronome and a light source that strikes the observer, the 4 square metres of the base covered with a layer of sand of around ten centimetres, a light atomised cloud of water sprays over those using the swing, who are given a transparent raincoat, room in semi-darkness."[32]

Bendini was rightly defined as a trailblazer of Arte Povera, and Renato Barilli in his account of the modern numbered him among the most brilliant artists to be attributed the true and noble paternity of the movement. Barilli also states that Bendini can be compared to Beuys and that "the example of the mature post-Informale artist was decisive for the debut of his then very young fellow citizen Pier Paolo Calzolari, in turn connected with other young artists who collectively managed the Palazzo Bentivoglio space."[33] Vasco Bendini remains a sophisticated and emblematic figure, a reserved and curious man whose research always pushed beyond his own time.

In the early 1970s–for instance in the works displayed at the Venice Biennale of 1972, including important multimaterial compositions from the *Gesto e materia* [Gesture and Matter] cycle–he returned to the bodily gesture, again transposing behaviour (and time) into the grammatical space of the painting and to pondering the writing of the self: the two works *Io che guardo* [I looking] and *Io che cammino* [I walking] date to 1970. In 1973, the year he moved to Rome, alongside bodies that petrify and materially stiffen elements of nature, he also returned to painting and its interior aspects. Dating to this period are the room at the X Quadriennale Nazionale d'Arte in Rome (1973), the important solo shows at the Institute of Art History of the University of Parma (1973), in the Sala Comunale of Alessandria (1973), the Museum of Modern Art of Saarbrucken (1976) and the Galleria d'Arte Moderna of Bologna (1978).

As Paolo Fossati declared in 1984, Bendini "was a key figure in the artistic events from the end of WW2 onwards".[34] In the works of the 80s and 90s, as indeed of the years between 2000 and 2015 up to the erasure of the word end from the finale, he carried out a compact and fairly disillusioned review of his entire past, from the great intuitions of the 50s and 60s to the clear experiments of reproducing on the canvas the silence (memory) of a face or a voice. In the presentation written for an unforgettable show at Fabio Sargentini's L'Attico gallery, Emilio Villa dwells on this:

"It is on the borders of the colours that the spectrum of memory emanates; it is memory that dares, without body and references, to become body and limbs, that flourish and interrupt, warped, transferred, and therefore in action, the branches of memory. It establishes itself as the habitat, as architecture, as the urn of the laceration and the flow of horizons, genealogy of savoured and deliberated areas, captured in accents, in timbres, in beats, in modules, in neumes, in *numina*"[35].

Filiberto Menna spoke of the artist walking continuously backwards in the time of his own existence,[36] and while Bendini's work is at times explicitly pioneering, at other times it is filtered by a nostalgic contemplative vision that appears to go back and regenerate the lessons of the past, understood as "infinite conversations" of the pictorial language, left suspended, open to the openness of the spectator's hallucination as a trace, remote imprint or poetic reconstruction of a face, of a void full of absences and fadings, of presences. All of Bendini's work, at least all the work that returns to the clarity of the surface from the

32
V. Bendini, "Appunti generali", in *Vasco Bendini.*

33
R. Barilli, "Arte povera", in *L'arte moderna*, no. 170, 1975, p. 70.

34
P. Fossati, "Foglietto per Vasco", in *Vasco Bendini. Sette stanze - un giardino*, catalog of the exhibition (Mantua, Casa del Mantegna, July-September 1984); now also in *Vasco Bendini. Opere 1950-2006*, p. 268.

35
E. Villa, "Apertura vocale per alto sigillo", in *Vasco Bendini. Stabilità dell'instabile/ memoria del futuro/ memorie*, catalog of the exhibition (Rome, Galleria L'Attico, 18 April-9 May 1980) Esse Arte, Rome 1980.

36
F. Menna, in *Bendini*, catalog of the exhibition (Rome, Galleria Senior, April 1967).

Trittico (21 June 2013, 1 of 3), 2013, oil on canvas, 110×90 cm, private collection, Rome

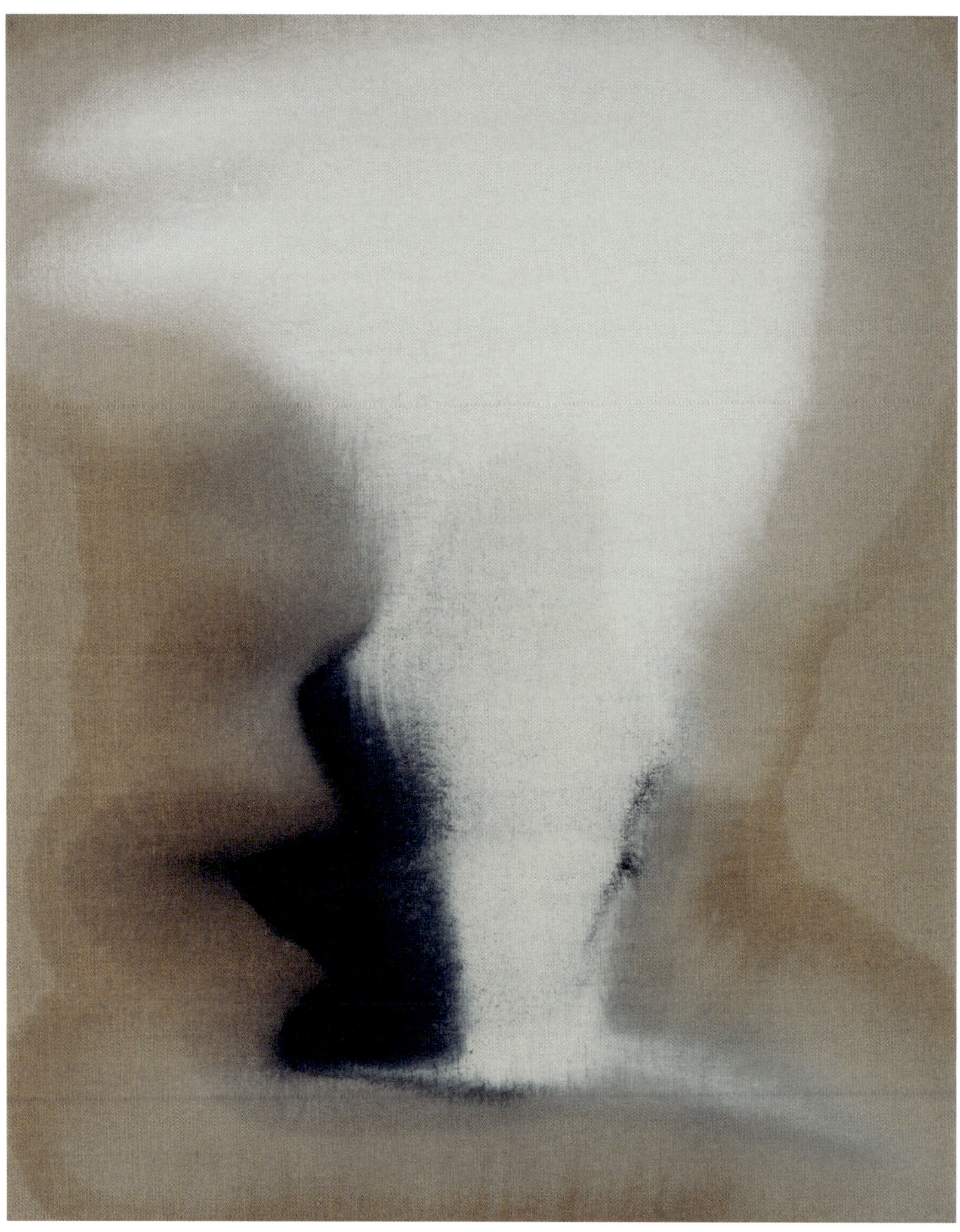

second half of the 70s–the 1981 series *Alchimia dell'immagine* [Alchemy of the Image], *Segni come sogni* [Signs as Dreams] of 1989, the series *Inquieti silenzi* [Troubled Silences] of 1995-1998, that of *Memoria del futuro* [Memory of the Future] in 2004 and *L'immagine accolta* [The Welcomed Image] of 2006-2008, as well as the numerous *Untitled*s down the years–reshuffle the cards of painting to bring out its strength, its being a mental act, rhythm of thought that thinks itself, place of slow and lucid reflection (of *luce lenta*)[37], stability of the unstable and psychic archetype[38], meadow of the mind, idea of the gesture and of the idea, homeland of consciousness and knowledge, pleasure in which the form is achieved every instant, perpetually ongoing in its warm interweaving of matter and manual memory.

"When I paint I abandon myself completely to what I am gradually doing. Just a few basic things happen in sequence: choice of the size of support, the quality of the surface, the colouring materials, the impastos, the tools, of where to spread the coats, the quantity of material and so on. All this with both restraint and fervour, assessing each aspect in the order and direction of my vital impulses. In this way I realise that my psychic process materialises, that my psyche lives in the matter, or rather with the matter. Thinking, feeling, is doing."[39]

37
See T. Trini (ed.), "luceLenta della cognizione", in *Vasco Bendini. luceLenta*, catalog of the exhibition (Florence, Galleria Frittelli Arte Contemporanea, 4 October-6 December 2008) Spaziotempo Centro d'arte, Florence/ Carlo Cambi Editore, Siena 2008.

38
See V. Bendini, "La pittura si immagina", in *Vasco Bendini. Venti disegni erotici (1956-1984) con una dichiarazione poetica*, catalog of the exhibition (Mantua, Galleria Gianluigi Arcari, 18 June-18 October 1986), Gianluigi Arcari Editore, Mantua 1986, p. 6.

39
Ibid., p. 5.

BUT. ON AN UNFINISHED PHRASE OF VASCO BENDINI

Irene Santori*

*Chair of the Libera Associazione-Archivio Vasco Bendini

First, let me confess my trepidation about having to make room, in just a few lines, for something that defies placement. "Placing" an artist is in itself already a most daring venture—and one that's not up to me. It becomes downright perilous when you're addressing the work of a master in whom congruent opposites secretly come to the surface, impact of a meteoric diachrony; ancestral and future condensations, exhumations and gestations, precipitates. Moreover, the attempt to "place" this manifestation looms over its direct or indirect witnesses, but any manoeuvre aimed at alignment or ordering must start by admitting its own inadequacy. When all this erupts weirdly into the most private life of an individual, no bulkhead can withstand it. When the master bursts into your home, no blueprint is proof against it, no truly load-bearing wall can bear it, can bear the paintings, no nail can nail them.

This is my encounter with Vasco Bendini: I hung my walls on his paintings.

I got to know Vasco about twenty years ago, and I first met him at his house in Parma where he lived with Marcella and his mother-in-law Alma. My husband and I went to buy a painting, the first, the beginning of what was to become a collection.

There were many works to choose from and we selected a painting from 2001 measuring two metres by two, before even knowing the title, which was for me both revealing and paradigmatic: *Nell'insidia della soglia*. This is also the title of the 1990 Italian translation of a book of poetry by the great French poet Yves Bonnefoy, *Dans le leurre du seuil*.

The point is, not that I discovered that the painting had a poetic title after I had already chosen it, nor that this strange coincidence made any particular impression on me. No, the point was actually the threshold; the point was the snare.

When that painting entered our house, when it crossed our threshold, the feeling I had was not that the house was embellished or enriched or even consolidated by it but, on the contrary, that it was falling down, that it was collapsing around me. The painting came in to ensnare it, to undermine it.

Since then, all the paintings by Vasco that have come into my house and settled there have undermined my threshold, always giving me that same sensation of subsidence, of danger and perilous foundations. This is why I became convinced that it wasn't Vasco's paintings that were hanging on our walls, but our walls that were hanging on Vasco's paintings and being held up by them.

I think that this is the critical and irrevocable crux of the encounter with true art and with a true master: everything else collapses and he remains as the only authentic "load-bearing" element that we have to cling to, participating in the feeling of ensnarement. Or, as Vasco called it, the 'moment of alarm' that precedes the creative act and bites into the work and is never deactivated, disbalancing those who perceive it. When a master pushes beyond the threshold, the limen, everything topples: every wall, every parameter, every blueprint, plan and scale... The same is true of every location—which, rightly or wrongly, we define as a display or host venue, whether of monumental proportions or tiny—as soon as it is touched by the real work it ceases to be bearer and is borne. It is, to all intents and purposes, hosted and generated by the work. I was Vasco's guest in my own home.

Speaking of scale, and of off-scale, brings to mind another aspect of *Nell'insidia della soglia*: when we got it home, we found it wouldn't pass through the inner staircase of our flat. Such was the raptus and rapture of seeing it and buying it that it hadn't even occurred to us to wonder whether it would pass through that other threshold. And it didn't. So, for several weeks it was lodged in a room next to the front door until a restorer friend of ours came and dismantled it before carrying it upstairs where he nailed it together again. This operation made a great impression on me. I had never seen the body of a painting treated like that. Chopped to pieces and manhandled, it seemed to me that it suffered a species of Passion. This allusion of mine should not be shocking or disconcerting:

true art is the descant of archetypes, the coded reactivation of their presence, latency or removal. It is invention as much as inventory and repertoire, the symptom and symbol of every primary image, effigy of the memory engram cells in our brains. Nor should it be shocking that I exemplify the artistic inversion of the bearer-borne relation in a Pietà, the *Rondanini Pietà*: can you like me see that here it is the deposed Christ who is supporting and bearing his mother?

So, *Nell'insidia della soglia* was hung on the upper floor, and something happened, but i'll relate that later.

That said, when you ask a poet to give an opinion about someone who has entered his life at a depth few have reached, it will not be his voice that speaks, but something other, since he will refer, will restate, other. So, I will not give my opinion about Vasco, I will give his, and I will give it as I understood it and—at the beginning—misunderstood it. I'm referring to a precise phrase of Vasco's, in itself so simple as to appear obvious, almost irritatingly so. But the tone in which he said it, his suddenly puzzled eyes looking downwards almost as if he were watching it emerge from his mouth, and the caught breath that left it suspended: but... That's the point, the *but* that dis-closed the phrase.

I frequented Vasco almost daily for nearly fifteen years. In the shadow of Marcella, I knew, suffered and reciprocated every mood swing of his temperament: rage and hearkening, jabs and playfulness, foolishness, the sweet absurdity of dining at five in the morning; never ever silence. But that was the only time I heard that tone and saw that look.

The phrase was: *I know how to make a painting, but...*

I didn't jump in with a "But? Finish what you were saying. But what?" Actually, I didn't make any comment at all, being almost confused by the banality of the phrase while also unsettled by the precipice of that *but...* over which he was leaning, almost exonerating himself from the statement. At that instant I saw him infinitely alone.

In that phrase there was no declaration about his *making art, how to make it, why to make it* of the kind to be found in many of his writings, even the most disquieting and searching, nothing denoting or connoting. It was just him alone, infinitely alone, facing a void, an unknown and a fear all his own. In that message there was no assertive pose—albeit precarious and problematic—anything but, and I realised it only later.

That interrupted phase was the very negation of any erect, presentable and respectable posture; it was a ban on all deportment. It was the deep stabbing pain of painting as un-making, as de-posing: it was the indication of an inner rupture between having to act and having to be acted on, a knife-edge felt to be traumatic and necessary, pivoting on a matter broken and to be broken.

It was the ostentation of a poetics of dis-ability.

A disability not feared but rather invoked.

At the time Vasco was ninety years old. His first ordeal came in 1933 when, at the age of eleven, his father challenged him to show that he knew how to hold a pencil, placing before him the image of a *Crucifixion* by Guido Reni to copy. Vasco drew only the face of Christ. The lad was good; the drawing was remarkable. From then on, his path was set: the signs on the paper were his destiny, especially the faces and the heads. Eighty years later, he also had full maturity behind him; the greatest Italian critics of the twentieth century had written that his mastery of the gesture was consummate—and was it ever! *But.*

Vasco perceived the *knowing how to make a painting* as a curse to be staved off even at ninety years of age. Going back to *not knowing how to make* a painting, waiting for it, was the appeal to a blessing that had yet, yet and yet again to be doubted. The vocation was to invoke that blessing every time, every time his hands took up the tools of his trade, and if the gift did not arrive, then the *well-made* artefact was to be violently destroyed, even many years later, even if it meant ripping it off the wall of the house of a dear collector friend, Beppe Brandani, and breaking it to smithereens before his terrified eyes.

Constantly revoking his own ability, zeroing it and being born again. Newbirthing every time. Or yet, dying every time? Entering the channel of birth that leads from the maternal darkness to the light and coming into the world: that channel, that dark warmth, that dusky glimmer that is one of Vasco's most cogent tropes. But then, don't the survivors of near-death experiences tell of how while dying they traversed a dark tunnel at the end of which they glimpsed a source of light? The fact that clinically birth and death have a disconcertingly mirrored quality matters little, as do the chemical, neurological and biological implications of death. What is at issue is the status of the subject in these stages: immature, depersonalised, totally exposed and traumatised.

To me, Vasco was no longer bearing witness merely to his experiencing the presence of matter—to be worked, thought, fought and dreamed—as an indeterminable obtrusion. Rather, with a giddy transposition, he was evoking how he had suffered, endured and expiated his very bodily and mental presence as an obstacle, insofar as it was the medium of an approach educated—or, still worse, well-educated—by the high priests Guidi and Morandi and, over the course of a lifetime, rendered able and "qualified" by his own expertise. Every time, the issue at stake in painting was how to succeed in dis-abling, in regressing to the source, in rupturing his own dexterity, just like the breaking of the waters at birth.

Every time, for almost a century, the wager for Vasco was the shrugging-off, the questioning of parental authority, the liberation from the paternal language of the masters and from any other historically-established school or grammar. Liberation from the latest naturalism, liberation from the informal, liberation from painting, liberation from the Povero object and return to the brush, liberation from the brush and the pouring of colour. And—still less—letting the colour shiver on the canvas, tilting it just a little, going off to sleep as it dries, rising in the morning to see how it has trembled: taking oneself off (from the medium) doing oneself in. As in one of the shortest of Kafka's short stories, *The Wish To Be A Red Indian*:

> "If one were only an Indian, instantly alert, and on a racing horse, leaning against the wind, kept on quivering jerkily over the quivering ground, until one shed one's spurs, for there needed no spurs, threw away the reins, for there needed no reins, and hardly saw that the land before one was smoothly shorn heath when horse's neck and head would be already gone."

F. Kafka, *The Complete Stories*, translated by Willa and Edwin Muir, Schocken Books, New York, 1971.

Losing the spurs, the reins, the head—those heads that visited and bedevilled Vasco his whole life—albeit without ever escaping the intellectual register, that sometimes cerebral air that flickers in some of his notes, without ever abdicating the act of awareness in a rash slip, but rather creating an antagonist force field (trembling on the trembling earth), presiding over one's own overthrow. Again, as in the near-death experiences, looking at oneself from outside.

Transforming matter into an atopic place, rendering it in grammatical ruin. These are his *heads* and this is the debilitating process that has marked them from the first self-portrait of 1946—dominated by a Guidi-like physicality verging on rarefaction—through to the latest, most extreme, including *Nell'insidia della soglia*, which is a self-portrait. "It's me" said Vasco when we chose it: white but, as in the white of negative images, with just a drip of gold in the centre. A shroud?

Seeking the antibody in matter, almost grasping a possible onomatopoeia, from the syllable downwards just as far as the breath, the primary gesture of the warm well of speech, through to the vibrato of his wonderful erotic drawings, explicit and provocative to the point of indecency, yet virginal as silence.

Bendini's *heads* that Arcangeli in a masterstroke called *Veronicas*, insofar as they are reliquial. *But*, in the reliquary of Bendini's art without flesh and muscles, the eleven-year-old Vasco had already banished the ostentation of limbs. Thus, in this urn of his, don't go just to the bone

Testa, 1952, acrylic tempera on canvas paper, 78,5×39,5 cm, Collezione Santori Lettieri, Rome

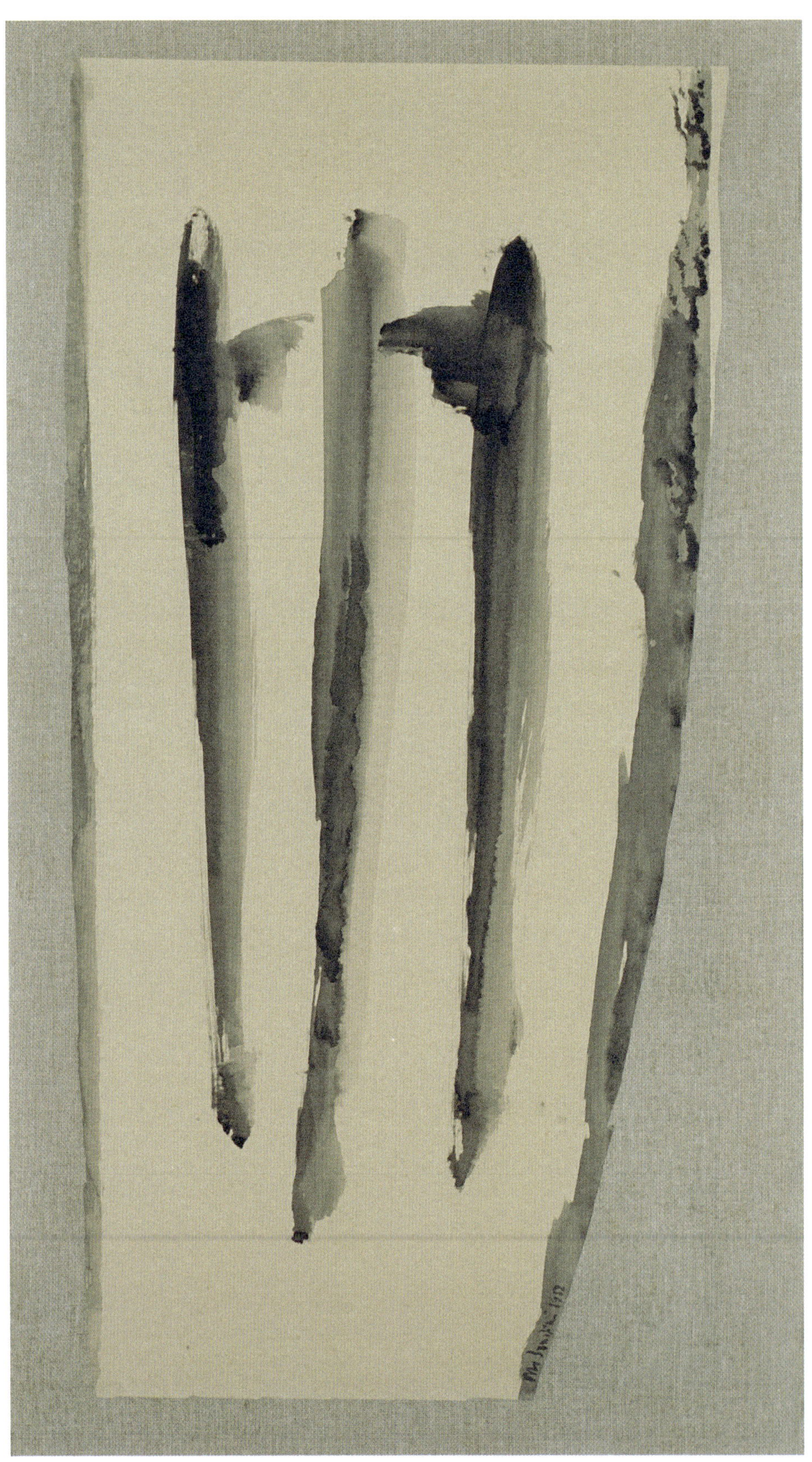

because even a fragment, a splinter of the mortal coil, is still too much for him. A remnant, albeit residual, is nevertheless still too physically implicated in the reconfigurable, memorable and hence subject to reappropriation; further, it is always replete with historical and cultural references that are easy prey to mastery and expertise, namely the cult of self. Strange to say, when the *Testa* of 1952 on canvas-backed paper entered our house, I couldn't look at it. As I passed in front of it, I tended to look the other way. There was something about that exhumed human fossil, deformed by the weight of ages, that concerned me profoundly, which was the very reason I couldn't look at it. Those three crooked spikes, those three black grooves, unpredictably dubbed *Testa* precisely because they are exempted from being "image and likeness", deviating from any even remotely recognisable, reassuring and hence satisfying, human figure. They drew upon that truth—first, last, and universal—of the crushing weight that everyone bears, that everyone takes on. Removing, eliminating, even deboning, Vasco allowed the fulcrum to flash forth, as if precisely by rendering latent the image of a face he had yielded it up in all its pathetic and unsightly pregnancy of a stigma-countenance. Similarly, by removing the arms and legs from the crucifixion in his youthful drawing, he had focused on the face alone his sentiment of the "true Cross".

From then on, as Vasco himself was wont to say, he painted nothing but heads and faces. But that is not to say merely that these were his preferred and obsessive subject. I rather think that it also meant that in his painting all he did was to repeat that original process of subtraction and amputation, which he carried out on himself too, as a dangerously skilled craftsman, in such a way that the painting would make even what was not visible ring out like an appeal and a call, would attract the ungraspable, what had been cut away, the unframed. Just as in the *Crucifixion* by Guido Reni that he copied, the crucifixion itself was offstage, veiled, making the face the unicum, the absolute trace and echo of a unanimous wound. And so, even if I turned aside, I still heard the pulsation of that *Testa* of 1952 like the resurgence of a voice entombed in an ancestral recess, like the line of a removed offstage, but mine, profoundly and intimately mine, and that of others.

And so, I venture to suggest: in Vasco's every sign see a Veronica, the wake of what is given by subtraction, a dawn that rises but sets, that dissipates, scattering blind vestiges to be auscultated and gestated. And then, again, in Bendini's reliquary go first to the bone, then think about its blind shards like the prongs of a tuning fork, and then think just of the tuning fork, and then just of its sound that encapsulates everything, so that everything goes back to that inept before, limbless and to be awaited. *But*, if possible, think of an antechrist Veronica—as it appeared to me in the poem *Self-Portrait*, the most disincarnate I ever wrote, in the collection *Hotel Dieu*, after his death.

Face of the prey
Leaning towards
The frayed stitching
You watch me inept almond
Just before the stone

And from there
At times you dawn
My four-syllable dream,
Ungreen
Unseeing
Antechrist

Postscript: *Nell'insidia della soglia* was hung in the house. I sat down to look at it and, for the first time in my life, I wanted to be a mother. A month later I was expecting my son. I called Vasco, "... looking at the picture... wanted a child... I'm waiting."

DEAR VASCO

SoHyun Bae

Dear Vasco,

I know that you live in your paintings. I picture you there in the wide open space full of light. Radiance comes to mind. No rigid forms, no demarcations, only endless space and time. How did you do it? How did you become so free?

Well, you were already 82 when I first met you, 45 years older than me. You had painted longer than I had lived. How did I work up the courage to approach you? I was a foreigner, barely able to speak Italian. "Mi scusi," I said, "Non parlo bene ma questi quadri sono bellissimi... They are wide open." I don't know how much you understood what I was trying to say. You must've found yourself in a strange predicament. Here was an Asian woman speaking in English, claiming she was American, an artist from New York. In any case, I did leave the gallery with an invitation to your studio.

You sat at a distance and kept your reserve. You had a solemn air about you. You spoke more like a professor and less like an artist. You told me that in order to see more of your work, we must go visit your friend, a great collector. So we did.

As I looked at your work, you were watching me. I knew exactly what you were doing because that is what I do when people look at my paintings. I watch them. You must've seen something in me that you recognized... that pleased you. By the end of the evening, we were both giddy. We were like two children, ageless.

What did I see? I saw you... in your paintings, coded in your secret signs, gathered images, gestures and materials. I had never met anyone like you. You were more wind and fire than water and earth. You were spirit.

Both you and Marcella embraced me. You have no idea how much that meant to me. You invited me to your exhibition in Florence and sat me next to you at the dinner. Like a proud father, you boasted to everyone that I won the Guggenheim.

You told me to pronounce my name Bah-eh, the Italian way instead of Bae.

I was determined to bring your work to New York City. It had to be seen by the rest of the world. You were a secret too good to keep. It took me seven years plus moving back to NY but I finally succeeded.

Do you remember you called me via Skype? You were thrilled about the show! I'll never forget the look on your face. Then you asked about me. My face told you everything. What is it like to question from the inside when the rest of the world questions from the outside? You saw your face in mine.

Weeks before our joint opening, you left us.

Your departure brought Marcella and me closer.
Then she, too, left us.
I know that you are together now.
Knowing that comforts me.
You are free Vasco. You are free.
With all my love,

SoHyun

CRITICAL ANTHOLOGY

Virgilio Guidi
Francesco Arcangeli
Giulio Carlo Argan
Maurizio Calvesi
Renato Barilli
Emilio Villa
Filiberto Menna
Flaminio Gualdoni
Fabrizio D’Amico
Paolo Fossati
Bruno Corà

1949 Virgilio Guidi, VASCO BENDINI – LUCIANO FERRIANI, Milan: Galleria Bergamini, 1949. Catalog of an exhibition of the same title, presented at the Galleria Bergamini, Milan, February 26-March 10, 1949.

Vasco Bendini is exhibiting ten works, and as he is very young, an introduction by someone more famous will be useful. That person is me, who detests this kind of literature, which has so many moral weaknesses that the person being introduced almost always appears superior to the person doing the introduction. I hope to salve my conscience. In the meantime, please read Bendini's own words in this catalog, to avoid distraction. I would simply say this: he is a real person; he feels, thinks, writes, paints and approaches painting from a human position. And when I say this, I also think of the rhetorical image of the man that is beginning to emerge today, an error worse than that of the past, when the man's presence was refused when judging his work.

All the critics' brazen errors lie in this failure to see the close relationship between the man in all his smallest actions and his work; in not knowing how to see how much of the man is present in the work, and only rarely understanding it because they have failed to judge the calibre of the person who produced it and have lost themselves in the external facts of painting that can be easily deceptive.

This painter's work is young, but if you look closely, it aspires to be a function of time, of its secret needs, which are always covered by the encrustations that each time has within. It aspires to the function of civilisation.

If it shows any weaknesses, it is that the concept is greater than his experience. Generally speaking, his painting contains a need for unrushed renewal at the margins of a tired Europeanism, going beyond those who ruminate in the midst of it and bring new thoughts inspired by European civilisation, in the desire to insert them into the Italian spirit.

1958 Francesco Arcangeli, "VASCO BENDINI", *Il Milione. Bollettino della Galleria del Milione*, 30 s.n.; reprinted with variations in BENDINI, Rome: galleria L'Attico, 1958. Catalog of an exhibition of the same title, presented at L'attico gallery, Rome, January 1958.

> "But the rising sun turned it into mere dark vapour, a doubtful, massive shadow trembling in the hot glare."
> Joseph Conrad

It was not until around the age of thirty that Bendini found a path that was decisively his own. He had been a painter for some time, but with long pauses caused by the war or harsh practical necessities, and possibly also by his own disposition and the fact that at times life itself seemed to him a sufficient spiritual adventure. For some years now Bendini has arrived at a pictorial quality that appears to me first-rate; but it is also clear to me (from the work and not only because I have known him at length), that before being a painter, he is a poet, in the meditated and suffered sense of the term. This is the primary reason why, even for his recent painting which is so conscious of the latest directions of western art, the cultural references are only legit to nourish his spiritual fame, to give body to his religious intentions, materialized in the severe approaches of a solitary man to poetry and to painting.

Solitude made his encounters almost casual; occasions into which he poured an almost boundless dedication. To sum up the young Bendini, we could say that at a certain moment he felt Italian "Metaphysics" pursuing him. Not Metaphysics in the literal and academic sense of illustrious poetics, but in the broader sense of a yearning towards universals and eternals, not straitened in the contingency of the technical product which is, also, a work of art. He was interested in Guidi and Sironi, apparently in their formal culture, but in reality in their aspiration to infuse it with another light or a grandiose drama. Soon enough, however, Bendini began to feel himself imprisoned by these forms, and anyone who is alive shakes the bars of the cell.

Towards 1950 he struggled with Masaccio in what was almost a final, and naturally unhappy, clash with an Italian tradition preached for decades and now interrogated at its most illustrious source. But immediately afterwards, almost as if life were no longer possible except in an unrestrainedly romantic liberation, he filled up large pages with pastel storms and floods, whirlwinds that I can only just recall, black agitated spirals that collapse in avalanche upon themselves. Nothing remains of them: yet the abandonment to that highly isolated and almost absurd anarchy was, albeit fairly uncontrolled in the medium, of an absolute earnestness. (It was in those same years that Vedova, unfortunately hampered by a geometrical style, generously hurled his *Esplosioni* [Explosions], *Aspirazioni* [Aspirations] and *Scontri* [Clashes], into a fray apparently without a future.) After this parenthesis of an almost apocalyptic bearing, in 1952 Bendini appears to approach other cultural precedents. However, no sooner had he discovered Picasso or Matisse (a fount not so very different, in terms of meaning, from that of Guidi or Sironi), no sooner had he sighted the most secret Morandi, but these cues were immediately dissipated, echoing just perceptibly within a new candor. As it turned out, I actually presented his work at the show in Florence in June 1953 and, to be precise, it was not so much that his painting met with incomprehension, but that it was practically impossible for there to be a full awareness of his novelty. Since some of those works, inevitably, also open this show, I want to call up the inventory, drafted at the time, of some of the themes which inhabited this highly personal limbo of his:

> "Still lifes where the objects breathe like flashes, but feeble, slowed, spacious; a few shapes of faces, almost dazed Veronica's veils, where the shaft of a nose, the orbit of a forehead, appear to hint at a grand and solitary architectural rhythm, or a slightly staring eye

weeps shadows: languid and wind-filled sails,
injured on the blue of stormy waters [...]."

But even earlier, or at most at the same time, Bendini painted several decidedly abstract temperas, which still have nothing to do with the forms of abstractism then known, not in Italy as a whole, but in a city which was fairly secluded in cultural terms such as Bologna. Cultural immaturity meant that I didn't grasp their entire significance, which was only apparently abstract: there was in fact a too earnest persistence of the human presence, mediated in forms candidly fluctuating between consciousness and vision, and delightfully, exquisitely emotive. Bendini was, for the first time, mysteriously free. His interior aspiration no longer forced him into paths that were alien to him, but by now coincided with the recollection, or the dream, of the natural. At times everything was distanced to the point of introducing him directly into a personal world where they are no more than larvae, impressions, semblances. In France, "Tachisme" had just begun to be spoken of (the name emerged in 1951), and dating to precisely the same time, with the backing of a culture quite differently continuous and potent, was the mutation of Tal-Coat. The same period witnessed the emergence of Sam Francis.

Bendini didn't know anything about all this. He was on his own. In the ancient and beautiful but harsh Bologna, he couldn't even get hold of canvases, and had to content himself with tempera on paper. Guidi had already given, and Morandi was now a retrieval to be made in secret; possibly only Mandelli was less distant in harping certain of his personal, fragile figures, albeit always sensibly sheathed within a shudder of truth. Bendini, instead, shapes his dreams directly, only just permeating them with sensible substance. A homegrown "Tachiste," through faint marks, glimmers, vagrant layers and sensitive walls he set up a collected dialogue between world and consciousness, shading at times into monologue, into ineradicable and individual presence. His works, apparently so ahistorical, so out of the blue, are instead one of the truly personal chapters of a new vision and, dialectically, of the antiformalist revolt that had by now, in 1957, diverged into a thousand streams. In Italy too, people began to come to terms (alas, at times confounding and deceiving) with a history of no more than fifteen years. With Bendini the deceit was useless, because the documents, and the independence of the documents, are even now available. It's also important to immediately stress that in him there is substantially no trace of that technicism, and that cultural dialectic sterilized in its mechanism, with which too many modern (or perhaps better, only modernist) artists turn events over and over. But in them the art, as Dante says, is "[...] like a very sick woman/who finds no rest upon her soft bed/but tosses and turns to escape her pain." For Bendini, a certain manner of execution signifies the conquest of a world, the true liberation of an aspiration; thus it is not evasive of the real, but as an inevitable presence of temperament and dream, activates the real.

A few months after Bendini's solitary Florentine show, Morlotti displayed a series of landscapes, right here in these rooms of the "Milione", generating the explosion of the "naturalistic" question. It is the image of a nature, no longer seen, but where there is an almost bodily and painful "participation" (Testori's definition) in its germination, birth and growth. The question of sex, beyond the obsessive and gelid poetics of Surrealism, is substantiated in nature, becomes human without losing anguish. But in my opinion, and in view of my own precedent and subsequent rumination, which could strike from Wiligelmo up to Monet, the issue had and has to be geared to a range of facts that it would be pointless to recall here, since they are still in progress.

Nature, in any case, appeared as new and "ultimate." "Autre" might now come more easily. It was inevitable, even though risky, to refer to a "Lombard" situation which startled many; the concept was immediately more or less deliberately misunderstood, and particularly by those who didn't know or couldn't imagine what "Lombardy" is and has been. It failed to be understood that the things that were naturally ageing were other: in the first place the myth of the superman and an Olympian and aesthetic concept of art. Modern man does not make art into divinity and museum, which is a site of conservation and repose useful only for better re-immersing it into our vital attrition. In any case there need be no regret for having taken part in an Italian effort to stay alive, since this effort will endure, or for having taken part in it mate if brought to bear on a personal nucleus which has already been clearly prefigured for some time. from the provinces, which when truly so, effectively represent a test site removed from overly short-lived dialectics, and taken right through to the ultimate investigation of ourselves and of things. In this sense Bendini is provincial, and for this too was not unwillingly involved in the "naturalistic" question, even if—in its essential formulations—it did not coincide with his most intimate constitution. Already between 1953 and 1954 he had felicitously compared his dreams to a breath of nature, and even if between 1954 and 1955 he frequently came to choose images of vegetation even too lush for his most personal soul, he did not fail to make them glisten with that secret sense of vision, that controversy of his between the opposites of dream and matter, which is both contrast and the background of the dream. From the immersion within a vision of landscape Bendini was able at times to extract singular works: Springs swollen with breezes, almost timeless, medianic evocations of Autumn, remote Winters, with sparse traces of life within a boundless candor. But it was legitimate that a dissatisfaction would arise within him, not so much with the possibilities that the question in itself offered, but with the poetics which it more showily represented. Bendini had been alone for so long that it was quite understandable that he should briefly entertain the illusion of finding succor in the attractions of a still dominant culture. However, the practice—moreover just touched on, and with his personal chromatic timbres—of an abstract-style post-cubism could not favour the new flowering of that "spiritual" quality of his which had already in 1952-53 made such a highly individual mark. It was, rather, the expansion of the naturalistic question and the new contacts with the practice of the painting of nucleus and of matter, that helped him. If the question was expanded, explored or confounded, this was still achieved through a fairly searing process. What is certain is that in this flow of events Bendini achieved a profound recovery of that truer self of the years 1952 and 1953. It is obvious that this exhibition, which attempts for the first time to present a more conscious image of his person, should provide a bridge between that earlier and this more recent period. From a dialogue with the matter of the painting which a few months ago had become almost suffocating, albeit sustained by an insistent and subtle engagement with the execution, the larvae and relics re-emerged, like before, as always in Bendini's truest moments. Certain resonances can be observed, here Wols, there Fautrier, and in certain rare and persisting gratifications even the later Zao-Wou-Ki. But these are names that can be cited without fear of quashing, implicitly, the artist we're talking about. More than ever Bendini lets us hear his mature voice, sets himself in a precise situation. As others struggle for new natural images, unique and possible preface to new real images, in the same way he struggles for new images of the spirit. With an almost medianic precision Bendini has taken up again his own re-evocation. Almost as if rippling it with hidden air, or capturing dazzles and fluorescences, he brings to the surface of the matter—which with the magnetizing attraction of opposites he had enticed into an obscure dialogue—the new image, once again, of a face. But by now increasingly relic, semblance, trace of man, veil-shroud of our anguished condition, the real and highly concrete symbol of our reality, more real than many realisms. Veering within the paste, subtly blundering, directing seas of colour (his old unbridled storms, now verified, no longer absurd), Bendini seeks the new phantasm of our hidden, eroded almost obliterated countenance. We still carry it within us, like the mirror of a conscience which at times appears to us irremediable. The image forms, expands, exhaling in suffocated flashes, sweating in dolorous leprosies. They are the images of a new poetry which we could not call other than Romantic, in a modern existential sense, both companion and thorn in the side of the new "natural" wave, and no less of every abstractly "autre" eventuality, every technicism, every irresponsible vacuity. It is an ineradicable element, religious in the primary and ingenuous sense of the word, within the great dialectic in course. These images, authentic indicators of a spiritual condition, have been paid for by Bendini to the point of sacrifice. This is why, when he faces the canvas, the warning of an unknown light, possibly a hope, blinking slowly within the layers of the matter, begins gradually to shine forth in his room.

1966

Giulio Carlo Argan, BENDINI. OPERE ESEGUITE NEL 1965 DELLE SERIE *SENTIMENTO COME STORIA* E *SENSO OPERANTE*, Rome: galleria L'Attico, 1966. Catalog of an exhibition of the same title, presented at L'Attico gallery, Rome, March 1966.

The current phase of Bendini's painting is, in its problematic substance, exceptionally lucid; consequently in the somewhat agitated and confused current situation, it is to be taken seriously into consideration. After the informal experience, pursued along untrodden paths and without any concession to fashion, Bendini did not pose himself the dilemma of the apocalyptic and the integrated. Knowing that he had reached a limit, he did not devote himself to futile retrievals; since there could be nothing beyond the experience achieved that did not comprise his motives, he undertook a methodologically precise analysis of the process of his own painting. He arrived at the conclusions that we see, and which, in the meantime, proved how the matter of the Informal was not at all a limit beyond which no other hypothesis was possible. Thus he has approached the boundary of the fifth dimension: the dimension beyond existence and which is posited (and could not be otherwise) solely as hypothesis. The experimentation thus is valid to the extent to which the hypothesis may become phenomenon.

Already in the informal phase Bendini had never let up probing the penetrability and practicability of matter, seeking in it a possibility of existence that would not be confused with that of the matter itself; thus he had found stratifications of images and profound signal itineraries. He continued to draw within the matter: his graphics, very abundant in those years, are the best guide to grasping the sense of his material research. After he had succeeded in clearing, piercing and going beyond the wall of matter, the first question had necessarily to concern the dimension, certainly no longer existential, which opened up beyond, and the extent of which could not be known. All that he knew of it, as a general concept, was that it no longer presented itself as synthesis but as a spatial-temporal *continuum*. Conscious of the limits of his own sphere of experience, painting, and of the necessity of dealing with the concrete data of the problem, Bendini identified that hypothetical spatiality with the pure and simple surface of the white canvas. For any painter, of whatever epoch and culture, the surface of the painting to be done is not simply a material support, but an initial problematic datum: it poses the problem of its own two-dimensionality, of a flat, solid and coloured extension which, nevertheless, is symbolically and conventionally conceived as virtuality, availability, and unlimited spatiality. It is like the land on which we are to construct a building: only a bad architect would limit himself to considering it solely in terms of its capacity to support the material weight of the walls. From Cezanne on, the story of space in painting is in the non-painted, in the context. In Bendini's case the white canvas is something achieved and found afterwards, beyond a disintegrated, dissolved, vanished matter. In fact, it no longer has any bearing capacity; it is a screen that gathers vagrant remnants of images and does not even appropriate them, because its extension is entirely beyond the coloured veils and the applied strips. That it is a screen or diaphragm is demonstrated by the fact that the painter has to move it, to display it in certain inclinations in order to allow it to intercept currents of signs originating from an as yet unknown transmitter, and otherwise undetectable. The division into diptychs and triptychs, inclined panels and different levels is not intended to decompose, but rather, by moving the screens, to reconstruct the unity or the continuity of the projection.

The imprecision of the terms "screen" and "diaphragm," provisionally used, is immediately apparent: the white canvas is, in fact, only the intercision of an inverted perspective depth which dilates rather than contracts as it recedes. The spatiality of this painting is, in reality, a spatiality in expansion, such as that described by modern cosmology. It is probably on account of this inevitable cosmological interest, and this passage from one dimension to another, that the most reliable historic reference for this phase of Bendini's painting is Kandinskij in the period of the *Improvisations* (1913-15). More than a screen or diaphragm, therefore, it would be correct to speak of a "threshold," of a zone of transition, because what actually interests the artist is the layer, of a certain depth, in which for an unspecified duration image that had a significance and a value in the existential dimension continue to present themselves. We have to acknowledge that we are on the border of metaphysical ambiguity, or at least of an eschatological theory: could these not be images of the hasty elimination of lived experience as soon as the "threshold" was crossed? I don't exclude that this may be one of the components of Bendini's poetics: the title of a work, *Sentimento come storia* [Feeling as History] suggests that it is. But the artist gazes out from the "threshold" with limpid, secular steadiness, determined not to record anything that does not offer itself with phenomenic evidence. Nothing that is not yet, and maybe only briefly, real can impress the sensitivity of his screens, colour the first layers of the new extension. Analyzing the signs that appear on the white canvases we cannot fail to recognize the mnemonic origin; they come from past experiences, and have deposited in transit the meanings they had in the dimension of existence. They have highly diverse origins, but this is no longer very important. The lines are straight and oblique, parallel, divergent, intersecting: they are undoubtedly the features of a three-dimensional perspective structure, but appear to be broken and bent like the famous stick immersed in the water. There are figurative fragments: a chair, a window, human contours, glimpses of sky. But I don't see the jubilation, destined to turn to tears, of the propagandists of the "new figuration": these vain shadows of persons and things, brought thus far by the caprice of an obscure current, will never take shape, they will fade much sooner than others because, in the dimension of the non-existent, their very physical nature renders them infinitely fragile and fleeting. Finally, there are patches of colour that preserve and pass on the last trace of a material impasto or a gestural action: but the matter is devoid of substance, the gesture devoid of strength. The relations too are inverted: the brightest and most luminous colour is the black, the sky that we see from the window is on this side of the wall.

Already in Bendini's previous painting Calvesi noted a tendency to the lability of the image. Now the theme of lability becomes a precept, a key. The spreading of the colours is thin, sparse; they only just adhere to the canvas, like films which could be detached, and sometimes are. We feel that the images emerge from a laceration, although we cannot tell where or when it has occurred, because in the work there is no sign of it. It brings to mind a childhood game: the transfers that always came out wrong, a piece of the figure would remain on the template, another would be transferred to the paper, askew, slithering on the veil of water. The critical moment, when the image tore and was no longer either here or there, was the moment in which the template was separated from the sheet. In the same way Bendini's images remain suspended, neither here nor there: the fragments can never be recomposed in line with any known syntax. In saying that this is a poetics of laceration or detachment, however, we are simply referring to an experience common to all men of our time: what in art has led to the irreversible extreme of the Informal. Bendini set out to seek what has remained beyond, and what has come this way, and found only fragments. A historic laceration never clearly separates the obsolete values from the current, the dead eras from the living, the closed spaces from the open. However, he did ask himself whether the images of his memory still had enough strength to impress the white canvas, to sustain it, to give a finite sense to its virtual, indefinite and entirely available spatiality. In other words, he wanted to ascertain whether the flotsam of memory was still sufficiently vital to nourish and elaborate imaginative activity. He replied affirmatively to the question in the triptych entitled *Senso operante* [Operating Faculty]. Read as it ought to be read, from left to right, it shows a still confusedly carnal image, a palpitating shred of memory, which is matched, beyond the pause, by a geometrical structure that is settling itself into a lucid combination of orthogonal co-ordinates. The memory-imagination relationship, which represents the problematic nucleus of Bendini's current research, evidently implies the theme of history. Interpreted in the phenomenological key most suited to this research method, it is the theme of the *Erlebnis*, which is not reduced to the immobility of the *So-sein*, nor is in itself sufficient to give the future the structurality of a project, but nevertheless opens up to that intermediate region which is the region of the *eide*, of infinite possibilities, of the imagination that prepares the materials for the future teleological choices. If this is the correct key for interpretation, then we must no longer speak of metaphysical ambiguity but of suspension of judgement, of Husserl's *epoché*.

1968

Maurizio Calvesi, "BENDINI '65-'68. OGGETTI E PROCESSI", in BENDINI, edited by Maurizio Calvesi and Giulio Carlo Argan, Rome: Galleria Senior, 1968. Catalog of an exhibition of the same title, presented at the Galleria Senior, INArch Palazzo Taverna, Rome, November 1968.

Bendini's recent activity should not come as a surprise to anyone with more than a superficial knowledge of his past. There is in fact a profound continuity of the discourse, even though it is quite clear that, from 1965 on, we are dealing with a drastic renewal of the media. There is no doubt that Rauschenberg, Johns, and Dine opened up a new linguistic horizon to Bendini: but this is true for Bendini and all those, frequently younger, who in Europe and in the United States carried forward the logic of New-Dada until they achieved different and ulterior results, setting up a new problematic which was to result in most of the current situation. In this going beyond, Bendini was second to none. In the summer of 1966 he displayed in Venice, in Ca' Giustinian, two works, *Come è* [As it is] and *Senso operante* [Operating faculty] in which representation was abolished: chairs, a mirror, other objects. "Taking a seat, today, on one of Bendini's works," commented G. Scardovi in the catalog, "acquires the sense of making us forget that the work is there [...]. I sit on the chair and achieve a toilette of the ego." At that time Bendini's research proceeded in parallel with that of younger or in any case very new artists, or rather with a certain indisputable claim to priority.

Fifteen years earlier Bendini had already found himself in the front line with the Informal movement. The gestural experiences of the temperas evolved into a painting of matter and sign. The 1960s opened up a crisis that was not resolved until 1965 through what had by then become an objective utilization of the canvas. "In the case of Bendini," wrote Argan introducing the production of the previous year in March 1966,

> "the white canvas is something achieved and found *afterwards,* beyond a disintegrated, dissolved, vanished matter. In fact, it no longer has any bearing capacity [...] its extension is entirely beyond the coloured veils and the applied strips. That it is a screen or diaphragm is demonstrated by the fact that the painter has to move it, to display it in certain inclinations."

Taking this research to extremes, in the course of 1966 Bendini was to use the naked frames, intersecting with one another and leaning against the wall (*A Johnson)* or, with a truly "povero" gesture, by hanging cans and boxes on them as in *La scatola U* [The U box].

The paintings of 1965 contained another precept: the reading took place in succession, as if following a discourse, and suggested a physical dislocation, not only of the eye. The new work of the *Senso operante* series, displayed in 1966 at the collective show mentioned above held in Ca' Giustinian, resumes the theme of the *Polyptychs* of 1965. However, by now this is "workable," inviting to an internal itinerary, with pauses on the chair, which is no longer painted, but placed before an upturned canvas and bordered by the frame; the other panels are covered with a large cellophane, beyond which it is possible to "enter." This precept of process embodies a significant intuition which emerges in the later works; nevertheless in some cases these are nothing more than the realization of projects already conceived at the time. More frequently, these projects have remained such, albeit evocative to read, and the reason for which Bendini found it easier to realise the "povere" works (here I mean those displayed at the Bologna one-man show of 1967, and presented by Arcangeli with a correct intuition of their high quality and their significance as extreme "self-portraits") lies precisely in his "povertà." Effectively, Bendini's poverty, far from being a metaphor, is a real condition against which he has to grit his teeth and struggle, like many young people.

In *Come è,* the other work displayed at Ca' Giustinian during the last Biennale, there is a clear abdication of the aesthetic aim, at least as traditionally understood. The chair is just an ordinary chair, as are the mirror and the mat. The difference from the models of the New-Dada is this: Rauschenberg's object is again just an ordinary object, but in the work it acquires value, is aesthetically adopted. Effectively it calls for a very precise placement, almost always fixed, within a plastic-pictorial context. Bendini's objects, instead, do not aspire to value, are not part of a plastic block, do not concur in the determination of a co-ordinated image, nor are elements of an image which the spectator can construct at his pleasure. They are mere tools in an operation that is referred to the user; their connection lies in the process of fruition. The "instructions for use" are derived from the description that Bendini provides of this work of his, and of others, in this same catalog.

We sit down; the mirror at our feet returns our image and the recorder (not present in the realization) our voice. All that this work aims to do is produce a parenthesis in the flow of our experience and our perceptive activity, forcing it to fall back on the only object that is always excluded: ourselves. Presenting this work along with Napoletano and Scardovi (September 1966) I wrote that "this philosophy of objects and appearances consummates, with that characteristic ineffable concentration, the complex but synthetic mechanism of thought" that is proper to Bendini. Even previously, in fact, it had seemed to me that the very informal experience had, in Bendini "a foundation at once speculative and poetic," and I had posited a juxtaposition of the first temperas with Zen thought rather than with the expressionism of action painting. The gesture in Zen painting, and hence Zen painting as a whole, has a scope that is cognitive much more than aesthetic; its rapidity is significant, because "grasping the truth means being quick, and painting rapidly means training yourself to grasp the truth," the truth as essence. In fact Barilli had already recognised a cognitive interest in Bendini's theme of the face and in his search for an "essential structure": "but if there is an essence that presides over his paintings" Barilli concluded "this does not mean that he falls into essentialism." In *Come è*, and in the works that followed, the old Zen root of Bendini's poetics is recognizable in the rejection of the aesthetic aim and in the condition of isolation and concentration that consigns man to himself. Once again, Bendini's search for essence is not metaphysical abstraction, but investigation of the "substance." His poetics has always insisted (and this too was already stressed by myself and by others as regards his painting) on the "reciprocal incidence," or rather, on the absolute convergence or identity of thought and senses. The essence that he investigates is not in heaven, but in the infinite capillarity of the perceptive circuits, which his recent works aim to stimulate; this essence is possibly in the "simultaneousness" of the sensory and mental stimuli, or rather in the consciousness of this condition, since every essence reascends to consciousness. If, therefore *Come è* reasserts the "ontological" vocation of Bendini's poetics, we are speaking of that "new ontology" which appeared to me a point of convergence between many current researches: an ontology of a Dewey type, understood as a reflection on human reflection and on the experiential conditions that solicit it. *Come è*, so fascinating in terms of data, marks an extreme in "povera" research that the subsequent works of this strand overleap to retrieve an even more explicit and rich aesthetic dimension. In the "solar" cabin the visual sensation of the light in progression is shored up by the thermal sensation and integrated by the olfactory. It is closed and yet recalls the open air, the beach, nature enjoyed through the skin; at the same time it is a closed space, of growth, where time has a purely organic rhythm; or, again, it is like the cranium where thoughts are elaborated and all sensations gather, forming perception. That is, a more ample margin of suggestion comes into play, while also stressing the archetypal profundity of a research that, poring over the phenomena to analyse them with almost scientific fanaticism, is at the same time conscious of the abyssal echoes that their perception may trigger within us. These are the polarities of external and internal that have always been dialectics in Bendini's pictorial exploration, in the very theme of the face, which now reproduces its own problematic, for example, in the "pad": lying down on it we perceive an internal-external, non-gravitational dimension of our body.

In any case, whatever the margin of suggestion of these works may be, their scope is revealed as markedly cognitive. The condition of the event and its very fruition is aesthetic, since it is "disinterested" action; above all the dimension of transference which invests the operation is aesthetic. The user, repeating the suggested action, draws on an experience which the artist communicates to him through this means.

It is no longer the language of forms that communicates the values contained in the work, but the relived experience.

1978

Renato Barilli, "IL PERCORSO DI VASCO BENDINI, in VASCO BENDINI", edited by Renato Barilli and Sandro Sproccati, Bologna: Comune di Bologna, 1978. Catalog of an exhibition of the same title, presented at the Galleria Comunale d'Arte Moderna, Bologna, November 1978.

The almost thirty years of Vasco Bendini's activity documented by this exhibition represent the exemplary career of an artist whom I would define as profoundly dedicated to the cause of informality. I have deliberately used this unusual term because I wish it to indicate three quite different phases of evolution, of which only one, the first, is identified with the Informal in the strict sense, that is the historic Informal. This is a phase, moreover, of which we are rediscovering all the significance as an authentic centre of gravity of the events of this second half of the century, already far advanced, while also reconfirming all the weight which the personal involvement of Bendini had within it.

But informality is something more far-reaching, it is an "open" thrust, a tension which goes beyond the precise and delimited structure of the historic Informal, to the extent that it re-emerged—albeit in a fairly altered garb—towards 1966-1967 within the complex of experiences which are by now conventionally earmarked with the label of "cold" Informal. This was an explosion which overflowed the old banks of the painting to reach the shores of the quite distinctly vast continent of aesthetic and behavioral animation. Bendini was one of the front-line protagonists of this breakthrough, and thus managed to stitch together in an exemplary manner the two successive phases of informality, what we might call the intracutaneous phase of pictorial editing, and the following phase of spatial invasion. However, he himself did not fail to foresee the limitations of this same phase of physical expansion, and after the climax of the 1970s, he gave himself to tracing out—always in an exemplary manner—a parabola of an opposite value, of implosion, clustering and densification of the materials previously used, almost analogous to the cosmic phenomenon in which the galaxies are victims of a collapse and converge towards the center, giving rise to those "black holes" that are so evocative to us non-initiates.

The importance of the historic Informal was that it took a definitive leave from the climate of the search for closed and rigid essences characteristic of the first half of the century. Exemplary in this regard was the way in which, at the start of the 1950s, Bendini latched onto the models typical of two domestic masters, Morandi and Guidi: still lifes for the former and seascapes and above all faces for the latter. Treated by the young artist, not yet thirty, these themes open up, in the sense that they dislodge and unhinge their joints; and above all they are read on the keynote of leanness, abandoning all claims to plasticity, being instead translated into stenographic signs, deliberately provisional, blatantly gestural. This process of transcription in an accelerated phenomenal key was implemented contemporarily by many other artists, in Italy and beyond, on one and other side of the Atlantic. As regards Italy, we can consider the accelerations and retractions of sign generated by Capogrossi (another former pupil of the Morandi school) or Vedova, without overlooking the Spatialists and the Nuclears. As regards North America, we can even go back to the early Pollock, or Tobey's *white writings* and the entire chapter related to the retrieval of the ideograms, with all the mystical magic that these characters represent for our western sensibility.

In fact, of Bendini too, we can say that in the very early 1950s he "wrote" the theme of the face or the seascapes: a few disarticulated and oscillating signs, which in addition leave disclosed and evident the hand that traces them, marked by the characters of what is almost potential calligraphy, with uprights that are thicker or thinner depending on whether they are upstrokes or downstrokes. The figurative motif becomes an airy and porous cage, ready to magnetically draw into it the most varied and prismatic phenomena. This launches what I have defined as a dialectic between "structure" and "texture." The masters of the twentieth century comprise only the first of the two terms: everything is structure, which directly guides the dimensions and paths of its manifestation. In the Informal, texture instead comes to prevail, that is the warp of the phenomena. But on the other hand, so as not to lose their way in their sea, they still need to have a guide, a criterion that can select them and share them out, or even earlier stimulate them and drive them out. The theme of the face was to have a similar function for many long years in Bendini's art: the function of a light structure, almost invisible or rather visible only through the phenomena that it succeeds in coagulating along its trajectory. In the same way as the lines of force in an electromagnetic field can be visualised only through the depositing of the iron filings, or the passage of a jet high in the sky is revealed by the trails of ionized vapour.

In fact what distinguishes Bendini's phenomenism from the very start, and hence also his participation in informality, is the desire to set himself very close to the limit, in the area where our senses have to be refined and become almost medianic, telepathic: from the solid state to that of gas, ever more rarefied. From the visible to the band of radiation, so fine as to be almost no longer perceptible to the senses. And the still ingenuous and naturalistic reference to the face may then expand to more general proportions, become the tension between a screen and the apparitions that it partially succeeds in framing, but that partially escape it. A "structure" that pursues fleeting exhalations, that engages in a fierce struggle with them, always running the risk of being overleapt. In the same way that the screen of an x-ray holds the radiation but the rays also pass through it. In the same way that the crystal ball and all the other transparent surfaces used by the devotees of the arts of magic are suddenly animated by mysterious presences, which are equally prone to suddenly vanish again. Nothing like the obvious and banal relation established between the thing and the reflecting image, when the illusion is linear and direct.

But returning to the strand of the actual evolution, this dialectic of appearance/disappearance is attenuated for a time (from 1954 to 1956) under the pressure of Arcangeli's "last naturalism," that is when the critic and the artist believed for some time that the promised land of the Informal could be the sphere of vegetable phenomena, the enigma of the chlorophyllic function. For a brief period, nature appears the appropriate term of reference in the march towards informality. But it was, as I said, only a brief moment, because after the *Ultimi naturalisti* Arcangeli wrote *Una situazione non improbabile*, where he acknowledges that it is necessary to take into consideration a broad international front. Behind nature gapes the chasm of matter and its correlate, the gestualism of the artist who wants to tune in on it. Thus Bendini too sees that he has to come to terms with the great European Informals, and first and foremost with Wols. The last years of the 1950s find him refining with extreme subtlety the dialectic between structure and texture, screen and apparition, the face and its magnetic function. No-one is better equipped than he to summon the resources of a varied and inexhaustible instrumentation, here dense with paste, here liquid and skin deep: curdlings, corrosions, erosions, broad flakes of veneer, rough and grazing flows. The face re-emerges, always the same and always different, in the same way as an electromagnetic field can cluster the iron filings in an infinity of patterns. But the great season of the historic Informal, around the turning-point of 1960, hints at a growing weariness, or suggests that, having probed all the interior possibilities, it is now obliged to restrict itself to a sterile exercise of variants. Moreover, there is the forceful thrust of a new generation which, as always happens, brings in new demands. Bendini initially appears to want to play the card of heroic defence: that is affirm with greater emphasis his faith in informal phenomenism, with the extremism of a fierce warrior loathe to lay down his weapons. This act of faith, moreover, has its *raison d'être*: we must not forget that the 1960s was a time of instances that were not infrequently divergent and ambiguous; by now we know that we have to distinguish between the first and the second half of this decade. Bendini, for example, can no longer adhere to the "new course" if this means returning to a need for geometrical and rational order (as more or less took place in the strand of the "programmed" and gestaltic optical researches); and nor can he accept it if this means placing the accent on the Pop side, the retrieval of icons and personalities. No-one is more congenitally adverse to the personality than Bendini, given that, on the contrary he believes that things and bodies are ready to exhale into energy, that they tend, so to speak, to a volatile state. This is why up to 1965 it is reasonable to nurse the impression that he is one of those not rare artists who, victims of generational limitations, persisted in an obstinate, albeit heroic and valid, exercise of the Informal.

The turning-point occurred when, in that same year, Bendini intuited that he could turn the new instances to account, applying not to those of the optical species which were unapproachable for him, but to the others of the New-Dada, apparently more retrograde but actually latent with a yeasty future. Rauschenberg and Johns had in fact taught to acknowledge the presence of things "in flesh and blood," of the plastic matter "as it is," in its artificiality. At the same time they did not passively surrender to it, or renounce investing it with a charge of psychism, which then, translated into visual terms, corresponds to an impetuous chromatic and gestural aggression, again of an informal stamp.

Having drawn on this ambit of "real" experiences in a three-dimensional space, Bendini appears to evolve two separate series, or rather let's say that it could help us in our exposition to make such a distinction. On the one hand, he gives us a whole series of isolated and minute objects. The titles are tautological, that is they say the same things in which the work resolves itself: *Basket*, *Bowl*, *Spoon*, etc. but they do not indicate the layer of sensible effects which is condensed on these objects, the coupling of psychism that invests them. As usual, like every other structural element, like the faces and the screens in Bendini's previous works, these operate as a magnetic pole to attract, gather and curdle sensitive charges that would otherwise be impalpable. Or even ultrasensitive, metapsychical: in particular, for example, *A memoria di gesso* [In memory of plaster], with that hand print like that of an ectoplasm which has deigned to leave a direct trace of its own passage. Effectively, these little objects have been, so to speak, creamed by immersion in a "soft" and viscous substance—wax or glue—in this way too creating a link with the work of Beuys, or entering into harmony with the only *ante litteram* phenomenon of "povera" art already existent at the time, that is Californian Funk Art.

The other series could, in a certain sense, be the opposite of this first one. If here, as we have seen, the concrete and structural element is inside, and represents a sort of kernel that is exposed to an external treatment, an electroplating of sensibility, in the other it tends to act as a container, or a structural element in the more strict sense of the term. Clearly however, it can't do it, does not manage to contain or hold in the diffused energy. This aspect resuscitates the link with New-Dada, considering that many works consist precisely in the disputing, demolition of the traditional framework (typical *A Johnson*): empty frames breathlessly pursuing the space in an attempt to delimit it, to constrain it, but only managing to reveal their failure. Like trying to hold a phantasm within the four walls of a room, which then amuses itself by striking unexpectedly printing in cut-out (like with a clicker press) the gigantic imprint of its own hand (*La mano di Vasco*, Vasco's Hand). Or the structure is adapted to a more subtle function, which does not consist in openly displaying the failure, the dismantling of its own joints, but rather that of providing an apparently sterile and neutral container. This is the most courageous apex of de-artification that Bendini achieves, entirely renouncing the plastic values of the object. A renunciation that, as mentioned above, the New-Dada and even Nouveaux-Réalistes never achieve; at the outmost, we could refer to those two very *sui generis* New-Dadaists, much stricter than anyone else in their adherence to the lesson of Duchamp, that is Klein and Manzoni. The former inevitably comes to mind in the presence of a work from 1967 such as *Cabina solare* [Solar Cabin], clearly erected to pick up an energy by now forced to the last degree of rarefication, beyond the limits of the visible. The latter instead can be evoked with reference to another of these sterile and anaesthetic containers, proposed this time *Per una essudazione totale* [For a total exudation], and hence as an act of homage to bodily secretions as physical and concrete as can be. Nevertheless, it is not incidental that, even when Bendini enters into such a mindframe of corporeal ransom, he still aims at the physiological manifestations most ready to take the path of liquification, or still better of aerial exhalation. Moreover the neutral and instrumental character of these devices, devoid of aesthetic value in or for themselves, implies the intervention of the behavioural dimension, that is demands that the artist-operator, or other person delegated by the same, or a volunteer from the public, offers his services in the capacity of actor, or to express it with the untranslatable English expression, generates a "performance." 1967-69 were the years in which Bendini proposed these performances of his, a "genre" that was not common in Italian artistic practice, nor even actually greatly cultivated at world level. Once again, perhaps, Beuys comes to mind... Overcoming his natural shyness, the artist presents himself in first person, in a garb that immediately plunges him back into anonymity—an irreprehensible black mime costume (*Il mio spazio*, My space; *Io, e io ora*, Me, and me now). But the performance of the human operator is not always present; in other cases what is set up, so to speak, is a performance by inanimate elements: a kinetic art then, we might literally say, were it not that this label is linked to the use of complicated, rigid and segmented "gadgets" which could not be further from Bendini's intentions. If anything, the kinetics that could interest him is, as usual, the subtle breath of certain invisible gases and fluids, in relation to which the solid bodies play the subordinate role of docile detectors. In *La memoria* [Memory], for example, the whirling polychrome fragments indicate otherwise imperceptible ascensional currents. At heart, even the pictorial elements used by Bendini throughout his previous career were none other than detectors, indicators of the passage of forces set beyond the threshold of the sensible. But, having reached the turning-point of 1970, Bendini takes stock of himself and his entire previous history, and is struck by a potent generational summons. We must be full of respect for this mysterious generational logic, almost an equivalent of genetic law extended to the ambit of cultural production. Each generation has its own destiny, or in more neutral terms, its own centre of gravity; it is reasonable for some particularly dynamic and intolerant member to push himself somewhat beyond the permitted range of action, to strain the equilibrium, but not beyond a certain point, after which there is a movement of compensation or sucking back towards the centre. Bendini's generation, or that of the historic Informal, was born and bred accepting the advantages and limitations of virtuality, of the illusory nature of the surface. It mapped out the possibility of breaking down that barrier, and in some cases made decisive contributions to this. As well as the case of Bendini, we can think of Dubuffet and all the spatial researches of the *Hourloupe*, pushed as far as the mastodontic proportions of the building and the monument; or we can also recall the much less well-known episode of Moreni's gigantic plastic watermelons; but in more recent years, these artists too perceived the call of the surface and its tricky fascination. Bendini was no exception: after the outward explosion, the inward implosion, the redensification of the fragments. Moreover, these diastolic and sistolic phases are almost an organic woof underlying the entire cultural production, and hence have on their side a sort of inevitability and necessity. It is not, however, a mechanical doing and undoing, or a pure and simple return to the point of departure: the pendular oscillation "inwards," the retrieval of the surface, brings with it the awareness of the use of new materials acquired in the meantime, and is bolstered by a boldness unknown in the stages of the classic Informal. We feel that the work now offered to us, despite being reduced to the plane, is still swollen with a quantity of action, only provisionally flattened, but ready to re-explode, to again emanate its depth. We could speak of a performative quality miniaturized and packed into a box, or traced out like a cartographic procedure. Attesting to this, in fact, are the "poor" materials aggregated to Bendini's canvases "after 1970," inevitably set in fine equilibrium with those of traditional pictorial origin; the Funk taste for waste, which had marked the years 1966-1967 evolving in an intense series of little objects "invested" with the most intense affectivity, is maintained and possibly even strengthened. Thus we find the cellophanes, the precious dribblings of wax, the coffee beans and tea leaves, the "found objects" of the egg box type, along with strips of cloth, crumpled and twisted almost as if the layer of pictorial paste was wriggling and twisting. It would be futile and mistaken to invoke the name of Burri here, because there what predominates over all is the severe sense of the page, of the composition, that is, a spirit of closure. Here, instead, we are dealing with the highly provisional fixing of a moment of action, of a probing, almost a survey conducted on the (physical, psychic and metapsychic) currents that circulate and give expression to the plastic materials at their will. All the works of this cycle continue in those adjacent, rather than closing themselves in detached magnificence.

The pendulum continues its progress towards the terminus of the implosion, that is, towards an increasingly more radical virtuality and immateriality on the return. In other words, if between 1970 and 1974 we have the works that I have attempted to describe above, where protruding "concrete" elements coexist with other superficial elements, afterwards Bendini goes back to exploring, as at the beginning, the paths of an exclusively intracutaneous, skin deep, art—or rather, if possible, even more liquid and rarefied than that of the 1950s. However, the trained eye continues to discern the signs of passage through the three-dimensional phase.

In fact the surface, although not broken at a material level, is nevertheless contradicted at internal level. In the recent works there inevitably appears a fracture, a barrier, a fault cleaving the space, cracking it, bringing about the coexistence of distinct universes, and in short fracturing the notion of a continuous surface. This is a novel retrieval of the New-Dada motif of the rod, of the chip, of which now all that remains is the trace after its removal: a flaying or abrasion, almost the shadow, the x-ray of the structural element. Possibly it was laid on the painting for a moment, but was then immediately worn and corroded by the pressure of the gases, the dissolving liquids. Yet, even if at the price of its own sacrifice, it has succeeded in fulfilling the structural function, distributing, guiding and containing the exuberant flood of the fluids; or even just, for the umpteenth time, in revealing their tensions. The structure, as always, at grips with the texture: maybe more often overcome than dominating, but in this case too still capable of "revealing," of witnessing the invisible forces unleashed by Bendini's art.

Translation by Lexis, from *Vasco Bendini. Opere 1950-2006*. Florence, Siena: Spaziotempo, Carlo Cambi, 2007. Catalog of an exhibition of the same title, presented at the Frittelli Arte Contemporanea gallery, Florence, February 10-March 31, 2007.

1980

Emilio Villa, "APERTURA VOCALE PER ALTO SIGILLO", in VASCO BENDINI, Rome: Esse Arte, 1980. Catalog of an exhibition of the same title, presented at L'Attico gallery, Rome, April 18-May 9, 1980.

Vasco Bendini reaches the thirtieth anniversary of his ideal, unreal journey; sometimes by indulging in the moody conglomeration of linguistic temptations (and unfortunately forced, albeit innocently, into the ordeal of inferior disciplines and gloomy public or eccentric, biennial, municipal or random rituals), and at others by crossing, piercing, animating and even distorting the veil of that superior intuition of the world, which in painting was called (with such an ill-advised word by the clueless managers) "Informal" or "material painting," or similar; Bendini is approaching what he was promised by his initiatory tension.

Mundus indolens
Mundus sed dolor
Mundus mutuus
Mundus absque dolore

A severe and secluded, absorbed insideration, whereby the world (and here we cite the world as *mundus*, strictly in the cosmological sense or in terms of cosmogony) nourishes the colour, and the colour nourishes the world, and the one and the other food, which are shared, are both recognition and disavowal, and a conspiratorial melee of mutation in its pure state, that is, in the paradigm of a meticulous, lonely, sober, besieged viewpoint. Thus the seeds of oscillation and vehemence of the afflatus are sown, to stretch the field of the energetic between two points of the blinded mirror, the two points of the inaccessible equality, labile and evoked, impossible scansion, unanimous positive-negative: of which the signal, or symbol (i.e., the marked picture, the degree of operation, the physical painting, encircled and accelerated by its most secret, most discordant, most mental symptoms) generates the notation, or nutation, the trembling and sensitive neuma, not as a secondary object, but as an abysmal nucleus, infinitely minimal apparatus, tenuous implant of the levels, layers, periods, of the agglomerations or knots or tangles of a larger mechanism: abstruse humours from condensate, the synoptic network of corymbs, or the wait for the harp that is full and smoothly silent, perfectly measured, protagonist of currents, trace of exchanges and spontaneous emissions. In each act, in each moment, the act and the moment of the world are laid down in a simple recumbency. Not by metaphor, but precisely by breathing, or even the exclamation of the mind; by brisk plots and interferences from the portion of physicality that presses and envelops the beyond, by transduction, by echoing passes and non-material degrees, veiling tears and clashes, gashes and threads of the obscure, arcane, fixed physicality.

It is on the borders of the colours that the spectrum of memory emanates; it is memory that dares, without body and references, to become body and limbs; that flourish and interrupt, warped, transferred, and therefore in action, the branches of memory. It establishes itself as the habitat, as architecture, as the urn of the laceration and the flow of horizons, genealogy of savoured and deliberated areas, captured in accents, in timbres, in beats, in modules, in neumes, in numina. Memory as a membrane, on which the anatomical figures are engraved (decided) at quotas of sparse and penetrated delirium, at sails and banners of sleep and devastation, at the transmutation of ever-resuspended terminals: magnetising absorption, from irradiation, of gravity, and anatomical grevity that is gradually fading; aspiring to the time of unlimited Formations, without trace, without enclosure, without form, without end; only Process of the decisive Speculum, of the thermal General Picture, of the degenerating mass. Therefore memory as a rarefied defluence of the Dispensation, duplication and doubling of the Enchantment.

Mundus (r)orem aperuit
Mundus in ore factum est
Mundum (r)os aperuit
Mundum (r)os genuit
Mundum mrors aluit
Mundum (r)os habuit
Mundum lux esit
Lucem mundus esit

This is how, from memory, we understand this painting. The arduous climb, the ascent in obstinate dimensioning towards the Moment (Moment-zero, Moment-infinity), by crossing or journey or trajectory, by taut line, along the sources of the world-generated, fabled and sown in the mind (the pictorial *mens*). Fragmentation, fracturing, crumbling of a single display of blind transfixion, anoptic extension of the body and of memorability, under an intermittent gaze, unique, united: margins of fusions, forms of emission and escape, of dilation, the search for the shareable luminous molecule, *currens emphasis* and at the same time *peremptio*, from carefully delineated thresholds, in emission.

Thus we believe in this brilliant *genus* of painting, as an unaltered testimony to continuous Excess, up to the point of exasperation, and all the way through to the final *exultet.* And certainly our present language, almost perished, can no longer translate the other nature invented by the pictorial initiative in a vocal sense.

So this agony of the air (whose victims are the obscure suggestions, the congestions accomplished), hermetic melee or race of destinations, and here, almost as if to say cosmomachy, protraction of the myth of the sectioned *Sopore*, in fringes, in branches, in veils, in *super facies.* The extreme game, the Great Game, the infernal *Ludus*, between the Absence of mirrors, the Annihilation of perspectives and projections, trajections, dejections, which prefigures *in re* the *ludus* between Lugubrious and Serene, the Entanglement and the Whirlpool, the Embrace and the Strait, the Movement and the Ictus, the Orphic and the Medeic of time; within the scenario of the abundant unconscious maternity of the *materies*, the heart of the non-limit, aorist directions. Omniverse anatomy, subtended like an Artery, the artery of trans-mutation *in se permanens.* The artery traversed by the painter, let us say, *pictor* of Tradition (*paràdosis*), born among those who intensify and consolidate in memory, in memorable testimony, in *introibo*, and hope in *flatus*, in the very essence of *flatus*, in the animated amalgam and in the majestic engulfment of *flatus* and dissemination. His journey, in grains and particles, we could define as participating, attracted, in the indefinite territory of *loksía*, the Apollonian area, the ubiquitous obliquity of the conspiratorial air, warm wandering erratic, diagonal connective; convocation and reception of stimuli of analysis, establishment of the ictus of signals, attribution of splinters and dross, wandering *fragmina*; and a poignant load of tight and transfigured anxiety (more in figure, beyond figure), thickening of atmospheres in nuclei, instantaneous semaphores without duration, which cloaks and recalls delicate incandescence. This is how the painter carries out his act: the system of Tear and Strip, hinged, diagonal, of the Obliques (always Apollo *loksòs*) of the Channels, of the Precipitates, of Subatomic Paths, the *Umbrosae Civitates*, *munitae* and *inconditae*, the infirm *periéchon* that embraces and connects everything. The apparatus, radiant and uncertain, intelligent and arcane in which the continuous onset and immediate disappearance of the Extremes is determined, in enquiry and request for settlement, or for a Front or a Spectral, flashing or eclipsed, in Outrage and Amazement, and in calm rejection of the Pliable and the Tonic. The colour, all the way through to the *subtilis*, *subliminalis*, unconscious, natural drafting; the colour-corpus, autogenous like the Orphic *corpus*, dispersion and perfusion, smile and din of the indistinct, hermitage of the absolute, only akin to itself, shattering of the indistinct. So that each one, when looking, recognises his own invisibility, his own light, his own abyss, without footprints: the *notio* and the *nutus* appear (or diaphanise) simple and of indifferent duration.

In the adolescent clarity, or the breathtaking candour of the expanses, a certain kind of disciplined, adhesive alchemy lies solitary, almost mute (without any reference to cycles of recovery, revival, or pursuit of themes typical of historical alchemy). In this, there was also a symbolically natural, almost didactic wording of a dominant *nigredo-albedo* conflict, *lux-in-tenebris, lux in tenebris lucet et tenebrae eam non comprehenderunt,* or the ultimate, eschatological solvency of corporeity within the layers of light: the "firmamentum" and its plenary metamorphosis; field of the *spatia calida*, interminable, in lost regions, inflictable terms: topology naturally similar to its source, to its superficial destiny, of sprinkled epidermis (*mundum ros genuit*), of the disconnected bed of unification, rarefaction and precarious continence of the *unum.* Therefore, whoever turns to look at the ample salt of these topological syllabatures, like the Lot of legend, may encounter the Transformation into salt, into topical White and iridescence and foam of the necessary Salt.

The painting of this *genus* cannot be defined as an existential condition: but a passage from one state of life to another, from honeycombs to hives; and the resting of existence in oscillating veils (*velum templi scissum est*), in the pattern, in the: very force of the white void (of "moving") where states of life and vital centres, the ecstatic patience of surfacing, the grasp of emersion, the unheard-of pressure of the world, are compared, in a single expert incessant (*perenniter extensa*) cohesion: experienced indifference, physiological trace, returned memory, surrection and destined solicitude: like an intensive destination and predestination; extensive, of tragic waiting: waiting is of the Homogeneous, and of the Hologeneous. Beneath a kind of: veil, banner, shroud, sindon, simulacrum, sown between a cosmological echo and the final interdiction; excited, coagulated, tight, shattering, atomised animations, (as of breaths, of souls, of perished wings), acrobatics of pure trails, fading or solution of uncertain imaginary power (and imaginary as: recovery, redemption, exemption, restitution, *expiatio*, autotome, citation, excitement, intervention, concision, excitement, intervention, concision, thoughtful and considered phrasing: phrasing of the great Tree of light, at the end of this long flight and tenacious reverberation); to create the immense unstable Curtain, inserted in the Intimate (the minimal Abyss), which the hiatuses quote and the impossible return of the Perpetual Larva irrigates; liquid *descensio*, between longing and obliteration, and the reciprocal radicals, and the imaginary fracture demultiplied into fragile shatterings of conjecture and blunder. The knot of light thus sows the field of Apollonian air, *sine loco*, *sine tempore*, *saeculum seculi*, transparent scraps of the millennium *immin-ens-eminens, immanens-emanens, immanans-emanans, minans pulvis*. Like the gaze touching upon a fraction of immemorial and causeless wind, without the *se cause sui*, the *se* spectrum that is both hospitable and adverse, where the consumed escape from the centre is the only effect of the non-cause, non-caused shadow. This shadow is research and image, enquiry and signal operated by painting: as if to create an unknown principle of minimum energy for maximum instability.

Fumus fuimus
Fumus fingemur
Fatum fingimus
Fumum futurum

1988 Filiberto Menna, in VASCO BENDINI. OPERE DAL 1966 AL 1970 DELLA SERIE *OGGETTO COME STORIA*, edited by Mirella Chiesa, Venice: Il Traghetto, 1988. Catalog of an exhibition of the same title, presented at the Galleria Il Traghetto, Venice; Break Club, Rome, June 1988.

But such an intricate relationship cannot but stand on a border between the two domains, on a threshold that divides and unites inside and outside. This place is the surface of the work where painting can assert all its rights, removing the risk of solipsism and intimist complacency from the path back to the inner self. Bendini's work therefore stems from internal motivations, so that "a chromatic lake is a lake of the heart" (Arcangeli) and the sign has all the vibrations and shifts of a sensitivity that is brought to extreme tension; at the same time, the artist's focus never loses contact with the outside world, with the objects and images that surround us and accompany us daily.

This Venetian exhibition, centred around a group of works from 1966 to 1970, reveals the other aspect of Bendini's work, the one that looks outwards and is therefore attentive to a recognition and collection of objects and fragments that enter the domain of the surface and contribute to a new definition. The transition occurred in the mid-1960s—in 1966 to be precise—with the work *Come è* [As it is], consisting of a chair in front of a frame, a mirror on the floor and a voice repeater: seemingly random objects, which were in actual fact skilfully arranged by the artist to pose a fundamental question for art regarding representation and the relationship between it and the viewer. A singular work, which is "poor" in nature and yet also "conceptual" in that it poses the problem of art's self-reflection before engaging it in a reconnaissance of the outside world. The empty frame allows the gaze to go beyond the window of the picture and look out, while the mirror refers everything back to the subject looking at it, just as the repeater refers to the subject speaking.

From this critical situation, the artist moves towards more direct contact with the outside world, using the surface of the painting, the pictorial material and the signs, for relating, as instruments capable of attracting, within the structural economy of the work, objects and fragments drawn from the outside world. The inward journey of the first phase, more directly involved in the informal adventure, now changes direction, moving outward with a new focus on the things that accompany us daily. But Bendini's interest is not directed at the objects and images that characterise the urban scene (high-tech products that artistic procedures take as a term of reference, like a "second" nature), but rather at fragmented things, on the verge of disappearing forever. The pictorial and extra-pictorial elements merge on the surface, interacting with reciprocal exchanges, each bearing news of its own linguistic and existential history: matter, colour and sign welcome external things into the work, mediating their message and integrating it with the flow of impulses from within; the objects keep the surface under tension, balancing the forces that push in a centripetal direction, tending to bring the painting out of the painting. The result is a very tight structure, steeped in a dynamism that is all the more engaging when it is apparently locked in a contemplative measure.

1992 Flaminio Gualdoni, "PERCORSO DI BENDINI", in VASCO BENDINI: OPERE STORICHE, OPERE RECENTI, L'OPERA SU CARTA, edited by Flaminio Gualdoni, Oscar Goldoni and Danilo Eccher, Bologna: Nuova Alfa, 1992. Catalog of an exhibition of the same title, presented at the Galleria Comunale d'Arte Moderna, Bologna; Galleria Civica, Modena; Galleria Civica, Trento, March-April 1992.

In recent years, critics have examined the complex story of Vasco Bendini in a conspicuous fashion, almost as if to renew the tension and richness of the readings that, intoned by Francesco Arcangeli and Maurizio Calvesi in the 1950s and 1960s, had made him one of the most important examples in the debate. Moreover, these approaches were free from the pressing discomfort of aggregations and critical definitions, more attentive to singularities and exceptions than to systematic clauses, and more relaxedly distant from the fervour of those years, those hopes and those mythologies.

On this occasion, it is necessary not so much to re-propose a reconstruction of Bendini's career and his exegesis, which are given due consideration elsewhere in the catalog, as to identify the strong moments, the radiant problematic nuclei that determined the trigger and guaranteed continuity throughout these decades. Furthermore, the changing and sometimes abrupt mutations into which his work has ventured over time, consistent in an incontestable way with the nervous system of expression, free to wonder and act in a non-strategically linear sense with respect to every stylistic rule, should immediately be perceived as a primary perspective.

The first nucleus, which is crucial to Bendini's rich season of the 1950s, is an understanding of the value of corporeity, and of the identity of apparent form, which is quite eccentric with respect to what our local history, still provincially bound at the beginning of the decade to the divide between figuration and abstraction, has determined.

In order to evaluate the radical diversity of Bendini's early years, it is good to be clear about the non-modal influence exerted on his training by Guidi: beyond the pictorial circumstances—and it is worth remembering Guidi's tangency with Spatialism at the time—he was a musician of chromatic clots of light, and an auscultator of a *vie des formes* of vital vibrations, of open and perilous formativeness. And Guidi is the intermediary of an interpretation that is certainly loving, yet anything but "domestic" and orthopaedic, of Morandi, and particularly of the Morandi who, in the 1940s and 1950s, offered the new generation the clues to a figurative tension that transcended its own historical premises in silent adventure.

Bendini bases his reflections on his sensory experience of the world, and on the poetic restitution of its expressive density, on these clear poles of triangulation. His reasoning is first and foremost about space, as a place of flowing between the first projective trigger of sensation and the abstract depth of consciousness that perceives it: space that is not established, postulated or conditional, but perceived right from the first genetic clot of the process as tension and relationship; as suspended drama. And of light, light/colour, which becomes the substance and identity of that space, not through transcription or translation, but through its own specific quality and vocation, which causes the differentials, the movements and the characters to materialise.

Bendini devises an image whose dimension is not locked, astonished, in objective metrics, nor does it proceed according to the fertile step of analogy, the rhetorical scheme of the screen of consciousness. For him, the place of the image is a sort of undefined mental climate, an alienated and suspended situation in which the otherness of painting can really attempt, a non-spurious relationship with the world and with meaning.

The image is an appearance, but not of another appearance. And its physiology, its physicality, is the genetic *phylum* that does not mimic the natural one, but equates it. The figure becomes extension, a "nonchalant substance", and draws upon a corporeity that has nothing to do with the deafness of matter, gravity, opacity or mortal destiny. It is the body of painting, light/colour that assumes a provisional, wandering, unstable, yet congruent and clear identity, emotionally and intellectually perceptible without misunderstandings.

What counts more than the integument of this body is the nervous system, the weave of energies, of the courses that, through internal and unforeseen ways, have decided its qualification. Thus, in years in which themes such as forming and shaping, naturalism and naturalness, material and sign, gesture and body, found a kaleidoscopic spectrum of contiguous intentions, often varying in their minimal yet substantial accents, Bendini sensed that he possessed—in the authoritative and final stance of the gesture that indicates, heir to ancient automatisms but, like a *jaku*, resentful of its ultimate implications; and in the luminous lightness of the dry materials, of a soft and simple thinness, which are characteristic of him—the key to a strong and typical expression, of precise autonomy.

Thus the series of *I Segni segreti* [Secret Signs] and *Teste* [Heads], with the substantial implications of landscape and figure that they excite, should not be read in terms of an *ubi consistam* between the ranks of the abstract, with Venturian veins, or those of an early *autre* atmosphere, of a stylistic, or even less so, strategic type. In their dry and severe experimentalism, in their rising on the breathing and climatic spaciousness of the canvas, the sheet of paper, they represent the radiant pursuit of a practice that discounts those theoretical positions in the name of a sinking without a net, without clauses, in the understanding of the world and in its springy expressive rendering.

Appearance, and the other body of the image, are therefore the real issue that Bendini decides to tackle, revealing a singular ability to place himself at the nerve centre of the artistic debate—to whose scope and positions he is anything but indifferent—and at the same time to maintain a sort of anti-theoretical, certainly anti-intellectualist *aside*, concentrated on a confidential and close conversation with the *act* of painting.

In the harsh, unconquerable, proliferating excavation of the early 1950s, he searches for the boundary at which the identity of the image emerges, the primary status of its being a form of space. In this sense, marking and tracing have a founding value and a conceptual priority that Bendini explores in the stupefied and obsessive serialisation of his works.

The birth of the *Gesto e materia* [Gesture and Matter] series is the natural consequence. The "concision" that Pallucchini mentions in his 1956 text for the Modenese exhibition at the Saletta, the naked emotional vibration of the *Segni segreti*, so introverted yet hopeful of a possible image, has a restraint, a suspicion. Bendini does not know the rigour of *less is more*, but the entire phase of those papers and canvases asks the neutrality of those backgrounds for a privileged condition of expression. The emotional immediacy of the marks—even when, in the *Teste*, the urgent brushstrokes invade the whole space—gains in analytical precision from the fact that the autonomous value of the material, dye, coloured paste, is placed in check from the outset.

Now Bendini knows that the misunderstanding and mystery of the corporeal must pass through that experience, with all the inescapable historical implications this entails, from certain expressionist chromosomes to the visionary Morandi of the 1930s to the seventeenth-century mythologies of those times. And he knows that the resolution must come from a rhetorical overturning of the approach: finding the typical resonance of the sign/gesture, its qualitative faculty of making the image be, starting from a condition of saturation, of quantitative siege of the material and its perceptible textures and captures.

In philological terms, Arcangeli rightly devotes—and with due caution—references to Fautrier and Wols, also warning of the risk of elegance that Bendini's talent might unwittingly raise.

Once again, however, Bendini has something else in mind. The axial centrality of the *Testa*, a favoured feature in many works, with the implications of naturalness and semblance that the thematic trigger allows to echo, offers him a structural system with a high density of meaning, while also being very simple. On this basis, he avoids being carried away not only by the distressing emphasis of pictorialism, but also by that sort of vegetal and animal, programmatically magmatic blow-up, which finds larvae and filaments beneath the intensive movements of the pictorial matter that feeds but also limits the most practised naturalistic Informalism. Not only that. Acting again from a vast spectrum of problematic triggers—the absolute and deaf blackness, of desperate hardness, of certain works; the polychrome clamour reduced to an astonished and panting silence, in others; the liquid and neurotic washout of tones, in yet others—it is still possible to resolve the emergence of the semblance of form by way of light.

The short, saddened, urgent brushstrokes, or the liquid and stratified spreading of the drippings, feature sudden raised patches, lumps like nuclei, which respect the filigree of the horizon and the vertical axis, making the outcropping of distant glimmers, of lights, of not disenchanted whiteness, resonate with this growing image.

The material is rich, with a turgidity that allows the sensual relationship with it to erupt, but instead of being excited, it is provoked to a physiological humility, a modesty that makes it a neutralised quantity, inert and inexpressive. Once again, Bendini does not admit the easy sensual capture of what de Chirico termed "beautiful coloured matter": if his painting is fiction, another experience close to the perceptible world, the image that is created is not illusion, nor is it theatre: it is an effective figure of the possible, with its own body, its own soul, its own life.

Certainly, the "material simplicity" and the "tacitly convulsive" motion of the gestures intuited by Calvesi are the primary trace of this moment, which is far more foundational than the climatic debt of occasional titles such as *Larva* or *Reliquia*.

Indeed, even during this complex phase, Bendini is acutely analytical. His primary condition is one of unforced expressiveness, of concentrated and introverted poeticism: but it is thought out, and unfolds in a relationship with language made up of profound and lucid scrutiny, free from emotional complacency, definitive verification and purification of every element, every juncture and every operational method. It is for this reason that his position, during those years, is incomparable except with that of other atypical subjects such as Scanavino and Moreni.

This leads Bendini to a further crossroads. On the one hand, he feels that the process allows him to rediscover a figural step that is not ambiguous or heteronomous: the short series of *Figure* [Figures], in the early 1960s, is the lofty but final outcome—given the premises—of this analytical and inventive course.

On the other hand, Bendini warns that there is an element of ambiguity remaining in the disenchanted and non-complicit approach to the quantitative value of pictorial matter. If it is material, inert in itself if not for the actively formative character that the artist induces in it, the expressive process must be able to extend to a more contaminating objective dimension; it must be able to make the process of the possible act within the world of things themselves, in the existential margin, which has already been opened up, in very different ways, by Burri and the European and American New Dada.

Again, it is a question of appearance of the image and of the body: a body now sought at the point of contradiction between the ordinary plane of experience and the perceptible, memorial, symbolic transfiguration that takes place within art.

The mid-1960s saw the most extroverted moment of Bendini's work in terms of modality. Wood, resins, wadding, plastics, fabrics, straw and so on appear. As regards forms and objects, there is the glove-hand, the spoon, the box, the cabin.

Compared to the grid of elevated references, Bendini daringly implements a further interpretation of polymaterialism, especially in the series of canvases in which the material is charged with a strong emotional intention, with a complex subjective transfiguration, and used in a linguistically pictorial way.

In the environmental operations, which make him a not unlikely companion during the most conceptual moment of the artistic debate—although Bendini goes through all this, and it could not be otherwise, in an anti-strategic way, only pursuing the internal paths of his own expression—strong formal and modal schemes to the point of stereotype prevail. The environment, the physical place, is activated by the physiological measure of the body, in an entirely anthropomorphic metric, which attempts with lucid contradiction—I am thinking of *Cronotopo* [Chronotope] or *Cabina* [Cabin] (1967)—an exchange with the other corporeity of painting. The object, on which the artist exercises a profound and restless recognition, is prevalently an evident form, an emptied *pattern*—the glove—or an indifferent and ownerless thing recharged by manipulation until it becomes an amulet, an alienated apparition.

Bendini soon realised the profound implications, but also the theoretical limits of this extra-pictorial experience with respect to his basic approach. Moreover, we can be sure that cataloging experiences this moment of Bendini's as a derogation from his previous attitude, and as a mundane adaptation to the debate, given the difficulty of seeing the profound congruity of reflections and intentions: after all, even in the case of the much more extensively studied Schwitters, the mists of misunderstanding have only recently dissolved.

So be it. From the late 1960s, and for a number of years, Bendini implemented his polymaterialism with objective contaminations in a more pictorial manner. The *Gesto e materia* series is still the problematic reference point. Now, however, the desire is once again building for the neutral, barely atmospheric confidence of the background, alongside the almost anxious wish to invest the materials, the drippings and the things with a luminosity that leads them to the threshold of imponderability, of the coloured and affective evidence of the signs of the past. And to a sort of desperate beauty.

Analisi e ipotesi [Analysis and Hypothesis], *Alchimia dell'immagine* [Alchemy of the Image], *Il ciclo delle parvenze* [The Cycle of Appearances], *Il tempo come creazione* [Time as Creation]. Bendini senses a further rhetorical risk in the radiant iteration of these works. More than that, he perceives that it is the possible moment to distil the rate of technical artificiality of the work, in the name of a more intimate natural vocation of the pictorial image: a naturalness that is now no longer even problematically understood within the encountered otherness of art.

He now sees a higher and more suspended condition of colour and light: one might even say a metaphysical one. Bendini is attempting not a lowering, an extenuating control of the sensory uptake, but a forcing in a hyper-aesthetic sense. The wager, the hypothesis, is that even sensory hypertrophy can be exorcised, and the ordinary expectation of beauty can be transcended and purified into a distant, icy warning, brought back to the flows and reverberations of the mental sphere.

Gold, which becomes the leitmotif of his works of these years, acts in this sense, starting from its historically dual notion, both symbolic and material.

The materiality of the layers is reabsorbed into an imprint, a pure veiling variant, in a sort of atmospheric stratification of tones. In *Alchimia dell'immagine* it is the aluminium support that accentuates the pure luminous condition of the image, whitening, secret, agitated by minimal events.

In *Il tempo come creazione* and in the last series of paintings *Ipotesi d'attesa* [Waiting Hypothesis], the thin colour and the light, overcome by exhaustion, or by genetic strength, now encounter the conditions for an enlargement, for slow and clamorous growth of the image, which actually becomes an emotional landscape, a state of mind made of light/colour, and figure, again: a pasture for the eye and the affections, a wonder that is now shadowy, now blinded, with a light and persistent feminine sensuality. As D'Amico writes, Bendini's work "spreads across the vast surfaces with a manner that is both proud and persuasive. The hand abandons itself to unprecedented altercations; the soul swells as it goes, doing; it is filled with turgid senses."

Bendini achieves a kind of definitive knowledge in these canvases: so rich, yet so simple and necessary.

1993

Fabrizio D'amico, "BENDINI: 1950-1964", in VASCO BENDINI, Fabrizio D'Amico and Flaminio Gualdoni, Rome: (continue) edizioni d'Arte, 1993.

It is in 1950 that Vasco Bendini's early and yet full maturity, at once dazzling and mysterious, established itself, unequivocally attested by works and documents. To understand those distant beginnings, it is useful to return to a well-known passage by Francesco Arcangeli, who reveals a comprehensive understanding of his path in the second essay on the "last naturalists." "Thus," wrote Arcangeli,

> "just as Mandelli ends up maintaining a very modern balance between the inner screen of consciousness and the outer screen of nature [...], it seems to me that Vasco Bendini can lay claim, in Italy, to a first (a singular, solitary, and almost candid first) in the shifting of this balance of a naturalistic kind towards a painting where a strange accentuation of the spiritual prevails, without destroying the other term."

There is much in this piece to be remembered; much of what was seen at the time by those who were intellectually close to Bendini would remain true throughout his career; much would be retraced by the critics who—very select, attentive, always deeply involved, to a degree that would perhaps suffice to establish the importance of this painting in the context of postwar Italian art—would follow the continuation of his work. First and foremost, Arcangeli's identification of a "balance"—fragile, unstable, shifting—as the privileged, essential "place" of Bendini's painting. And it will always be this way: never a possession, for him; or rather a possession immediately cracked by doubt or further hope, will be the trepidatious way in which Bendini approaches his painting.

Then comes Arcangeli's description of the "accentuation of the spiritual" in Bendini. A "strange accentuation": which is already different, less defining and more elusive than a presumed prevalence of the abstract vocation over the naturalistic one; but even if still confusedly intuited, the knowledge of a particular inflection of the soul within that part which tended towards the abstract. A leaning towards a term in which the systematic and unequivocal nature of prose would have to doubt itself in the face of the less certain, or less demonstrable, reasons of poetry. And this second "point" of Arcangeli's would also be retraced and developed. This was particularly true of Maurizio Calvesi, on several occasions, starting from when, speaking of Bendini's image, he identified its "secretly dreaming nature" and its

> "wholly interior origin: where the relationship is established not between the self and reality (be it natural reality or that of dreams, vision and emotion), but between one part and another of the self; between the thinking and sentient self and the self that acts and realises, as if trying to dissolve the figurative insolubility of that relationship in a figurative hypothesis."

But in the face of these intuitions, which should be said to be still in the making in Arcangeli, something is already full, entirely true and definitively illuminating as regards both Bendini's soul and his painting; and this intimate comprehension descended at that time not only from a sharp understanding of the work, but from the moral solidarity between artist and critic. And it seems to me that this "something," this profound understanding of the reasons behind an aesthetic adventure in its infancy, is contained in the triple adjective with which Arcangeli defines the "first" he attributed to Bendini: "singular, solitary, and almost candid first." Bendini happened to record a number of firsts in Italy, which are remembered or accepted now; on the other hand, he also went back on his own steps and along paths opened up by others, in search of his own truth; it may be much less fundamental today than it was assumed to be then, to have recorded priority points in the book of time. But, singular, solitary and almost candid: that this was already attributed to him then, and that this is how Bendini's path has always remained, still counts today; this has that path an essential one, which cannot be exchanged with other experiences in the map of Italian art. Singular, first of all because little or nothing, at least in Italy, and at least within the sphere of things that could plausibly be known to him, could have been imagined by Bendini in 1950—or even in 1952 or 1953—as supportive of his research. Regarding our figurative history in that still anachronistically post-war period, we know the tiring diatribes, the fences that abruptly lacerated it, the forts equipped with ideology that gave asylum to opposing theories on art; and we know of the spurious hypothesis of the abstract-concrete, which imagined bridging those distances with an impossible dialogue. Bendini seems, mysteriously, not to have suffered from the *aut-aut* of his years: perhaps due to his brief distance from the generation of both the "masters" and the younger artists.

The first fruit he is able to draw from this discomfort is that which delivers him to his "solitary" modernity: the painting—or rather, during those months, the paper barely dampened by tempera—is not an indifferent occasion for the projection of an external objective or mental reality; it is, consequently, not a screen of an obligation that is servile with respect to pre-established intentions, to programmatic postulates. Rather, it is a place where, like an insect in a spider's web, they become entangled, still unaware of themselves, in the impulses of thought, soul and memory. Impulses that take on an almost unassuming figure on the paper, dressed in the fragility of growing life, in the mobility of the hypothesis, in the vague indeterminacy of the dream.

Apart from a few rare gouaches ("but produced using the tip of the brush, with the intention of drawing") in which there is a fairly recognisable echo of Matisse, conjugated with memories of an "old" abstract code, somewhere between Arp and Magnelli, veined with surrealism, the tempera paintings done between 1950 and 1953, then again in 1956, seem to distance themselves from any authoritative support, and to dispose themselves almost *sotto voce* to their own solitary, "candid" word. They are the interrupted paths of a black sign, which rejects both Hartung's rhetorically assimilated syntax and Kline's definitive gesture: "dashes deconstructed in black" which, instead of declaiming, whisper anxiously about their almost tentative search for space. Or liquid descents of irresolute colour, tonally tuned (blacks and greys; pinks, whites and greens spread out on the soft yellow of the sheet); impalpable, diaphanous spatial infiltrations; grids, with no body weight, pulled over the sheet so that the light leaks through.

To explain them, the correct assumptions made at the outset do not apply: Tal Coat and Sam Francis, "certain trends from Klee's final years," Bram Van Velde and Michaux, "certain drawings by Bissier," Italian Spatialism (on which, perhaps, one could linger further, pointing out the Roman activity of Tancredi, in the 1950s, and the first works of Mario De Luigi, both in relation to Guidi, Bendini's master). Because these are tangencies, mostly unknown to Bendini at the time, and devoid of any charismatic capacity for a young man who, even if he had spotted them, would hardly have been able to recognise any possible normative authority in them. It is better, then, to accept Bendini's research in the early 1950s for what it was: a solitary, introverted path, without any other dialogues than those that still linked him to Guidi and Morandi.

From Morandi came that profound ethical measure that marked his relationship with his work from the very beginning: made of silence and distance, of absolute concentration on a single theme, of listening to his own inner world, of welcoming—in it—the world of "the other," necessary and possible only on condition that he had first purged his emotions of all randomness and intimacy: of all existential arrogance. This method remained fundamental to Bendini from then on, even though the years were different: those years of his greater involvement with an ungoverned nature, or those in which his moral revolt against injustice led him to give a harshly symbolic name to some of his paintings. But it was only a matter of different baptisms: his longstanding need to found painting in the shadows of consciousness remained identical.

This was to be the time of what Arcangeli called "the fierce extroversion, strong at times to the point of stridency, determinedly ostentatious, of a persistent and obsessive introversion." And he was referring, in 1964, to the clamorous and sorrowful painting of the beginning of that decade; to which we have just come for a moment to note the substantial continuity of Morandi's teaching. Bendini, on the other hand, immediately distanced himself from it: in his completely different way of conceiving the "form" of painting—not an untouchable and tetragonal goal, entirely prefigured; but an uncertain and united landing place comprised of design, hypothesis and destiny. And in significantly varying the pretext, or the iconographic obsession, within which painting is concretely exercised. From the "still life," the silent and objective presence of the world, to the "face," a phantom that stands obscurely before consciousness like a fragile diaphragm between self and other than self, where the distance is almost immeasurable. Bendini travelled the path in its entirety, and poured the consequences of this long step "away" from Morandi over every other "theme" that he explored in his painting, following on from the long and dominant theme of the "face": from the similar one of the "figure" to what, with a margin of imperfection, we can term "landscape." The chronological and stylistic introduction of the "face" motif is linked to Guidi: but after the experience of the *Diluvi* [Floods], which is difficult to reconstruct today and yet certainly essential, that "face" rapidly deteriorates in nature and goes from being a certain simulacrum of a reality to an elusive semblance, a ghost, the imprint of a life that is now distant in time and space.

An imprint evoked by a memory that is not a consoling, lyrical evocation of a truth thus stripped in that way of the turbulence of its flagrant life, but a way—the only one possible for Bendini—of knowing: about himself and about the world that obscurely presses on that face.

At times the features that occasionally belonged so clearly to that face are so concealed in the weave of the signs, in the fluid descents of colour, in the serpentine movement of the brush, in the dense ink hatching, that the iconographic motif seems to be on the point of dissolving.

Other problems then more urgent for Bendini: that of the surface as the single place of a painting that thinks of itself, no longer bound to mimesis; that of the automatic gesture: wide and spacious; that of light, which has to reach the surface slowly emerging from behind, hidden by the blanket of colour. These are aspects of his research of a linguistic nature, and of a prevalently abstract structure, which also had full citizenship in Bendini's painting in the 1950s (and not only), peaking at the beginning of the decade, and then again in the "first half of 1956, fertile with silent abstract experiments." And yet, the suspicion of a distant, merely formal exercise never falls on these tests of his: even when thought guides the hand more than emotion does, the image that emerges is—in the same way as his other work—always pregnant with tension, damp with trembling, uncertain of its destination, as if disturbed by the very act of its birth. Thus, it may be that in this abstract vocation of Bendini's painting, the reasons for the absolute importance, and above all the singularity, of his experience in those years are found more clearly than in the other foundation of his soul. But it is certain that, rather than hypothesising a hierarchy between Bendini's two modes of working, it is necessary to recognise their close congruity, the common life blood in which they originate; and to recognise how it is in their coexistence that there is another indication of the anti-programmatic nature of this research.

It was certainly during months and days, perhaps in the middle or towards the end of 1953, that he developed the still chaste and wandering traces of this work from *I segni segreti* (Secret Signs) series and, immediately afterwards, the long, excited, uninterrupted brushstrokes of the *Marina* in the Zini collection. The latter is one of the surviving and best-known works from the period of Bendini's greatest involvement with the poetics of Arcangeli's "last naturalism."

> "The internal tension that had made the tempera paintings of 1952 so vibrant and some of the faces of 1953 so macerated was already loosening in him; he was attempting to match his speculative interests with the powerful matrix of nature,"

wrote Roberto Tassi some time later.

> "But in a group of works that still remain, in which the voice of nature was in tune with his ancient anxieties, his desperate tremors, the subtle and rigorous poetry of his indistinct staining, of his volumes corroded and corrupted by the light of his dissolved spaces absorbed by the image, it was reborn with silent immediacy."

This was certainly Bendini's "borderline" experience between 1954 and 1955: an experience upon which, among other things, the painter's severe self-criticism certainly fell, more so than during other seasons of his work, leading him to want to destroy much of what he had done at the time. And yet also a season (his first, after all, in line with the times!) that provided him with a certain, unassailable boundary within which to hold back the impulses of a part of his soul. This was a season whose fruits, after the brief and sudden shift in 1956 towards the opposite pole of ideograms of oriental purity, were to be seen in his truly informal period, from 1957 to 1958. This two-year period was occupied by the irruption of matter in Bendini's painting, which was completely new. And there is no doubt that this period, like the previous "naturalist" period, was influenced by the prevailing climate of the time. These were the years of the discovery of Fautrier, of the belated acceptance of Wols by Italian culture, and also Morlotti's greatest years. Bendini is seduced by all of this; he is uninterested in an entirely external race towards the new; and just as years before, without having sought it, he had opened up a path of extraordinary foresight on his own and as the first to do so, once again he is not afraid to link his path to that of others. In the matter that grows and spreads on the canvas, he does not seek an onomatopoeic effusion of the organic, nor an easy triumph of pictorial translations; but he deposits in it his ancient signs, his always equal obsessions (those of the "face" and the "figure"). He hopes that in his obscure assembly, in that place which is now physically more ascertained than the diaphanous veil of paper of the past, his truth will become entangled and remain more durably, sought in the encounter between the secret impulses of the soul and the objective identity of the world.

That he soon doubts this path is due to the constant pressure to which Bendini—then as now—is accustomed to subjecting his research: certainly not to the qualitative results of his very particular "Art Informel." The fact remains that at the same time as he seems to be linked, through his confidence in the material, to the work of an entire generation, he harbours different thoughts and tensions: at times, as early as 1958, he returns to tempera and, instead of the new series of *Gesto e materia* [Gesture and Matter], he assigns some of this year's works to the previous series of *I Segni segreti*. Gradually the paste of the paint crumbles, the clamour, the sudden lighting, the gems and the burnt lights that had made the image sumptuous fade away; the "solid" is replaced by the eroded and vacant space of the bare canvas, on which the signs are arranged sparse and wandering

Above all, it is a quest for light that sustains his works of 1959 and 1960. Light which, as in some of his works on paper of 1952, leaks slowly out at points on the surface, permeated with halos and infinite transparencies. Again and again, they are very certain epiphanies of ambiguous and fluctuating images; once again indicators of an inner dimension that, between dream and memory, trembles on the edge of life. Sometimes the lack of colour, tuned to those pale lights, is enchanted by a sweet, almost exhausted transition of tones; sometimes, more dramatically, a tremulous glimmer of light emerges from a united abyss of darkness, as if from an unbridgeable distance.

This is true of the lean temperas of 1959 (although some date from 1958, and others from 1960): very high moments, moments of extraordinary concentration, of absolute poverty and chastity and yet of equally definitive happiness and fullness. Bendini certainly arrived there almost as a counterbalance to his previous incursion into the jubilation of matter. If he sensed, then, that he had reached a pinnacle of his painting, perhaps he did not suspect that he had drawn on one of the highest points of contemporary Italian painting. Nevertheless, he must certainly have been painfully aware that he was once again alone on that road.

And it was probably this existential malaise of his that prompted Andrea Emiliani, although aware of the value of that once again solitary experience (but perhaps for the first time, painfully solitary), of that "deliberate impoverishment of a landscape of grandiose spiritual architecture," to celebrate the new method that—right in the middle of 1960—took hold in Bendini's painting and would last, with a few variations in style, until 1964.

> "With the end of the hard Lenten period of lean and rarefied tempera, the ancient colour of 1957 [...], now dissolved in a dense slurry, seems to stretch out in the broad gesture of the spatula with an almost absurd, paradoxical moroseness,"

wrote Emiliani, reconnecting the season that was being inaugurated at the time of Bendini's first informal painting.

This is something different and new that is now grafted onto that older stump: that Bendini assumes the significance of his "Art Informel" as the possibility of a "new image," in a timely and certainly consolatory concomitance with his younger years. Within that return to the "image" and the "figure" that attracted many to its "centre" at the start of the 1960s, Bendini positioned himself with an originality that would have explained his very singular evolution in 1964-65 in its entirety.

He brought something with him to the new season from an experience that had now stretched for over a decade: the sense of light that is not a sudden, external dazzle on the surface, but issues from deep layers of space and matter. But much more changed for Bendini in those years: for the first time he admitted that shouting, revolt, violent gestures and a sometimes clamorous chromatic explosion, far removed from the complicit knowledge of tone, were possible and necessary for him. A nature that grows in flames until it enters you; a symbolic urgency to which the image is forced by the need to oppose the pain of existence (the *Ciclo di Cuba,* Cuba cycle; the *Serie dei personaggi*, Series of Characters): this is what tears Bendini away from himself for the first time; this is what pushes him towards the world.

1996

Paolo Fossati, "UN APPUNTO PER BENDINI 1983", in VASCO BENDINI: LA BALLATA DEI DIECI CIELI, edited by Silvia Pegoraro, San Giovanni in Persiceto: Aspasia, 1996. Catalog of an exhibition of the same title, presented at the Pinacoteca Comunale, Loggetta Lombardesca, Ravenna; Rocca dei Bentivoglio, Bazzano, May-June 1996.

La ballata dei dieci cieli [The Ballad of the Ten Skies] that is presented again in this exhibition dates from 1983. It is a series or, as Bendini himself notes, a polyptych of ten elements. Ten canvases of identical size and shape, painted over a short time, between the summer and early autumn, during a period of singular freedom and creativity for an artist who is "singular" in every point of his work.

In short, it is singular because it is disorientating and unsettling with respect to the dates and references in the contemporary art handbook of our years. And singular, impossible to label, a work to be taken and followed point by point with due intelligence and responsiveness, because by decentralising his work from current events, he has imprinted it with very special characteristics that are neither automatic nor mechanical with respect to its own development. Indeed, they are divining and wandering, since Bendini's shots, passages and affirmations (turbulence, if we can introduce a meteorological measure) utilise painting to make use of it elsewhere, to process it in another way.

So what Bendini is asking of his viewers is not contemplation but participation with him in the art space that his paintings and actions have determined and continue to provoke and illuminate. (Ginestra Calzolari has happily commented on this approach to putting himself forward for rejection in a report in verse that begins as follows:

> "There is no irony in not taking possession / not even sadness or pain / in recognising the impotence of the artist who / only in this way can 'inhabit' matter / [...].")

What a presentation should prompt most, I believe, is the unique nature of the reading that Bendini calls for. That is, saying what not to bear in mind when starting out with him, and what, at the same time, to bear in mind. Not to bear in mind, for example, the average rhetoric of his friends and contemporaries, while having a clear idea of the season in which our artist and his friends and contemporaries grew up, matured, decided on their future work: decided where to place themselves. His formative years, Bendini's *Bildungsroman,* were decisive, and not only for the obvious tautological reason that they were his years as a young man on the way to maturity, but for two reasons as obvious as they are specific to Bendini. The first is historical: the Art Informel season played a central part for the century's figurative arts. And Bendini soon realised this. In his excellent reading of the painter's early years, Andrea Emiliani clarifies the matter as follows:

> "Morandi and Guidi (1946-1950); the three-year period 1951-1953, during which Bendini freed himself from every school; the last naturalism 1954-1955; the *Informel* or rather Wols and Fautrier (1954-1956)."

I think it is important to say this, to invite the visitor's attention: that one must start from there even to read a work of thirty years later, because what has to be established is that Bendini's way of working is poetically, existentially what it is because it is also charged with a long-term historical focus.

Bendini immediately realised the importance of the season of the so-called "Informel" and, on having understood the non-contingent reasons for this, he played his cards: that is to say, taking note of this and of the clarification entailed by this series of experiences during the century and of the reshuffling that ensued for the painting of each artist to come.

This indication is sufficient once and for all, while awaiting more convincing research: how during the "Informel" season painters carried out a double movement, aware of all the contradictions. On the one hand they loaded the support, as if this were already a painting without any other inventions and variations, with the weight of coloured and viscous materials, as if weight and viscosity were revealed in their "natural" inertia, surprises of meaning and portions of sense. At the same time, despite intentions and formulas, this carefully placed weight offers itself as a moving image, like a map, in which all the elements of the composition drive the viewer to turn his back on the weights and crusts of the materials and look elsewhere. (With a consequence that Bendini grasps very well, that, going back to the branches of the hitherto ill-supported Futurism, it is not contemplation that one must ask of the work, but participation and action, sliding to the limits of the art space indicated by the paintings.)

Faced with this wavering between the mobility of the action and the fixity of the mask, Bendini behaves, as Emiliani has just warned us, in his own way. From the literary vulgate that pursues an ultimate naturalism and strives to find situations that are not improbable, he chooses the path of decentralisation, of what he does pictorially, from psychological introspection and the projection of the spectator onto the painting. He masks the *ôtage*, the stain, the lump: but, as Apollinaire warned, if it is true that our story is as noble and tragic as the mask of a tyrant, subjection is immediately broken, no drama and no psychological intention will make us indifferent to other stories.

Bendini behaves as suggested by the texts of *Alice in Wonderland* or *Through the Looking Glass*, creating a representation that denies itself comprehension and moves towards the "autonomous image, independent of the artist's consciousness."

Lewis Carroll tells us how the White Queen remembers things before they happen. The Messenger is in prison before being judged for the crime he will commit after the judge has passed his sentence. So time stands still. In the Mad Hatter's house it is always five o'clock, it is always tea-time. And the cups are filled.

"For me, it's no longer a question of metaphor, but of metamorphosis," wrote Braque, hinting at a secret regarding workmanship, a focus on the processes of transformation on which the auscultation of the pictorial organism is based when the organism shifts the attention of the painting "further over" ("all images bear the words 'further over'," Montale did not fail to postulate).

"After all, the myth itself is the reflection of an accomplished act, and what has been accomplished is a continuation of it," explained Caillois in turn; and Canetti: "bad writers point out the traces of metamorphoses; good writers highlight them and pursue them." Metamorphoses, or internal flows, to go back to Montale, or, sticking with the same poet, movements: flows, or metamorphoses of what? and movements towards where?

The work, the painting, the sculpture, as if they were a more or less comfortable waiting room, the next room, once again a decentralisation. And once that waiting room has been passed through (we read in *Arsenio*, for example:

> "a refrain of castanets. It is the sign of another orbit; then elsewhere: a broken mesh in the net / that holds us, again, in Delta: the tugboat's whistle / that out of the mists arrives in the bay; etc."),

here are the feelings, or the prime motives, sometimes religiousness, indifference, suspicion, curiosity, cynicism, in other words, the functions that are more proper to painting or sculpture: the little garden to be set up and kept tidy; the gardens to be looked after, the *new Elysian fields*, if we listen to another poet who, in dechirican fashion, did not fail to assure us: "I saw the muses."

"A painting," Degas wrote to a friend, "is an artificial, unnatural work: it demands as much cunning as the preparation of a crime." It communicates a break-in, proposes an exercise in dexterity dipped in savagery. The painting in front of us, is the result of a calculated and well-executed event ("criminal," insists Degas) through which the author wanted to get rid of something.

"The universe, oh, if it were to suddenly disappear, / failed ghost! / A new alchemy would create dawns and sunsets / artificial magnesium, / season of Bengal and acetylene," clarifies Soffici. Palazzeschi keeps up with him, more radically: "God, have mercy on the last of your children, / open a hiding place for me / outside of nature!" Cardarelli's invitation belongs to the same order of positions: "we would like to say, let us be set straight by history, which, if it has any sense, will forget us."

(The explanation given by Leonardo Sinisgalli, in a book whose title is not accidental, in so many returns to the earth, *L'età della luna*, proposes another path to the same point: "he who loves nature too much risks losing the sense of the world," he writes. "The poet must reject the motions of creation. The child, like the poet, is the enemy of evidence.")

In order to arrive outside "nature"; to make the picture, therefore, a similar coming out ("look for a broken link in the mesh / that holds us, you leap out, flee!" Montale writes in the prelude to his *Ossi di seppia*), that is, jumping from the train in motion, turns out to be an obvious and extreme resource that preserves an important feature of the psychology of those who commit a crime. It passes through the compulsion to reveal. And if not of the crime revealed there, in and of itself, then certainly of its protagonist.

Where do I want to go with these indispensable indications? I want to establish that the decisive point for Bendini is his decentralisation of painting away from existential burdens (for respiration, or even exclamation, of the mind, as suggested by Emilio Villa regarding Bendini), painting as vision from action that continues beyond contemplation from the experience of self-representation, creating between the two spaces, of painting and of the painter's action, a virtual and symbolic short circuit, in the "transposed and specialised form" of figuration.

Here, too, there was no lack of warnings. Palazzeschi had written: "I put a lens / in front of my heart / to make people see it," and had ended one of his poems with his battle cry: "and let me have fun!" To be doubled with Savinio's usual tight commentary:

> "the poet is no longer an inspired person, who in some cases, and let us even say in the most sublime cases, is reduced to the completely receptive, completely passive condition of the pythia, but becomes himself a 'producer' of poetry. The poet no longer listens to the muse but only to the voice of his own heart. The question that the informal years did not fail to pose was where, in what practicable place, that voice led."

(Ginestra Calzolari comes to our aid again, placing the possibility of inhabiting matter in the artist's impotence. And Dario Trento has every reason to remind us how that short-circuit we are talking about becomes—in the years that are paintings in this exhibition—"a contribution to the renewed founding of the symbolic field in figuration.")

As we know, *La ballata dei dieci cieli* is a series of paintings, a polyptych of: ten canvases of identical size and shape, 190×190 cm. The series is not a forced repetition. The freedom of these ten paintings from one another is evident. The format and use of oil and gold pigments, are repeated. The polyptych repeats a single text, as in the repetition (stylistic? formal? material?) the work frees itself from the given language to offer spaces, possible scenes. Exercises, operations, possibilities. Again a balancing of different spaces, exercise (living), between invention (intoxication) and realisation (industrious, worthy, to return to Trento's text, of an "operator aware of his own aptitudes as a shaman of technological drift"). Mallarmé suggested,

> "exercise, as invention, involves an inebriation of art, and at the same time an industrial realisation. *Haystacks I, Haystacks II, Haystacks III; untitled 1, untitled 2,* [...] *, untitled 5; Baume am Gein; Homage to the Square I, Homage to the Square II, Homage to the Square III; New York Boogie Woogie I, New York Boogie Woogie II, Coca Cola bottles, Marilyn,*" etc.

(the authors are all too well known to recall them one by one); then, by Bendini himself, *Gioco come gioco* [Game as a Game] (1990), or *Ipotesi d'attesa* [Waiting Hypothesis] (1990-1991); and the additional "series" that is the subject of this exhibition. There is no point in attempting an argument on the theme here. Let us stop at two suggestions. Firstly, the series and the time. Ten times we see a presentation within a given dimension, ten times we suggest, in the unity of format, a tension, varied, thought out and painted in a short time, with a quick draft. (Each time it is the time of drafting, of elaboration, the nucleus from which the series extends forward and returns to its base). The series therefore ascertains a space of time and of an opening of the image.

Are the figures (i.e., the territories) of these ten canvases skies, open, flowing and fast-moving? Cloudy, airy skies in accordance with a symbolist tradition ("I love the clouds, the clouds that pass, there, over there, the magnificent clouds," of Baudelairian extraction, to be associated with the Cézanne of "it is always the sky, things without limits, that attract me")? Nothing exacerbated, if we are to believe it; since the lines of the path followed by the ten panels of Bendini's polyptych assume the design of a possible cosmogony, birth, growth, fall.

Skies, then, as a re-elaboration of images; but also as a production of interiority? We ask Moretti, accepting the answer: certainly, but above all in the sense that the artist's emotion before his image is great. "In emotion there is no key to the image," adds Moretti. The figurative coincidence, the time-image counterpoint, of each of the paintings in the series as a warning of a ductility and also of the possibility of language. Its symbolic nature. Second warning: the series and the ductility of language. The viewer should note that in our case the series does not lead to rituality (a rituality that is professional, which confirms the artist at work in his world, grappling with his craft). And less than ever, by trying ten times in a row, does he aim at experimentality. Bendini does not abandon himself to language, he does not take risks, he does not hypothesise risk. Bendini uses painting, he makes statements, he says without denying himself. Bendini, a painter who has always been figurative, a painter who has never strayed from figures (less than ever during the period of Art Informel), pictures, depicts, places, affirms.

The series takes the various paintings back to the identity of the format, the space it offers and in which it aims to place the viewer. A possible comparison? The series takes them back to the identity of the format, as the door returns on its hinges to open again, to close: a compulsory passage, a necessary step, and it is not necessarily the case that the compulsory nature of the operation forces identical solutions, proposes the same passage at every opening, opens onto the same sky. Lastly, by forcing, the series affirms: it affirms variety, mobility.

2008

Bruno Corà, "VASCO BENDINI: DIAFANE MALIE DELL'ENIGMA" in MALIA DELL'ENIGMA: VASCO BENDINI, Parma: Galleria d'Arte Niccoli, 2008. Catalog of an exhibition of the same name, presented at the Galleria Niccoli, Parma, February 16-April 10, 2008.

This unexpected visual "pentateuch" that Vasco Bendini has "provided" with poetic freshness, suitable for every meditation on our future, comes to light again from painting, in that manifestation of airy spaciousness that angelically combines it with chromatic *nuance.*

Within each painting in this new cycle, with its geometric golden ratios, offered up with a different metric repetition, by virtue of admirable spatial articulation, the five canvases disclose Bendini's complex meditative parable that flows from the memory of *ghenos* to the expectation of *thanatos*. In this tight and essential paradigmatic organism of pure evocation, the gestural "lightness" of each phenomenal episode brought about by the individual chromatic drafts is surprising. By assigning the emblematic title of *Malia dell'enigma* [Bewitchment of the Enigma] (2007) to the entire epiphany, thereby naming the feeling that aroused it, Bendini suggested that each of the five works, and all of them as a whole, can be read as a hermetic cipher of life. If this is the case, in each canvas the washed-out layers of oil celebrate moments that are as unrepeatable as they are indefinable. In this endeavour, Bendini's pictorial language, structured grammatically and syntactically from the outset in figural zeroing, proves to be one of the most eloquent and lofty of those capable of placing significant seals on the *Oscuro fremito (Nascita)* [Obscure Tremor (Birth)], on the *Bellezza dell'incontaminato (Infanzia)* [Beauty of the uncontaminated (Childhood)], on the *Malia dell'enigma (Adolescenza)* [Bewitchment of the Enigma (Adolescence)], on the state of mind *Fra il nulla e l'infinito (Maturità)* [Between Nothingness and Infinity (Maturity)] and finally on *Attesa dell'ultima eclisse (Vecchiaia)* [Waiting for the Final Eclipse (Old age)], segments of the common existential path, on each of which the illuminating opening of an image capable of welcoming our expectant pause unfurls.

The event is significant, although to the artist it seems like the usual breathing space that oxygenates his days. Nevertheless, it offers itself to a series of considerations that indicate the truly exceptional scope of this nucleus of works.

First of all, divided into five distinct works like the fingers of a hand, the cycle appears to be inwardly balanced by a single sensibility, even though it was generated by impulses that emerged at different times. It confirms that faculty of implementation through the simple acceptance on canvas of a colour distribution typical of Bendini, which is at the same time a restrained momentariness and an immediate implementation of the image.

Almost thirty years after the conception and birth of those oils and enamels on aluminium that gave life to the corpus of *Alchimia dell'immagine* [Alchemy of the Image] (1980), in which Emilio Villa had recognised

> "a severe and secluded, absorbed consideration, for which the world (and here we quote the world as *mundus*, strictly in the cosmological sense, or cosmogony) nourishes the colour, and the colour nourishes the world,"

Bendini returns to pronounce with even more resonant accents the arcane formulas that, through painting, tend to recall before our eyes the indistinct, the boundless, the abysmal presence-absence of the living, the "stability of the unstable" (Bendini). It is his *lectio magistralis,* in which, in the role of the great celebrant of the pictorial liturgy, he invites everyone to participate in the process of feeling, in that attitude of perceptive listening that in him accompanies, without rational intervals, the process of working the material and the conception of space. The transparency and lightness of the visual *verbum* pronounced by Bendini derive from the "momentary feeling" that is never designed or autobiographical and is therefore free from any conditioning that does not stem from the unique dedication to truth that painting—a sublime artifice—is able to display. In that state of poetic trance in which instantaneous gestures and technical skill are poured into the generative act of the work, Bendini is the sensitive catalyst, the conscious and available instrument through which—as Rumi's verse evokes—the breath of life becomes sonority.

The state of tension and the desire for industriousness drive the processing of that oil colour, diluted in varying degrees with essence of turpentine, to expansion on the canvas. The different degree of absorption of the wet deposits distinguishes the works in this new cycle from those of the 1980s on aluminium. Here, the damp gore and chromatic nuances, which reach imperceptible intensities, create a spatiality marked by a more intensely reverberating luminosity.

In the first oil painting, *Oscuro fremito (Nascita)*, on the vast neutrality of the canvas, sparsely covered by sweeping washes, nebulous milky regions emerge, surrounding and embracing golden deposits. In Bendini's post-creative interpretation, that colour-metal imaginatively exerts the significance of the prodigious source of life.

From that source-like work to the next one, *Bellezza dell'incontaminato (Infanzia)*, Bendini develops the notion of the *aetas aurea* already dear to

Medardo Rosso with an alternating dilution of colour, which is more transparent in some parts of the canvas and denser in others. To delimit the very diluted black, a diagonal sign-gesture of the same colour descends from the left apex and expands in different areas of lilac and grey.

In the following canvases, *Malia dell'enigma (Adolescenza)* and *Fra il nulla e l'infinito (Maturità),* both with an emphasis on the horizontal nature of the formats, as if to imprint a variation of more neuralgic sounds in the spatial-exhibitive rhythm, we can distinguish indigo and light ochres, but also diluted whites and blacks and blues.

The final canvas in the cycle, *In attesa dell'ultima eclisse (Vecchiaia)* incorporates floods of gold, accompanied by red and surrounded, like the first painting, by a neutral field achieved by mixing thinners. This last work has an oriental feel and, although it symbolises Bendini's state of senescence, it is the most sumptuous and ideally marked by verticality. It almost seems to want to veiledly confront, with a self-substantiating poetic tension, the expectation of the unpredictable thanatological event. It is in this sentiment, despite the fact that Bendini picked up on it subsequently, as a reading of his own work, that I have identified one of the ethical values of this cycle, on which it will be appropriate to dwell.

However, not before pointing out how the current nucleus of Bendini's works establishes a dialogue with the temperaments and aspirations of other postwar masterpieces by other painters. I believe that we can evoke Rothko's works for the Byzantine Fresco Chapel of The Menil Collection in Houston (1964-67), Fontana's "spatial concept" series *Trinità* [Trinity] (1966), Francis Bacon's *Three Studies for Figures at the Base of a Crucifixion* (1944), and Alberto Burri's *Annottarsi* [Nightfall] cycle from 1985-87.

Far beyond the "narrative" mode generated by the sequence of works belonging to a single summary intention, and despite the differences between these works, what they share is a plurality of parts that are thematically, morphologically and poetically coherent, in order to account for a single "feeling," a single dramaturgical entity. This is evidently iconographic and fiercely corporeal in Bacon, mystical and tragic in Rothko, sidereal and distanced in Fontana, gloomy and dramatic in Burri and, lastly, elegiac and endocosmic in Bendini.

After the first manifestation of that spatiality, observed since 1958 in the oils of the series *Gesto e materia* [Gesture and Matter] and then in the works of the 1980s, especially in the *Alchimia dell'immagine* series (1981), it is however after works such as *Cose ultime* [Final Things] (2000), *La memoria conserva* [Memory Preserves] (2001), *Nell'abisso* [In the Abyss] (2002), and in the series *L'immagine accolta* [The Received Image] (2003-2006), that Bendini descends into the sublime yet abysmal neuralgia of chromatic nuance in a drift that is as humid as it is aerial.

What happened in the space between Turner's visions of sea and sky and that which Bendini's painting announces today? Unlike Turner's consciousness, Bendini's is tuned to the frequency of the instant and of phenomenal and temporal discontinuity.

"If the work has the task of reconciling permanence and flux, it never achieves static completion [...]" (Bendini, *La pittura si immagina*).

Every moment is a recovery of contact with infinite reality. The distance between himself and the world, including nature, which Turner could consider a "subject" for his painting, has dissolved in Bendini's consciousness, which is now "immemorial and alone" in the phenomenon and within the perceptive moment that his painting is preparing to visualise. The physical space has been greatly reduced; almost annulled in a macro-entity adhering to thought, while that of consciousness has floundered in an endocosmic odyssey.

There is a dynamic material imagination at work in Bendini's painting, similar to the force in the expanding nebulous drags of the universe.

However, connected to the aerial imagination, regarding which Bachelard declared that "the poet's first task consists of unearthing within us a substance that wants to dream" (Gaston Bachelard, *Psicanalisi dell'aria*), there is the material imagination for water and in a broader sense for wet, vaporous and liquid compositions.

For the past thirty years, Bendini's painting has used a highly sensitive and highly volatile fluidity. The diluted colour has the same mobility as desire and emotion. Thus Bendini's painting is driven by a tension and an operational desire that finds release the instant the colour is used and in the invention of spatiality equivalent to the emotional dimension.

The cycle exhibited at the Galleria Niccoli in Parma seeks to sum up Bendini's entire previous career. In fact, each painting has an unmistakable identifying aspect and yet shares material and chromatic measurements and components with the others.

That this group of works belongs to a rhetorical moment, as poetically defined by Bendini places it within a sphere of conscious reflection on our anthropological condition. Although these works belong to painting, they increasingly seem to want to strip themselves of all its conditioning to become images of the intensity of a questioning sentiment, agitated in metaphysical painting by the Dechirician slogan "Et quid amabo nisi quod aenigma est?," but never satisfied except with silence or with the repetition of the same unanswered question. But if they take on the dimension of questions regarding the unfathomable, with the secular awareness that no answer can come from the horizon of events that precede the incessant dissolution of life, then they also appear as emblems of fine poetic lightness and considerable ethical integrity.

In the face of the euphoria of excess so distinctive of our time, thinking about the origin as well as about the "ultimate things" still comes across as an invitation to meditate on the edge of the edges. The latter appears to be one of the reasons why Bendini wanted us to look at his canvases in a half-light, so as not to be distracted, and to face their diaphanous, questioning irradiation.

Vasco Bendini

UNPUBLISHED WRITINGS
1965-2013

ETHICALITY OF ALIENATING "DOING"

Humankind is excluded from social activity, not by its own will, but because society passively cashes in, exploiting its "doing" as an economic investment, without meditating on the exposure entailed in the work. The artist's work thereby becomes "a stock market action," maintaining only a commercial function. The logical consequence is that the agent remains alienated from the surrounding problems, despite being able to evaluate and express them; the only response received from society is a pronounced interest in publicising the work (or the movement), carefully eliminating the content by means of a compact silence and absolute indifference.

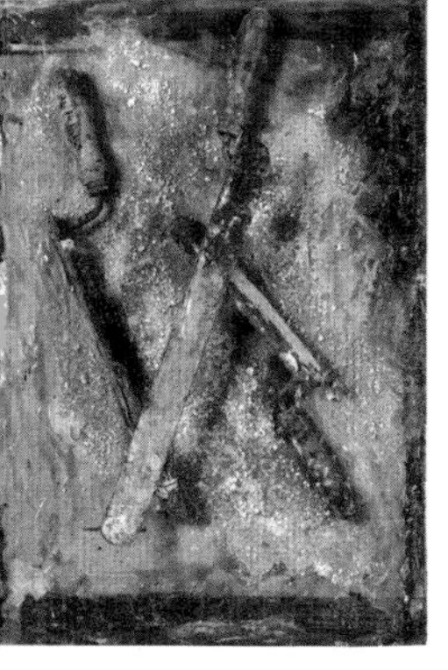

. T., 1964-66, from he *Object as History* eries, palette knives, aint, glue on board, 1×50 cm, Collezione 'rancescopiero Calzolari, 3ologna

Artists who realise this maintain their positive ethics by continuing "to do," or to act, but the content of their work is the same alienating situation that surrounds them. In their works, they act by creating spaces inhabited by objects: for example, their tools, which in this situation are no longer of any use, and therefore have no primitive meaning. They can be used in any other context, however extraneous or absurd in what becomes their new situation, they can take on numerous and various values, it does not currently matter which ones, as long as they are different. New values which can be attributed with a precise function or not, everything is possible but nothing is realised, there is a forced coherence between incoherent things. These are the reasons why objects can undergo any kind of mutilation or deformation.

Despite the real and apparent uselessness of these organisms, viewers are continually stimulated to act on or in the works themselves. Objects, or rather known patterns, (usually familiar) spaces, virtual or real trajectories really push them to intervene physiologically; the excitations affect visitors as a whole.

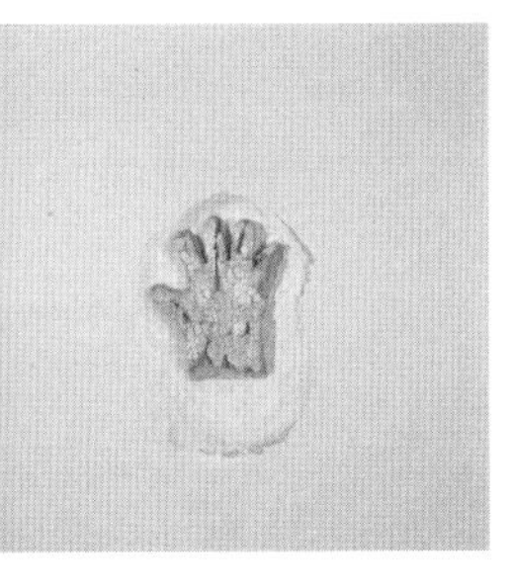

)ita divaricate, 1966, 'oam rubber, glue, vhite tempera, 20×100 cm, private ollection, Rome

The painter shows that he is already using potential elements for a new positive construction, but there is no situation suitable for receiving it; the result is necessarily an internal alienation from the construction process.

Nevertheless, this process indicates how old patterns that have historically consumed their value can be used if they are employed to construct new ones. These are negative data that have the possibility of becoming positive as long as they are no longer used negatively. Otherwise there would be no point in "doing," we would have rejection, "not acting," but instead there is a constructive proposal here. This is therefore not a moment of suspension, but a moment of waiting, already loaded with instruments that could lead to positive developments from the current situation.

The informal now demonstrates the reason for its disruptive function *vis-à-vis* what were known data. This operation of rejection that eliminated the value of patterns, which proved unsuitable for overcoming the difficult problems of the twentieth century, means that they are now still used but with completely new availability, both as object-images and as images of images of objects.

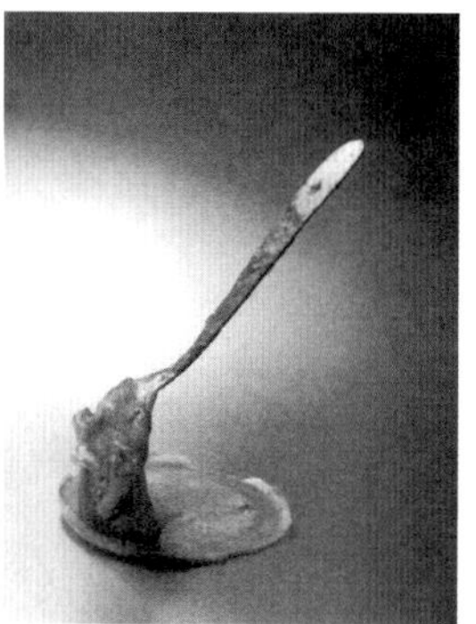

Cucchiaio, 1966, from the *Oggetto come storia* series, spoon and glue, 16×10×10 cm, Collezione Brandani, Bologna

The painter almost seems to be implementing a form of sadism, or revenge, in those spaces or surfaces that attract the viewer, inviting observers to act, to penetrate, to be an active part of those works which, after all, are there for them to enjoy. But anxious viewers find, for example, a cellophane that prevents them from doing what the painting itself seems to lead them to do. Viewers find something in front of them, something seemingly insubstantial, but concretely alienating. A similar situation to that in which the painter finds himself. The content, the relationships, the values, the very meaning of the clutter, which is in itself sufficient to make a painting negative for the majority of private buyers, may not even be understood by viewers. All the better. In this case, they will be perfectly involved in the new context; an object among objects without any function, they will wait passively, as they are used to doing, for others to give them a new value as they please. There is no need for their conscious participation.

One cannot say that the meaning of the paintings is symbolic, that would be to misunderstand them; they are simply a fiction of reality that is much more real than the fake realities we are given every day. They are reality because they are real for those involved.

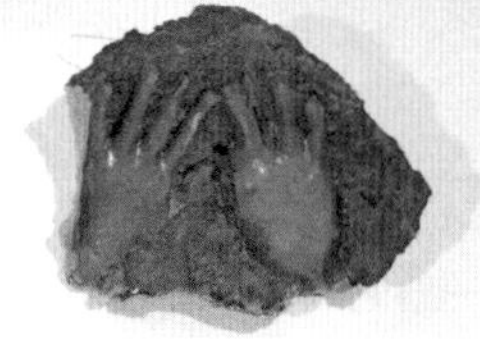

A memoria di gesso, 1966, plaster and lacquer, 8×30×30 cm, Collezione Calvesi, Rome

In this contextualised synthesis of his way of perceiving external and internal events there is no place for refinement or pleasing sensitive visions, let alone lyricism; but neither is there any place for a taste for the crude. These two opposite directions would lead to the same altering results for such a context; they would deny alienation itself because they would be a revaluation of already eliminated patterns and would give a positive meaning precisely where there must be a meaning of denial, while the constructive value of doing would become gratuitous.

The objects and situations are given as objectively as possible, without undergoing any qualitative alteration. Objective data, the only data that can help to create a tangible situation for visitors, just as the painter's position in society is real and tangible for him, albeit alienating as are the objects and situations.

Rome, 1973

LANGUAGE
"Language" signifies any means of communication that binds together the communicating and the receiving subject, but at the same time prevents immediate mutual contact. There are multiple communication tools in artistic language, but all are equally indispensable and of equal value. Engels, anticipating the fundamental principle of Konrad Fiedler's theory of art, declared that the hand is not only the organ, but also the product of labour at the same time.

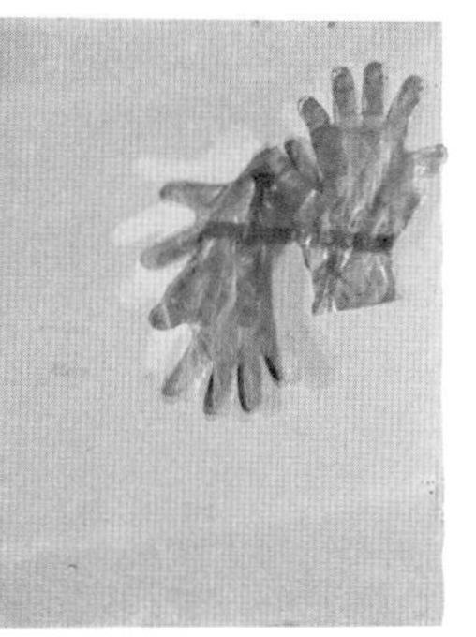

Polvere e plastica, 1966, mixed media on canvas, 90×70 cm, Collezione Tegoni, Parma

The dialectic in which artistic creation is enveloped clearly descends from this circumstance. The artist is not only the creator, but also the creature of his art; he is not just standing there nice and ready when he sets to work, rather he develops as his artistic creation is born and develops. Fiedler explicitly stated several times that in artistic creation "the hand does not execute something that has already been fully formed in the spirit," being fully aware of the inseparability of "spirit" and "hand"; something that escaped Lessing and Marx alike. He goes on to say: "Even in the most elementary attempts at pictorial activity, the hand does not do something that the eye has already done; rather, something new arises and the hand takes up the development of what the eye does and continues it."

THE "HEADS"
Restricted variations on a basic theme: self-portraits or more generally "heads." Some painters continue to work on a single basic theme throughout their artistic career, varying it from time to time. Often a complex phase is followed by a simple one, as a reaction, and then a complex phase emerges again as a further reaction, and so on.[1] There is a surprising affinity of approach between the simple brushstrokes indicative of a structure in the works of the 1950s, the more complex elaborations obtained with mixed media from 1965 onwards, and the portrait photos taken by chance by photographer friends. Take for example the work from 1950—large external brushstrokes that balance the rectangular structure of the sheet of paper, hint of an eye socket on the left, with a snapping line that forms an ideal connection with the other end of the sheet, while the opening of the "forehead" on the right allows the structural lines of the face to leave the delimited space of the sheet and connect to a virtual external space. The same (modified) solution can be found with the line extended at

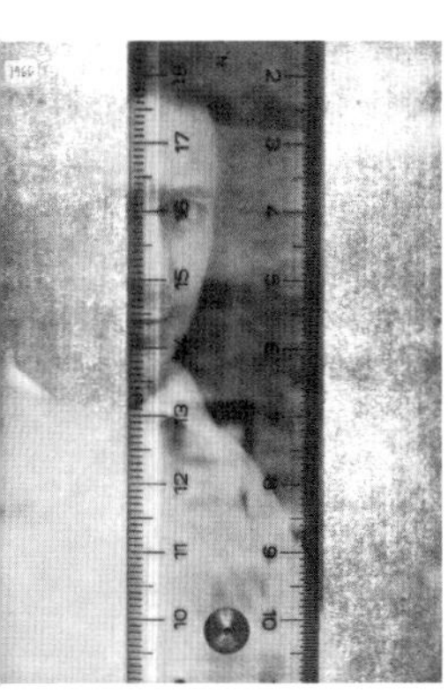

Cover of the catalog *Bendini: opere eseguite nel 1965 della serie Sentimento come storia e Senso operante*, L'Attico gallery, Rome, 1966

the bottom left, which offers a new connection with the external space. In addition to muscular factors (the movement of the hand and arm is pleasant and "satisfactory" from a motor point of view) and optical factors (the visual arrangement is pleasing to the eye), there are also evident psychological factors that have allowed such an "individual" pictorial variation within such a general theme as the "face." Proof of this also lies in the use of black, which suggests the "mental" approach of the work, namely the psychological factor ("Since there are much bigger individual differences in individual psychology than in the musculature of the arm or the structure of the eye, it is not surprising that the greatest pictorial variations and the weakest iconographic universality can be found among adult professional painters, where muscular and optical factors are completely suppressed by the intellect").[2] A further clarification of the mental structure of the face-portrait can be found in the drawing of 1951: the same emphasis on the eye socket and the eye on the left of the viewer, the same dolichocephalic setting of the head with elongated nasal septum; the hatching is nervous.

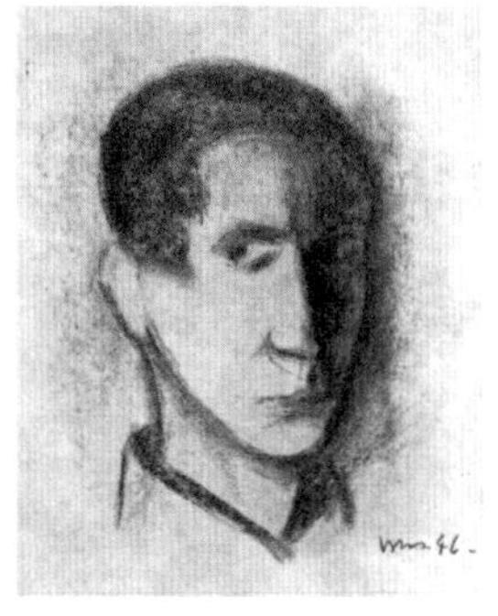

Eugenio Riccomini, *Disegni di Vasco Bendini*, Edizioni dell'Attico, Rome, 1965, plate 1

The juxtaposition with the photo on the cover of the L'Attico gallery catalog no. 78, 1966, is surprising:[3] the photo was taken with its particular elongated slant by the artist himself: the forehead, the eye and the nasal septum are all in evidence; the mouth evades capture. The juxtaposition can be continued with the black charcoal of 1946 (Riccomini's catalog).[4]

In this case the figurativeness (at least in the traditional sense) is more evident, but the essential structures are comparable to the previous one (of a later date): dolichocephalic structure, one half of the face (the eye above all) in evidence, nervous lines, the elusive mouth. There is a drawing from 1950 that takes up the same approach as this charcoal of 1946, but it is much more abstract.

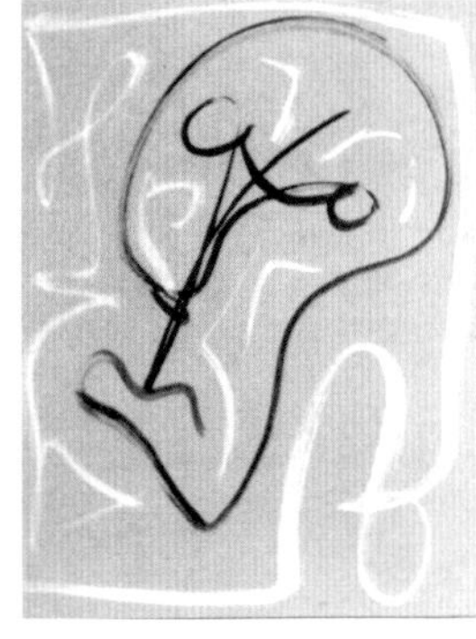

Testa, 1950, synthetic tempera on paper, 50×40 cm, private collection, Bologna

The severe eyes, the bitter crease of the mouth, and the elongated nasal septum are hinted at by a single, continuous, nervous line. Here the structural lines are not only black, but also white, implying the secret nervous structures, the fluid branches of energy. One guesses at the fast, tension-filled movement (which reveals an urgent needs for release) of the arm and hand; the action is continuous, with few interruptions, and the severe and terrible face that emerges is the face that we carry inside us like the skull, of which we have a vague awareness, like an intuition of the "truth" that still survives after death for a short time (truth is always relative), but dismays us (Plate III in Riccomini's book). The eye and its socket become increasingly obsessive in the drawing from the Calvesi collection.[5]

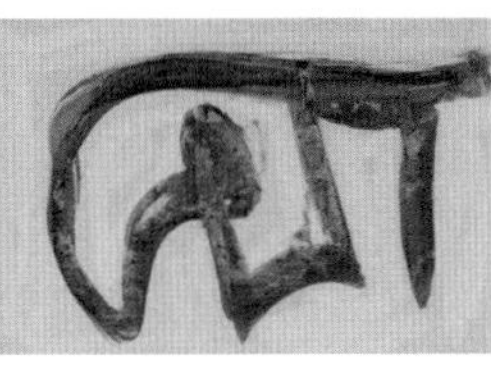

;.T., 1951, from
segni segreti series,
ynthetic tempera
n paper, 44×70.5 cm,
Collezione Calvesi, Rome

All that remains of the face now is this structure reduced to the bone, severe and ferocious in its rapid appearance. These self-portrait faces almost always take on two aspects: either the terrible aspect of self-consciousness or the melancholic aspect of the clown. The similarity between the self-portrait of 1947 and B.'s photo of 1967 is surprising.
B.'s photo was taken during a behavioural action inside the "sauna" (1967). The general impression of the two heads (one painted, the other photographed) is that of the introverted clown who is no longer on stage; the white plastic material of the photo also seems to suggest the rotating white of the Pierrot. What is striking in this casual (and then deliberate) juxtaposition is B.'s inner awareness of his own characteristic and psychological structures, which emerge from a few strokes. We are aware of our own voice from the inside, never from the outside (we listen to ourselves with our throat and not with our ears), except by chance when we hear our own recorded voice and discover that we are "different" because we have another "intuition" of ourselves; it is precisely this type of intuition that leads us to more general considerations about art: "[...] I work," says Davie "with the conviction that art is something fundamentally natural to humankind [...] it is difficult to free oneself from the false concepts of Art based on knowledge and intelligence [...] one must learn to have faith in the intuition that 'knows' without knowing."[6] B.'s intuition about B. is perhaps an intuition common to every individual about him or herself and which goes beyond psycho-sociological discourses (for which people reflect the models that society shows them like a mirror and filter them through their biological and cultural structures), even though they cannot totally disregard them.

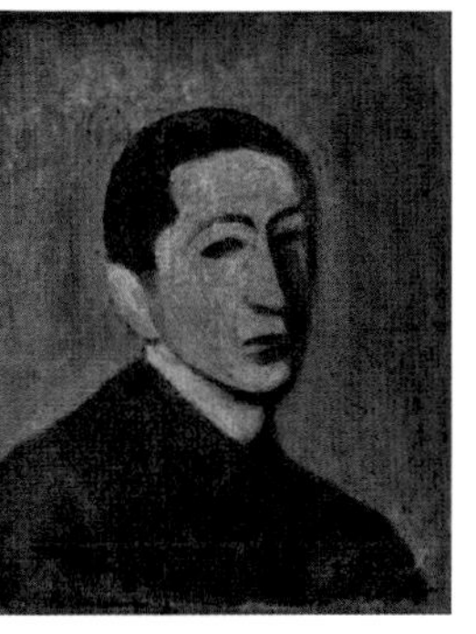

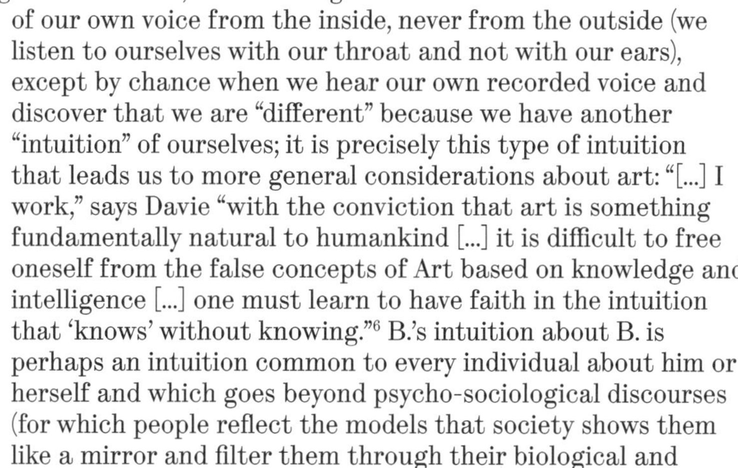

lutoritratto, 1947,
il on canvas, 50×40 cm,
rivate collection, Rome

It is like listening to oneself from the inside, the continuous conversation of subjectivity with oneself to which each of us is accustomed, but which represents an unfathomable mystery if only referred to the "other." Arcangeli himself said: "Shaved completely bald at the edges, a lean and ineradicable bone and spatial structure, a white iris that subtly stares at you, an intense red gaze nourished by silence, anguish, a flame that has burned for long years, and which it was now unbearable to repress within itself [...] an obsessive 'face' to the point of hallucination [...]"[7]
It is interesting to compare this work from 1953 with one of B.'s photo from the 1960s: same hallucinatory fixity of the eyes, same anguished severity.
There seems to be an unconscious "magical" desire to relate to the most intimate and radical part of himself.

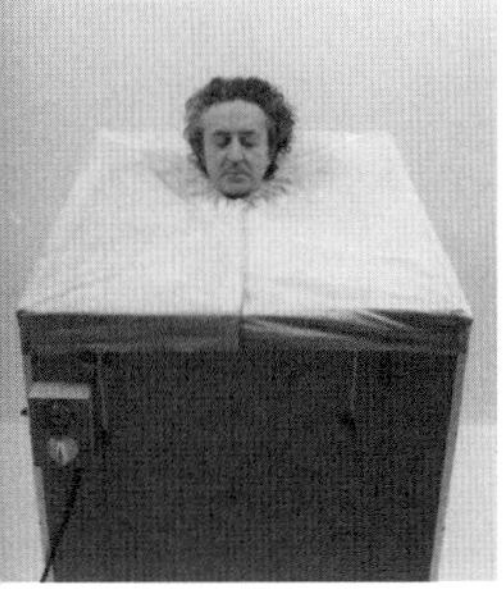

Per una essudazione otale, 1967,
erformance, Lux model
xudation oven,
05×76×96 cm

Rome, 1980s

ABOUT “ZEROING”

My figurative annihilation of the 1950s should not be understood as a destructive outburst, but rather as a primary and inevitable search for the optimal and basic conditions to be able to operate. Since annihilation, like venerating, is a reflection of one’s own state of nullity. I want to present the object, in my case for example the face, with a fundamental characteristic that defines it. Not, therefore, my face or his face, but the face, everyone’s face, the archetype.

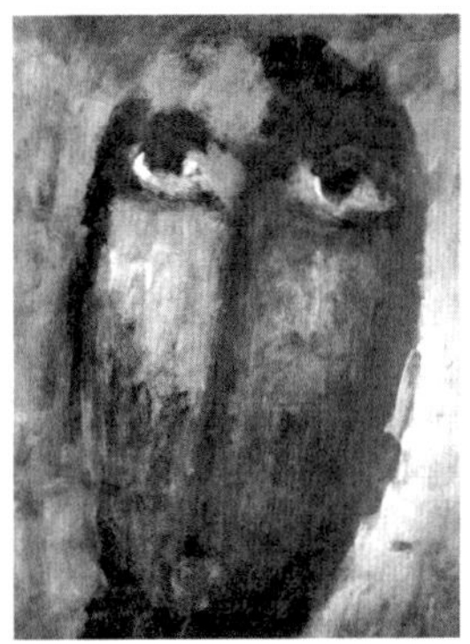

Testa, 1953, oil on paper, 68×49 cm, private collection, Switzerland

I became aware, or rather I began to doubt, that my reflective experience, at its deepest level, was not verbal, but an imaginary experience, simulated with the help of forms, forces, intersections that constituted an image in the visual sense of the term.

Using figurative language, I had to directly translate the result, or more radically, the mechanisms of the operations of my central nervous system, a logical instrument, ancestral centre of information.

Introspection, with its dangers, tells us something more. It is only through constant practice that we will be able to detect not only the results of our knowledge, but also to follow the smallest and most secret stages of the entire process (results=conclusive information).

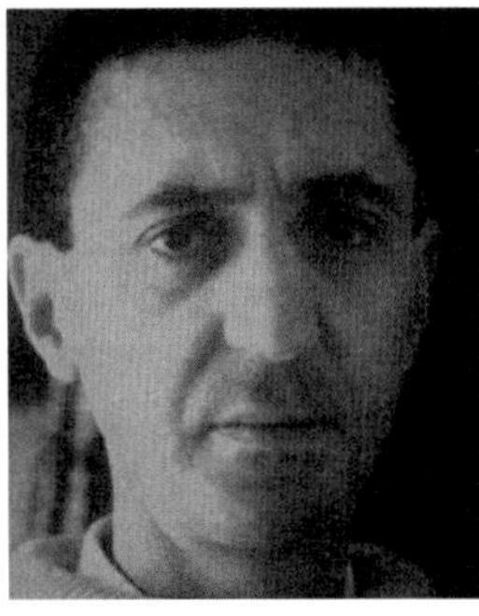

Vasco Bendini, catalog of the 6th Sao Paulo Biennial, Sao Paulo 1961

The artistic artefact does not receive its macroscopic structure through the intervention of external forces (by imitation of external structures), but constitutes itself autonomously through internal constructive interactions.

The discriminating property of the artist’s central nervous system is measured by the degree of orientation, regularity, and coherence of the artefact. Chance is captured, preserved, and reproduced by the mechanism of invariance and transformed into order, rule, necessity.

The artist and the world are each other’s instrument and causes of surprise, of novelty.

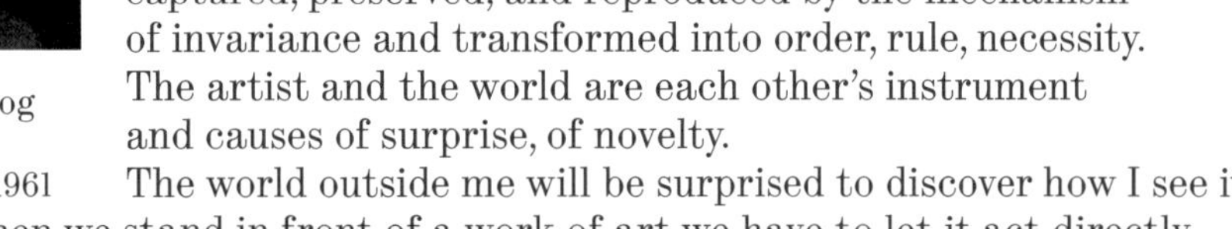

The world outside me will be surprised to discover how I see it. When we stand in front of a work of art we have to let it act directly on us, and wait for the moment of alarm, when our perceptive faculties, having come into contact with it, react.

Title emblematic of all my work.

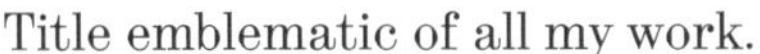

“THE STABILITY OF THE INSTABLE”: the term, structural fixity, in the absurd reconciliation of permanence and flux.

Rome, 1983

Painting: a dream driven by reason towards joy, towards pain.
The worst qualities: fanaticism, falsehood, prevarication.
I feel expelled. No longer in play. A double shadow on the wall that flutters, flutters like the butterfly, then dies.
The last generation: the transition from an active and innovative attitude to a predominantly receptive and retrospective one.
There is something inside me that I must remove. Perhaps provoke. Otherwise it remains unknown to me.
Every time, my work is an attempt to provoke an organic concrescence of real elements, thus symbolising the uninterrupted flow of the process of reality, with a single aim: to achieve self-creativity.
Concept of perception as global and non-analytical. Awareness of the relativity of space and time and their interrelationship.
(organic realism)

Rome, December 2013

From the early 1950s, Andrea Emiliani, Eugenio Riccomini, and Roberto Tassi, who were critics in the early stages of their careers at the time, frequented my home and wrote promptly and extensively about my work. The relationship seemed to develop into a true and deep friendship, but my restless and rebellious work in the early sixties distanced them with tacit concern from me and my experiences.
At the end of 1961 other needs were already emerging in me, and this new *Senso operante* [Operating Faculty] led me to produce large canvases that I exhibited in 1966 at L'Attico gallery in Rome, presented by Giulio Carlo Argan. A key text, in terms of its lucidity and concreteness of reading.
It is still difficult for me to forget Arcangeli's hesitation in front of these works, a diffidence that led him to my studio on the first floor of Palazzo Bentivoglio only a year later, in August 1967, where he came across my "poor" works, including *Finzione 1* [Fiction 1, now lost], *Come è* [How It Is], *La Tavolozza* [The Palette], *Due soggetti* [Two Subjects] and *La Scatola U* [The U-Box at MACRO in Rome] in 1966.
This is also where *Cabina solare* [Solar Cabin, at the MACRO], the *Ruota* [Wheel] and *Quadro per Momi* [Painting for Momi] were born in 1967.
It was in this climate of harsh contrasts and loneliness that he developed an intense relationship with a number of young artists, poets, and critics working in the city: the two brothers Pierpaolo and Lamberto Calzolari, Maurizio Mazzoli,

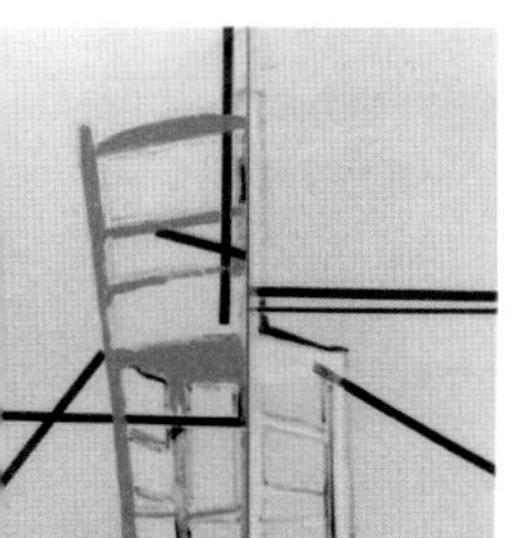

S.T. (diptych), 1965, from the *Senso operante* series, acrylic tempera and adhesive tape on canvas, 190×380 cm, Collezione CSAC, Parma (detail)

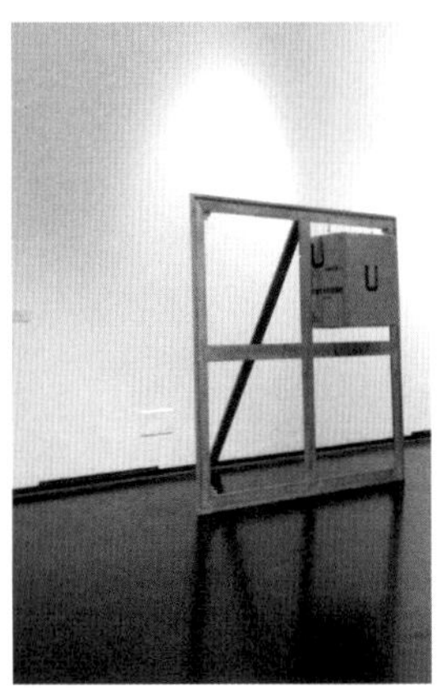

La Scatola U, 1966, from the *Oggetto come storia* series, frame, wooden support rod, cardboard box, 190×190×100 cm, Collezione MACRO, Rome

Antonio Napoletano, Nino Ovan, Bruno Pasqualini, and Giovanni Scardovi, to whom we can add other very young artists.

In May 1967, this association led to the birth of the Bentivoglio Studio, with its entrance on Via delle Moline 1/b. During the nights spent together discussing and working in this space, numerous projects were created and developed that could not even be imagined in optimal conditions of time, place, and means.

A hostile diffidence isolated us within our city, but we were united outside by the enthusiastic participation of artists who came to meet us from the main Italian and foreign cities: artists who exhibited their first "poor" works at the Bentivoglio Studio, where the first behavioural works and the first avant-garde films appeared. And it was precisely in this large space that Arcangeli, albeit after days of feverish contacts with me, offered to present my first "poor" objects, born out of a meditated and suffered coexistence that "was founded again in concrete acts of consciousness."

The exhibition was followed and received with unexpected clamour. There was a more violent and almost hysterical reaction among "authoritative" painters and critics in and outside the city. A tenacious hostility, although above all an emotional one, which ended up overwhelming and repressing Arcangeli himself.

But by then, at the end of the 1960s, time was running out and the city "exploded," participating with individual interventions in the unforgettable action of dissent promoted by the Board of Directors of the National Federation of Bologna Artists, organising the first exhibition of cultural protest. As a citizen, in January 1969, in a room of the Museo Civico in Bologna, I manifested my definitive estrangement from sinister European events with the action *Io. E io ora* [I. And I Now].

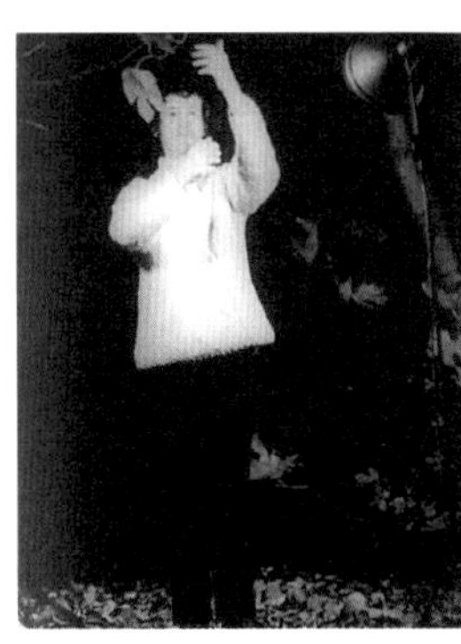

Io. E io ora. Reproduction of the performace in the courtyard of Bendini's studio in Bologna, documented by Nino Migliori. The original was given in a room of the Museo Civico in Bologna, 17 January 1969

1. Desmond Morris. *The biology of art: A study of the picture-making behaviour of the great apes and its relationship to human art* (London: Methuen & Co., 1962).

2. *Ibid.*

3. Giulio Carlo Argan. *Bendini. Opere eseguite nel 1965 delle serie Sentimento come storia e Senso operante* (Rome: L'Attico, 1966). Catalog of an exhibition of the same title, presented at L'Attico gallery, Rome, March 1966.

4. Eugenio Riccomini. *Disegni di Vasco Bendini (1948-1965)*, (Rome: Edizioni dell'Attico, 1965).

5. Maurizio Calvesi. *Vasco Bendini* (Parma: La nazionale, 1973). Catalog of an exhibition of the same title, presented at Palazzo della Pilotta, Parma, June 1973, plate 3, b.

6. Cf. Albert Camus. *A Happy Death,* (London: Penguin Classics, 2002), p. 86: "Just as there is a moment when the artist must stop, when the sculpture must be left as it is, the painting untouched–just as a determination not to know serves the maker more than all the resources of clairvoyance–so there must be a minimum of ignorance in order to perfect a life in happiness. Those who lack such a thing must set about acquiring it."

7. Francesco Arcangeli. *Personale del pittore Vasco Bendini* (Bologna: Studio Bentivoglio, 1967). Catalog of an exhibition of the same title, presented at Studio Bentivoglio, Bologna, September 23-30, 1967.

PERFORMANCES

IO. E IO ORA
[I. AND I NOW]

An action expressed with ritual acts, like an imaginary consolatory game. The choice of an artificial place of action, the only one possible to escape the contagion of collective madness. In this state of mind and with these convictions, I entered the room of the Museo Civico on the morning of the 17th, the day after Palach's death.

I made all the beacons of enlightenment converge on me, as if to unflesh myself in a certain sense, and with my right arm outstretched, bending to the rhythm of my heartbeat, I traced a circular line enclosing myself in an uncontaminated space, another space, as the only possible defence of the self. I imagined myself moving like someone who, for the first time, discovers they are the object of this world, the object of experience. The same eyes, a means of knowledge, are suddenly seen as a fragment of matter. I thus slowly resumed my initial position with my arms outstretched at my sides, and, always at an equal and slow pace, I moved each of my limbs (head, eyes, mouth, tongue, hands, arms, legs, feet) as if I were revealing them to myself, as if I were becoming aware of them for the first time. A pause of a few minutes followed as a preamble to meditation.

Then, I virtually traced the image of a broom. A very slow sway of the legs simulated flight. Having reached the "first circle," I slowly climbed an infinite ladder that led me to the "supreme circle," where I found myself ascending a rope. Towards what?

I stopped still and as if dazzled for a few minutes. The rediscovery of promise?

Then, with steady step, I left the circle.

Rome, 2013
Vasco Bendini

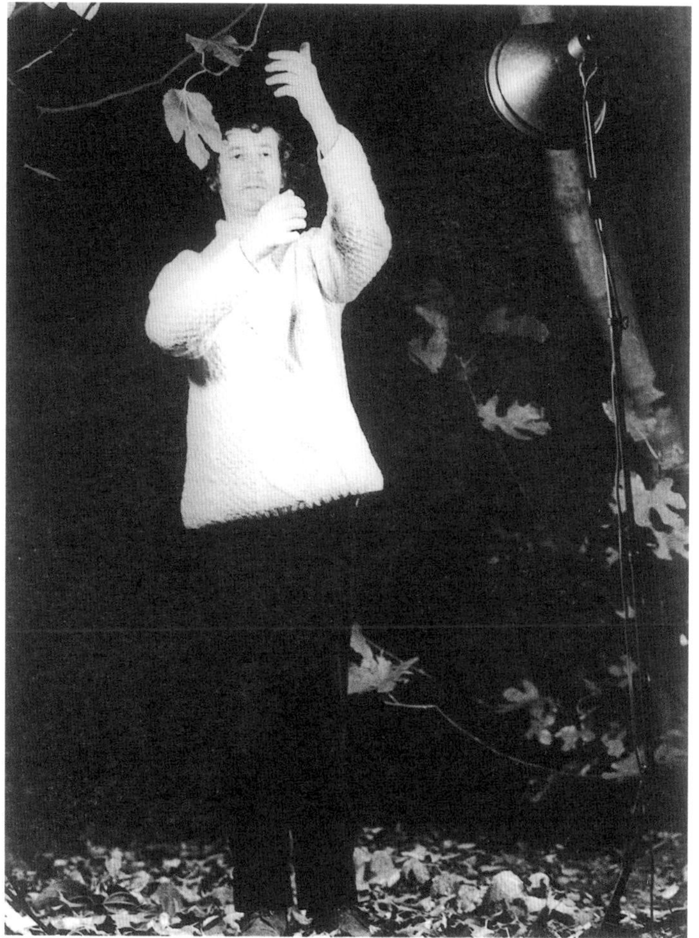

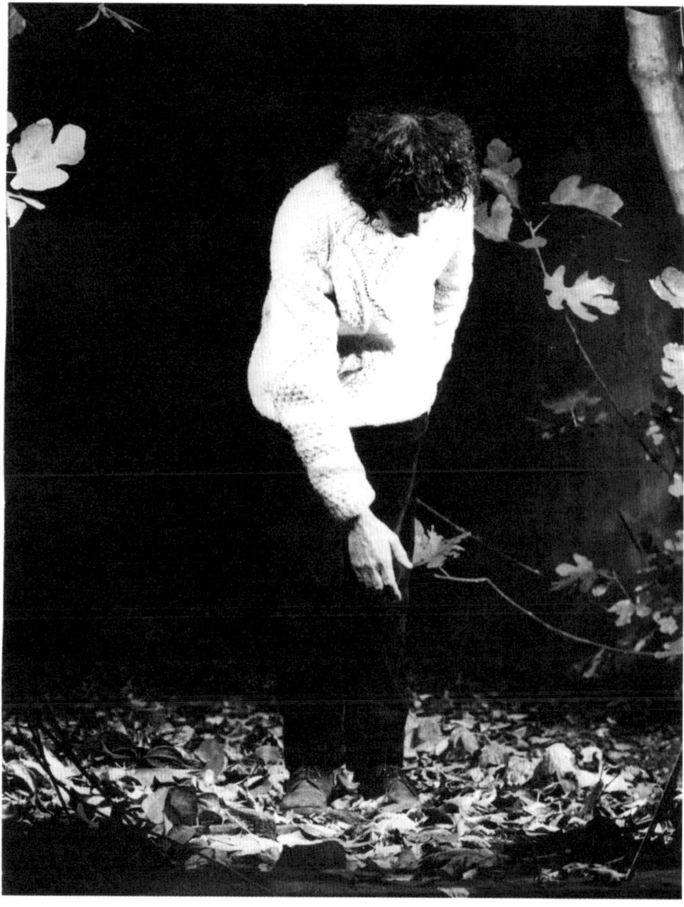

Io. E io ora, public performance by Vasco Bendini in a room of the Museo Civico in Bologna on 17 January 1969. Images of the reproposition in the courtyard of the artist's studio in bologna, deocumented by Nino Migliori.

PER UNA ESSUDAZIONE TOTALE
[FOR A TOTAL EXUDATION]

Room of any size.

Floor covered with a thin layer of gravel with a lux-model total exudation oven in the centre, comprising a rigid cabin with highly reflective, mirror-polished aluminium interior walls with four rows of four special carbon-filament bulbs at the sides.

Dimensions:
height 105 cm, width 76 cm, depth 96 cm.

Four adjustable heat levels,
equally distributed throughout the cabin
(bottom, middle, top).

Daylight.

Visitors will enter a dressing room to put on the sheet given to them.

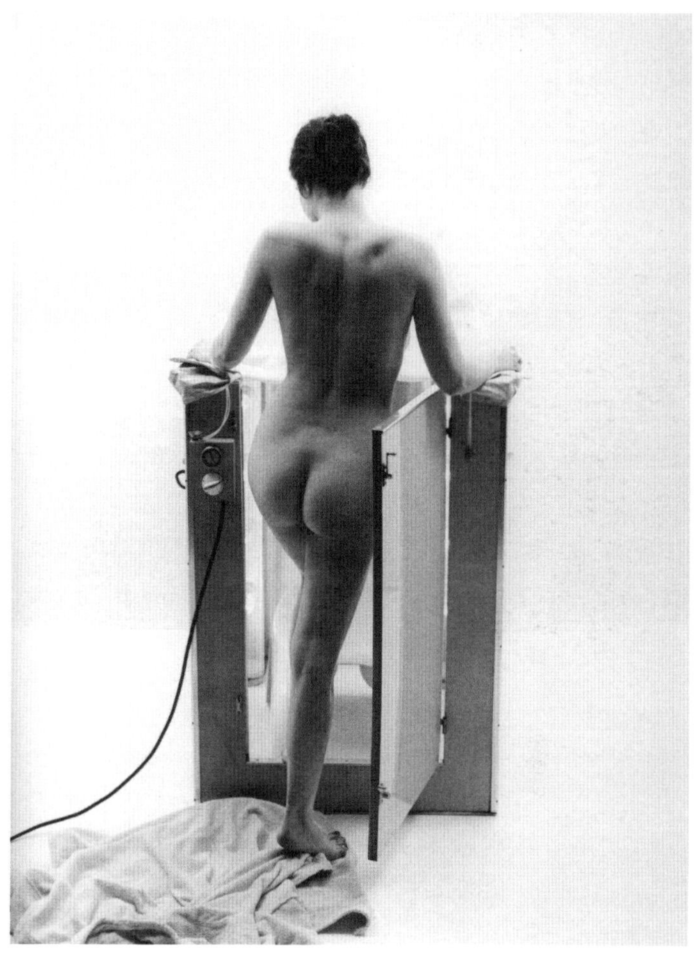

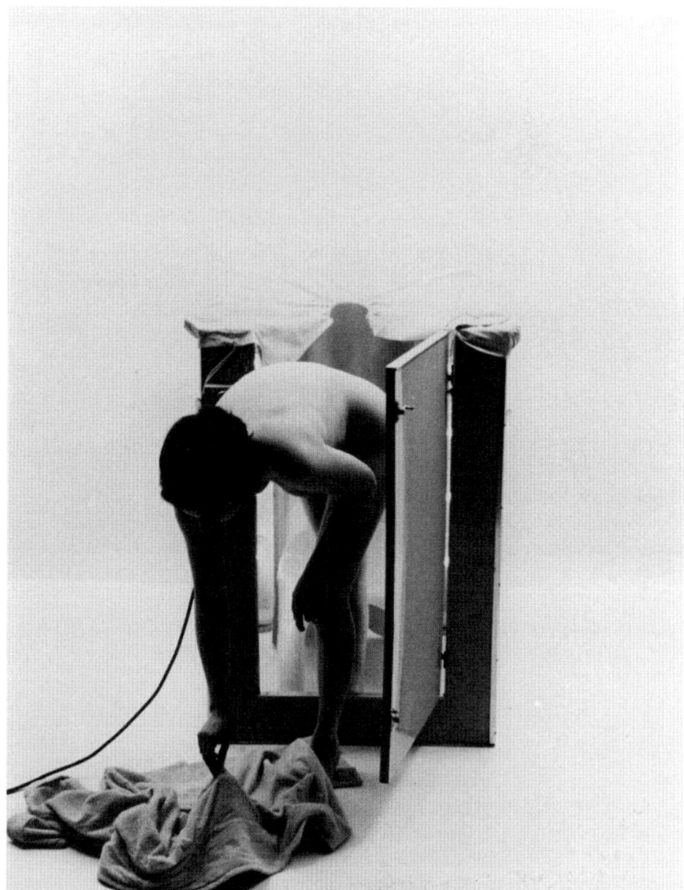

Published in *Bendini*, edited by Maurizio Calvesi and Giulio Carlo Argan, Rome: Galleria Senior, 1968. Catalog of an exhibition of the same title, presented at the Galleria Senior, INArch Palazzo Taverna, Rome, November 1968.

APPENDIX

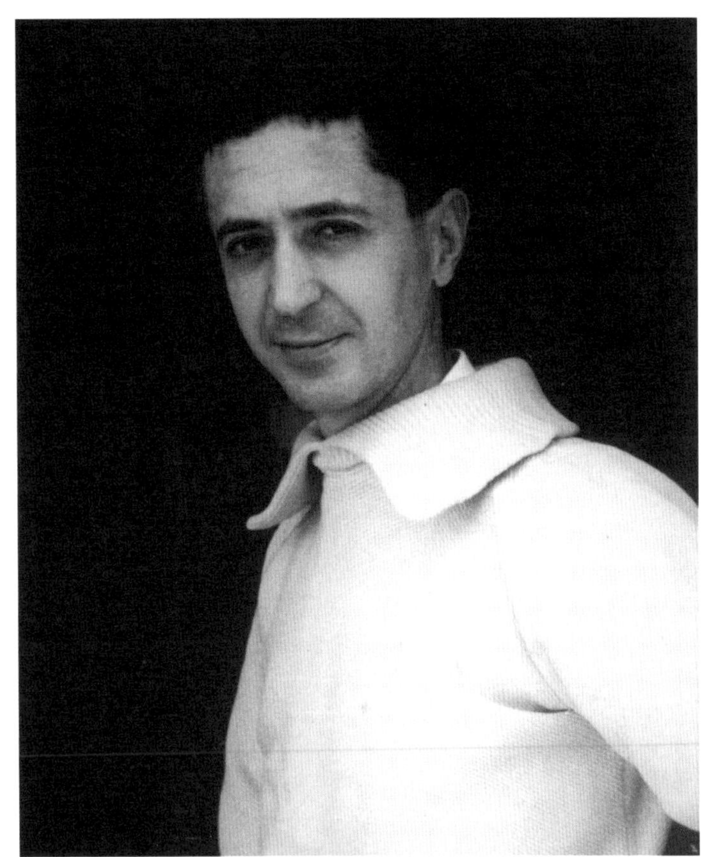
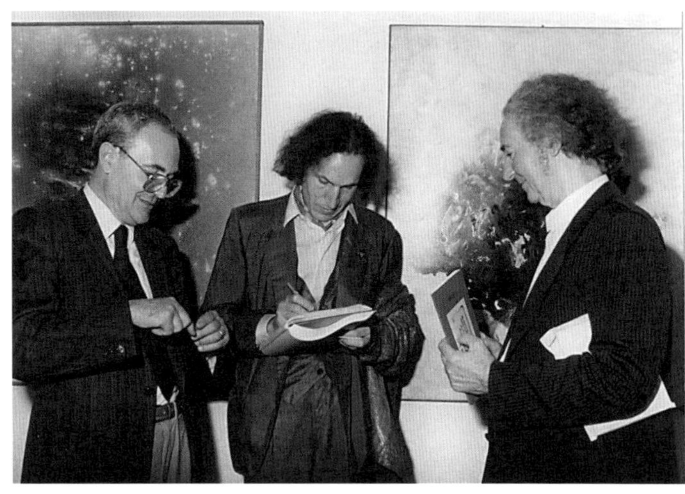
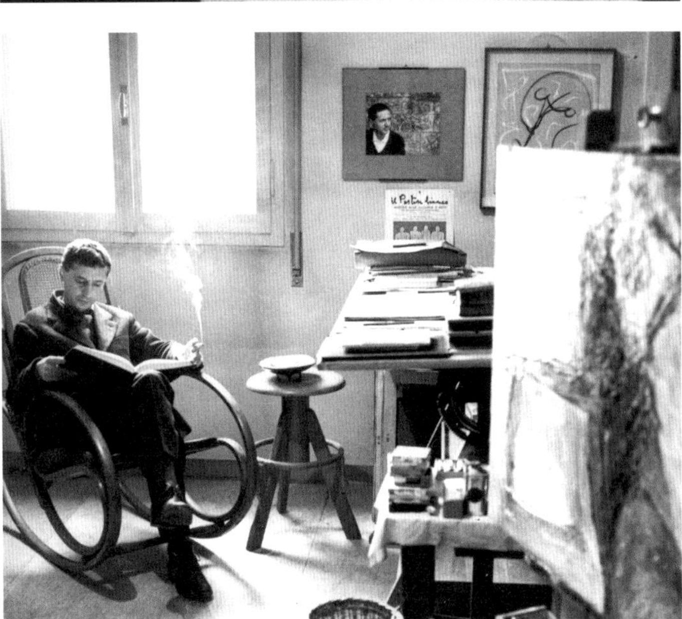
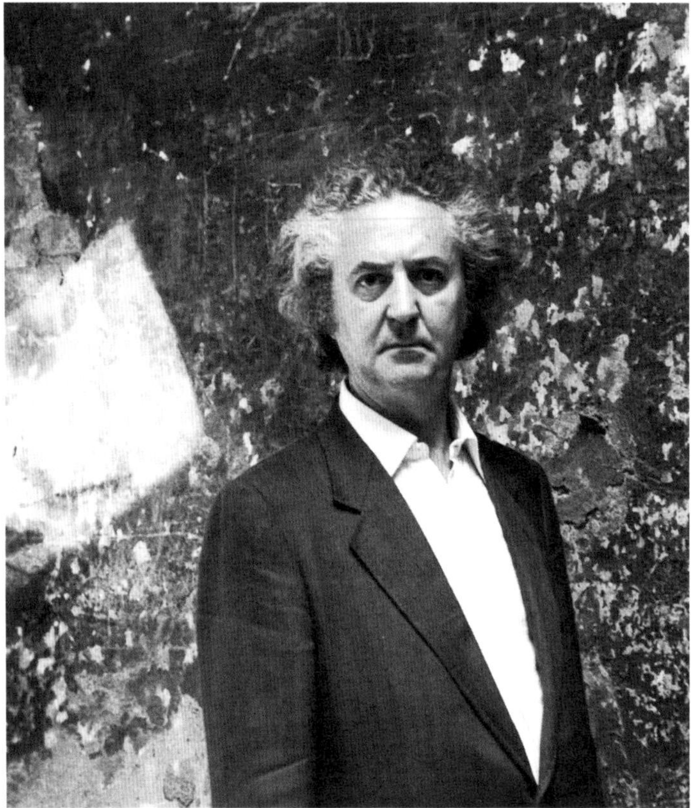
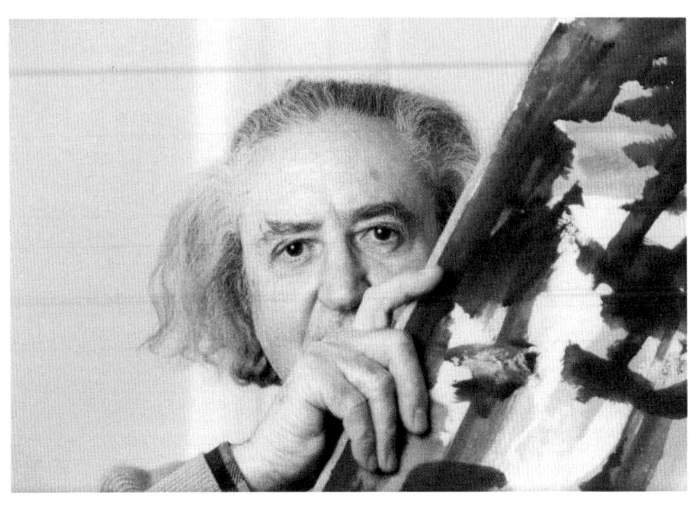
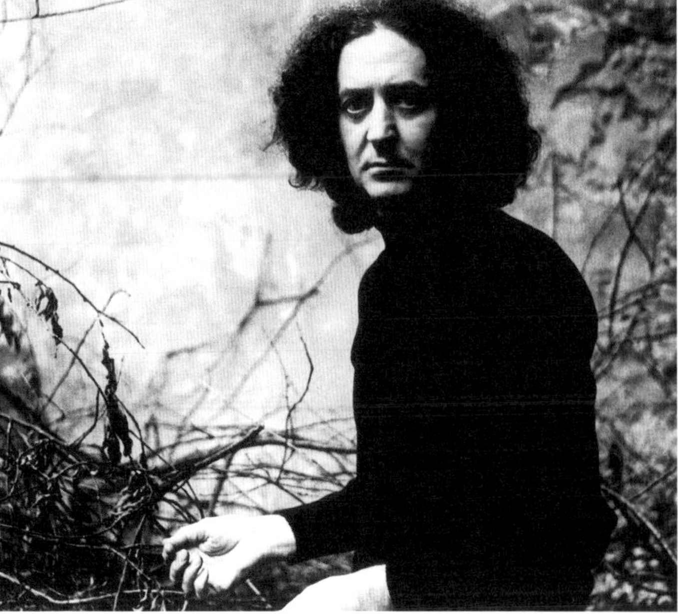

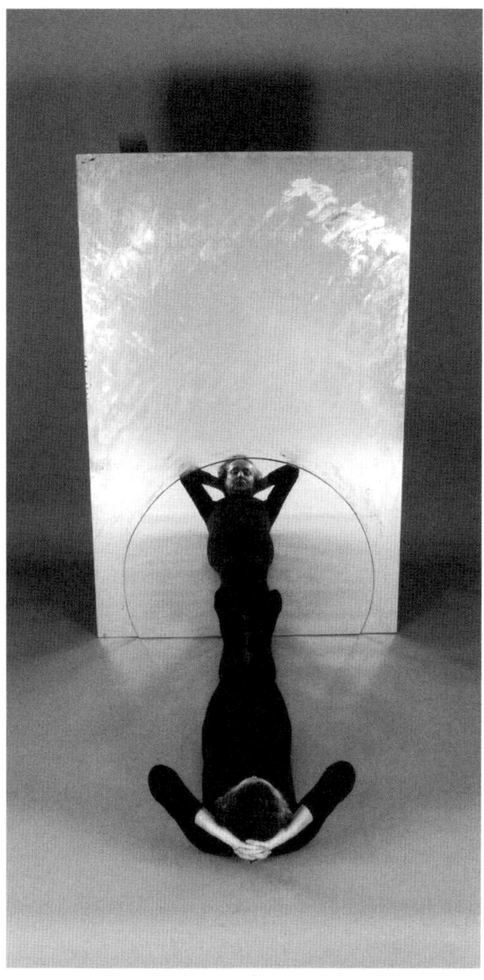

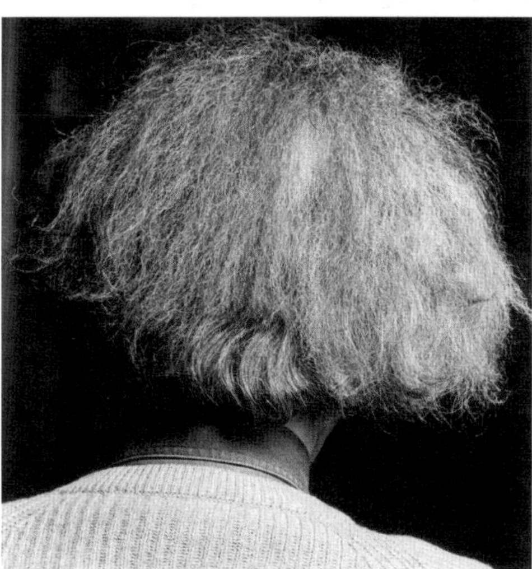

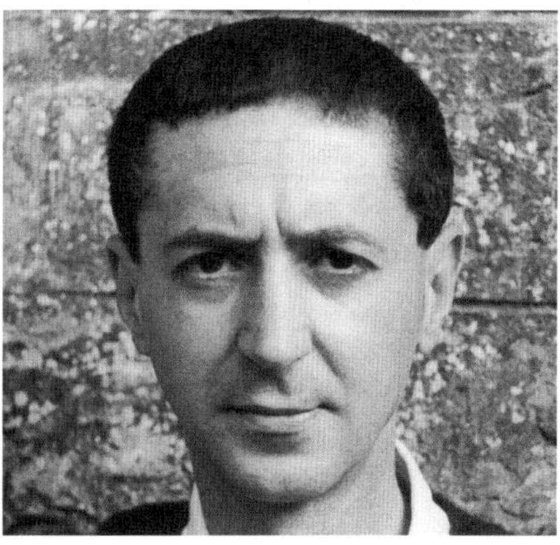

AUTOBIOGRAPHY

I was born in 1922. I was seventeen years old when the Second World War broke out and I was twenty-three when, on August 6, an American bomber dropped the first atomic bomb on Hiroshima.

Between 1949 and 1955 we experienced the negative effects of the Cold War: "peace" was entrusted to nuclear bombs carried by special aircraft or assigned to intercontinental missiles installed on nuclear submarines. The newspapers said that it would only take ten minutes to launch the new H-bomb, and in 1966 the time it would take to destroy humankind was reduced to two minutes, which became the title of a work of mine (*Due minuti*), created on March 24, 1966.

In 1956, Russian tanks invaded Hungary, followed by Czechoslovakia in 1968. In 1968, I was particularly struck by the publication, in Prague, of *The Two Thousand Words* manifesto, called for by numerous intellectuals anxious to achieve a true process of liberalisation to which I ideally adhered, with the execution of a work of mine entitled *Duemila parole* [Two Thousand Words].

I was fifty-one when the Allende case exploded. He was killed while defending the freedom of the Chilean people, who had been sacrificed for the interests of the USA, and I created *Un giaciglio per Allende* [A Bed for Allende] in 1973. And then came the long and tragic Vietnam War, followed in 1979 by the Soviet invasion of Afghanistan, not to mention the Arab-Israeli conflict, 9/11 and the war in Iraq. Nor can I forget the latest dramatic and inhuman resolution to erect more than 15,000 kilometres of barriers separating peoples on our planet.

These are the facts. It is impossible not to lose oneself. It is in these moments that my *neri* [blacks] are born: songs of the night, matrix of hope. And my *bianchi* [whites] arise, which are natural images of expectation.

BIOGRAPHY

Vasco Bendini (Bologna 1922-Rome 2015)
Between 1941 and 1942, Vasco Bendini attended the Accademia di Belle Arti in Bologna, where he was taught by Giorgio Morandi and Virgilio Guidi. It was on the basis of their lessons that the artist took his first steps in the direction of a painting style that could be defined as metaphysical, although the figurative element was to become increasingly abstract by 1948, with the sharp incisiveness of a conscious gesture that, in its simplicity, sought to arrive at the load-bearing and universal structure of the self. He began to create his faces and heads, which Francesco Arcangeli termed "veronicas" and Vasco Bendini described as "secret signs."

The artist read texts on Zen meditation practices, as well as *Chance and Necessity* by Jacques Monod and *From Being to Becoming* by Ilya Prigogine, respectively Nobel laureates in chemistry and in physiology and medicine. Upon reading them he became convinced that matter is nothing more than an illusory trace of mobile compounds made of waves and particles. From the mid-1950s, figures began appearing on the canvas that revealed themselves or dissolved in

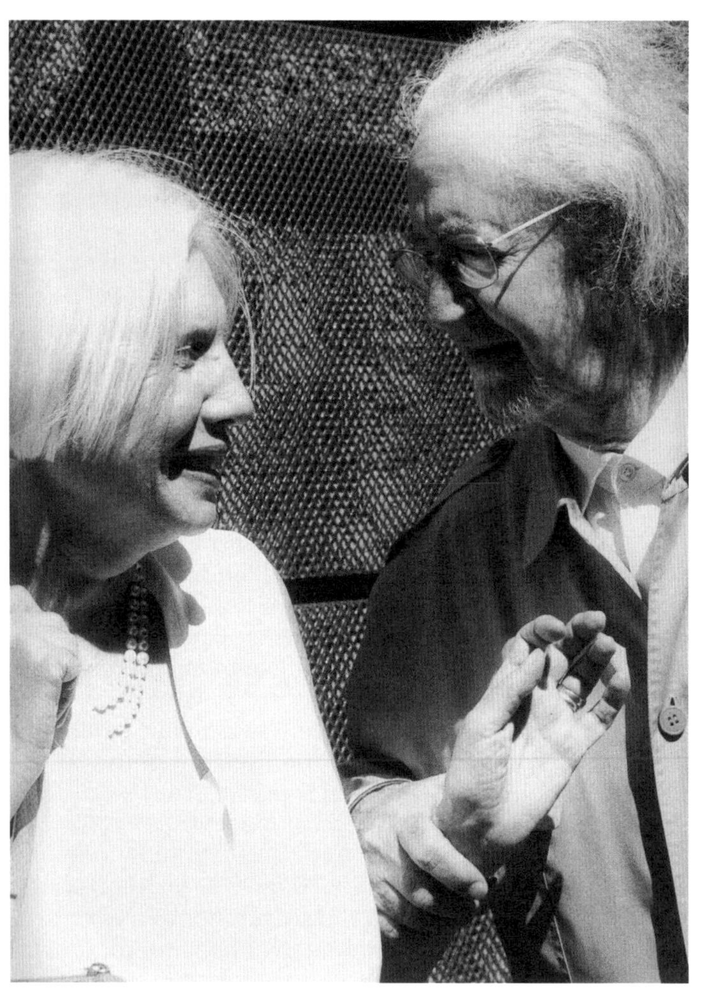

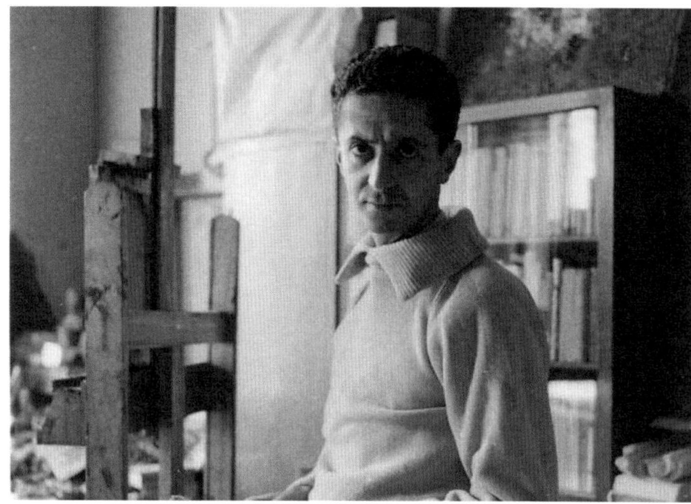

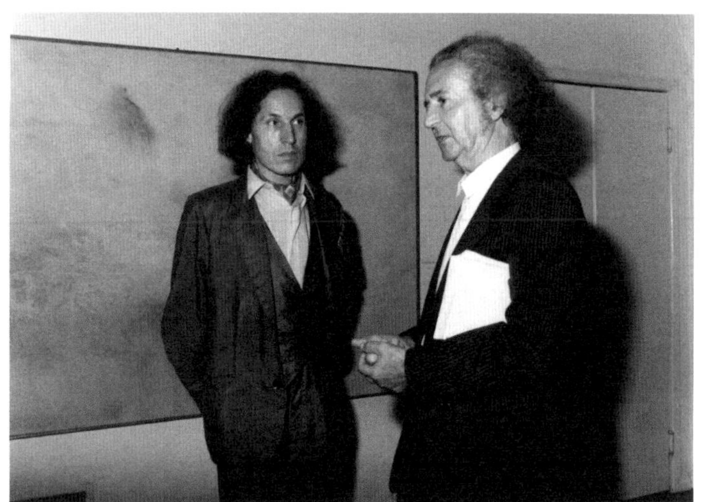

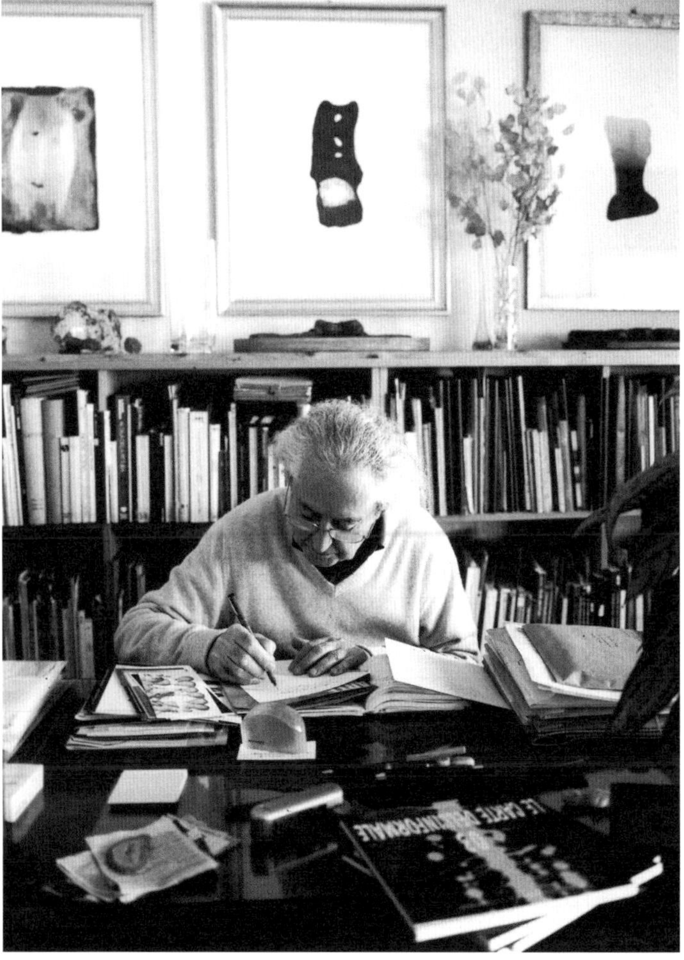

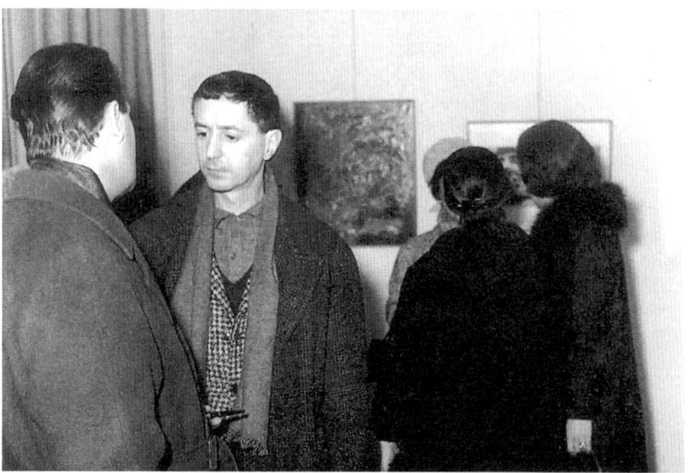

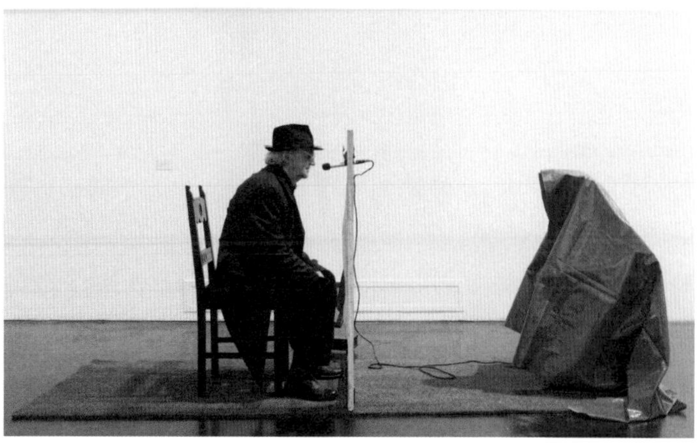

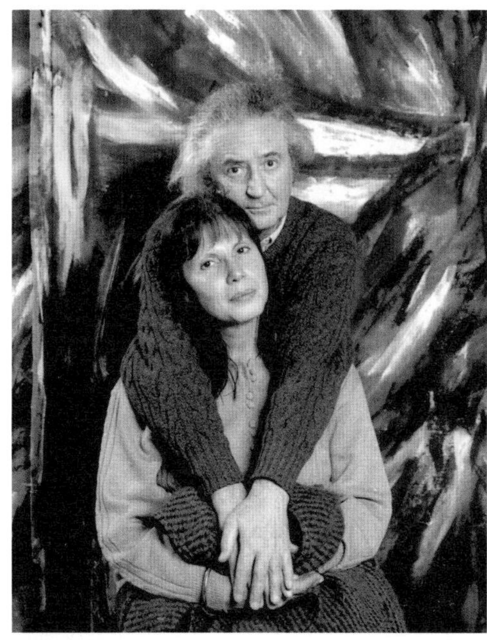

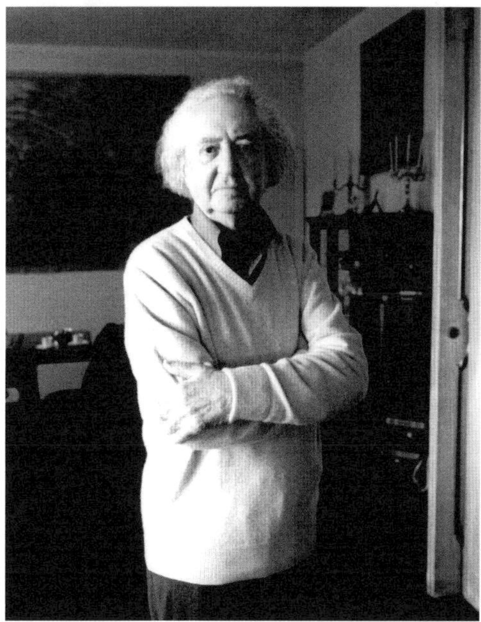

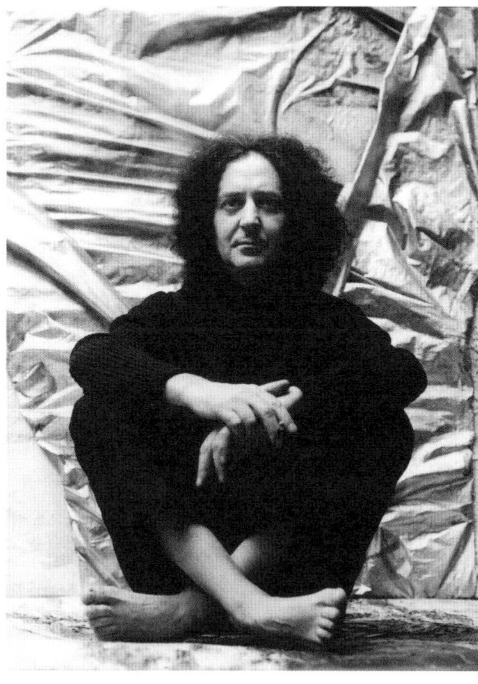

an uncertain light, with bodies that were increasingly dematerialised and fluctuating.

In the 1960s and 1970s, after participating in the 32nd and 36th Venice Biennales with solo exhibitions in 1964 and 1972 respectively, the artist sought to explore the vibrant darkness of matter in order to grasp the gradual unveiling of light. This gave rise to the series *Sentimento come storia* [Sentiment as Story] and *Senso operante* [Operating Faculty], through which he first undertook a methodologically precise analysis of his own painting process and then examined the lowly objects in his studio, transforming them into tangible acts of conscience, marked by a concentrated and haughty moral tone. Once again, in the second half of the 1960s, Bendini produced a self-portrait in the form of one of the *faces* from the early *Segni segreti* [Secret Signs].

In 1973 he settled in Rome, going back to live there again in 2012 after a period spent working in Parma. The 1980s and 1990s saw the creation of large-scale works such as the polyptych *La ballata dei dieci cieli* [The Ballad of the Ten Heavens, 1983], or the canvas-covered papers arranged on the wall like tapestries, belonging to various series such as *Segni come sogni* [Signs as Dreams] or *Ipotesi d'attesa* [Hypothesis of Waiting], exhibited at the Loggetta Lombardesca in Ravenna or currently at the Galleria Nazionale d'Arte Moderna e Contemporanea in Rome.

In 1994, the FAO acquired the large-scale oil on canvas *Il ciclo della natura* [The Cycle of Nature, 200×800 cm] and installed it in its headquarters in Rome.

In the 2000s, Bendini moved to Parma, where he created a real synthesis of his great pictorial experience, a happy season of informal painting, better defined by the artist as "Organic Realism," which bears witness to his incessant search for a universal identity recognised in the organic arrangement of matter.

During his last years of life, when he was in his eighties and nineties, he received numerous awards and prizes for his career, such as his inclusion in the *Novecento: Art and History in Italy* exhibition at the Scuderie Papali in the Quirinale and the Mercati di Traiano in Rome, curated by Maurizio Calvesi in 2000; the 2002 Lissone Lifetime Achievement Award, with an exhibition held in tribute to him in 2003, curated by Flaminio Gualdoni; and in 2010 the Guglielmo Marconi Lifetime Achievement Awards in Bologna, curated by Claudio Cerritelli, and Marina di Ravenna—together with Georges Mathieu and Arnulf Rainer—with an exhibition in tribute to him at the MAR in Ravenna, curated by Claudio Spadoni. He also received the Paolo Volponi commemorative plaque, courtesy of Casadeipensieri of Bologna, which organised the event.

Elected as an Academician of San Luca in Rome, in 2012 he presented his last monographic exhibition, curated by Flaminio Gualdoni and Ivo Iori, at the Accademia Nazionale.

Finally, in 2013, when the artist was in his nineties, MACRO in Rome held an exhibition in tribute to him, marking his definitive return to the capital. The exhibition called *Vasco Bendini 1966-1967* was curated by Gabriele Simongini.

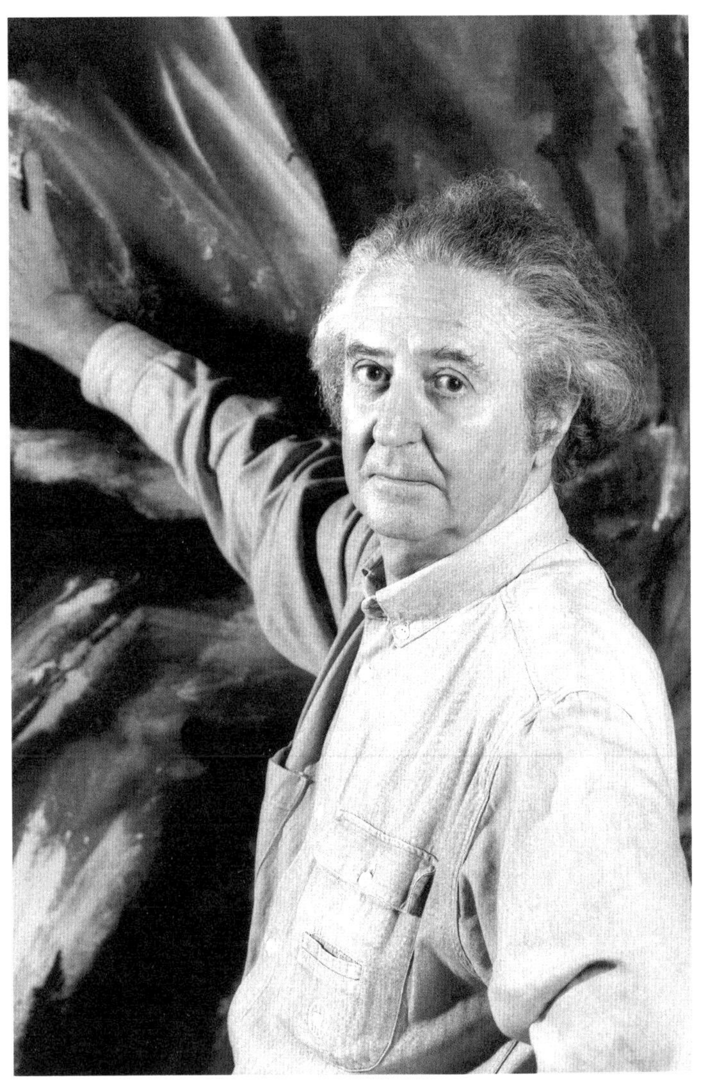

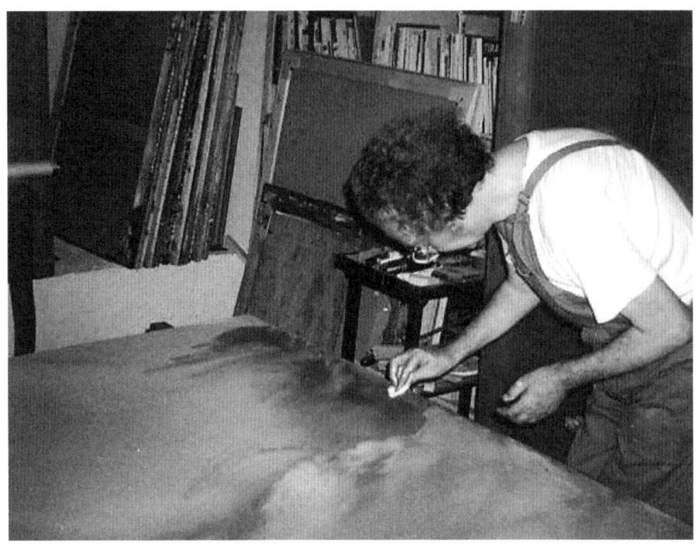

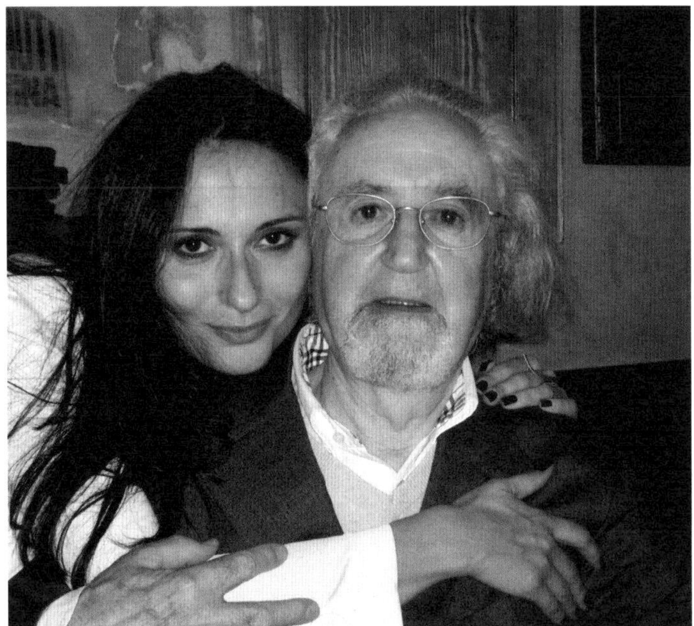

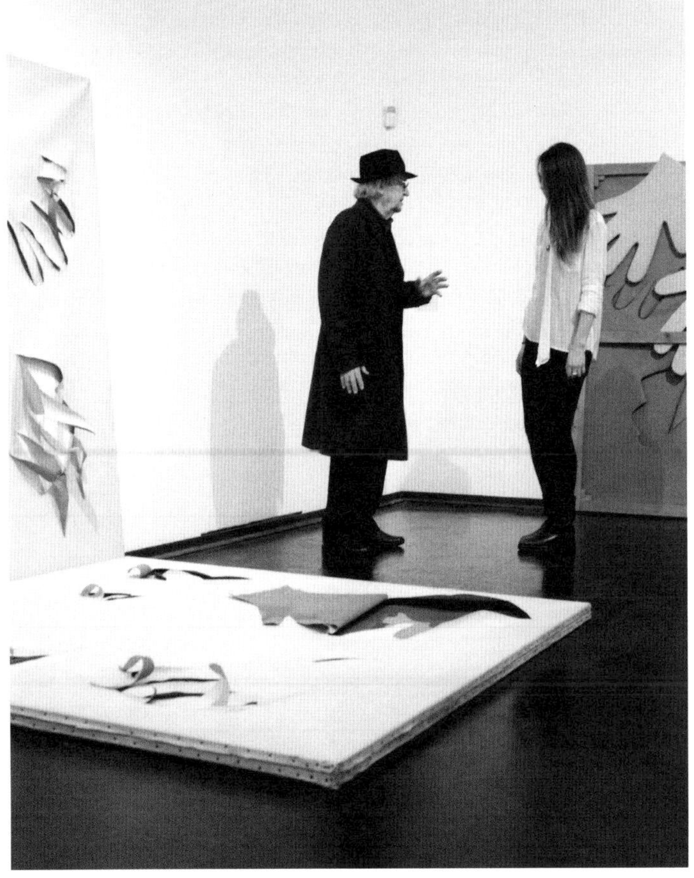

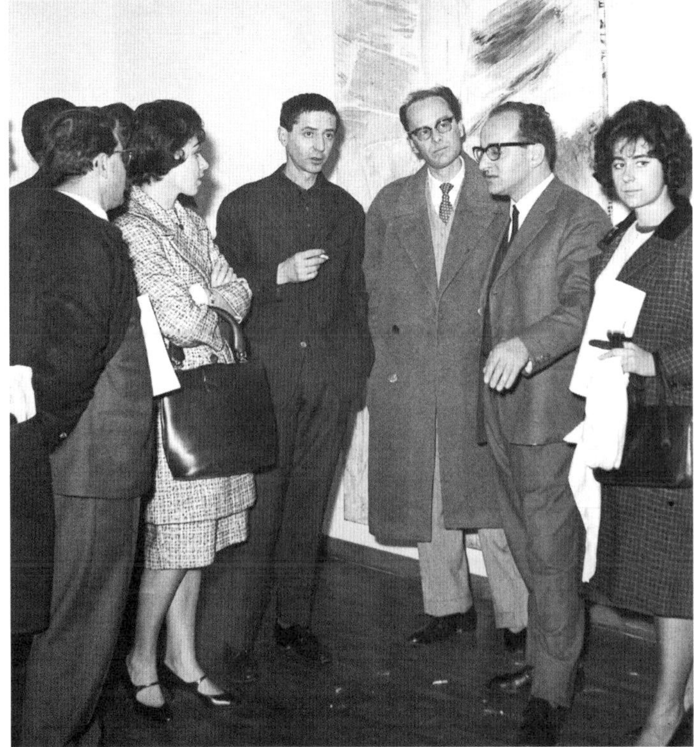

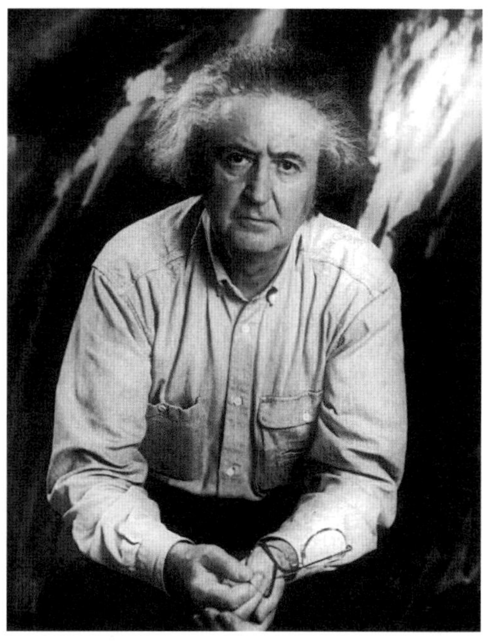

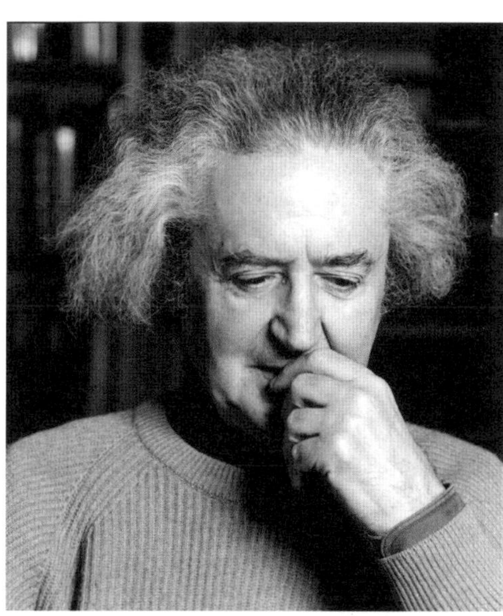

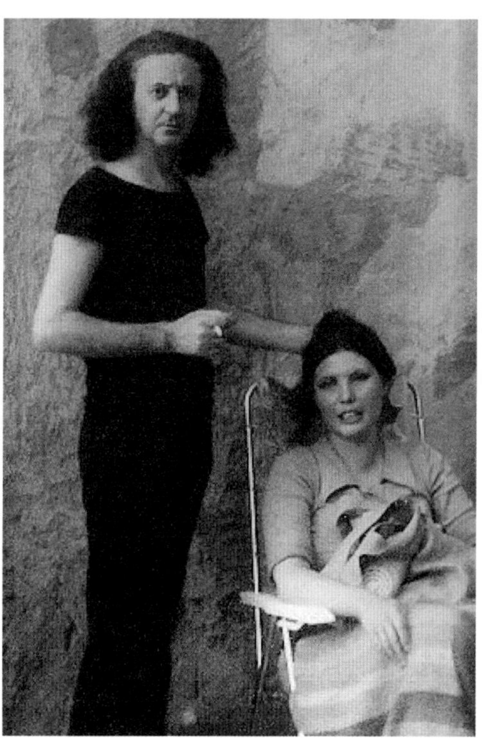

p. 128, clockwise

Vasco Bendini, Bologna, 1957. Photo by Nino Migliori

Ennio Borzi, Luigi Ontani e Vasco Bendini at the opening of Bendini's personal at the Break Club, Rome, October 21, 1988

Vasco Bendini in Rome, early 1980s

Vasco Bendini in the garden of his studio in Bologna, in via San Felice 77, 1970. Photo by Nino Migliori

Vasco Bendini in his roman studio of via Benaco 6, 1997

Vasco Bendini in his Studio in Bologna, via San Felice 21, 1964. Photo by Nino Migliori

p. 129, from the top

Vasco Bendini in a black overalls repeats the action of *Cronotopo*, created in 1967, in his roman studio

Vasco Bendini's hair in 1990s. Photo by Roberto Bossaglia

Vasco Bendini in Bologna, 1960s. Photo by Nino Migliori

p. 130, clockwise

Marcella and Vasco Bendini in Florence, August 28, 2008. Photo by Aurelio Amendola

Vasco Bendini in his studio in Via Barberia, Bologna, 1957. Photo by Nino Migliori

Vasco Bendini with Luigi Ontani at the opening of Bendini's personal at the Break Club, Rome, October 21, 1988

Francesco Arcangeli (from behind) and Vasco Bendini, L'Attico gallery, Rome, February 1958

Vasco Bendini sets up his personal at the MACRO, curated by Gabriele Simongini, Rome, February 2013. Photo by Luis Filipe de Oliveira do Rosario

Vasco Bendini signs an autentication in his home-studio in Parma, 2003

p. 131, from the top

Marcella and Vasco Bendini in his studio of Rome, 1990

Vasco Bendini in his home-studio in Parma, November 2003

Vasco Bendini in Bologna. Photo by Nino Migliori, 1970

p. 132, clockwise

Vasco Bendini in his roman studio, 1990s. Photo by Roberto Bossaglia

Vasco Bendini painting in his studio of via Benaco 6, Rome, summer 1987

Vasco Bendini and Irene Santori at the opening of his personal "Vasco Bendini. LuceLenta", Frittelli Arte Contemporanea, Florence, October 2008

Vasco Bendini and Maurizio Calvesi at L'Attico gallery, Rome 1963

Vasco Bendini at the MACRO of Rome speaks with Benedetta in front of some of his works of the late 1960s, March 2013. Photo by Luis Filipe de Oliveira do Rosario

p. 133, from the top

Vasco Bendini portraited by Roberto Bossaglia, Rome, 1966

Vasco Bendini portaited by Roberto Bossaglia, 1996

Marcella and Vasco Bendini, Vignale Monferrato, 1973

Main solo and anthological Exhibitions

1949 Curated by Virgilio Guidi. Galleria Bergamini, Milan, February 1949.

1953 Curated by Francesco Arcangeli. Galleria La Torre, Florence, June 1953.

1956 Curated by Franco Russoli. La Loggia gallery, Bologna, January 1956.
Curated by Franco Russoli. Galleria Il Milione, Milan, February 1956.
Curated by Rodolfo Pallucchini. La Saletta degli Amici dell'Arte, Modena, April 1956.

1958 Curated by Francesco Arcangeli. Galleria Il Milione, Milan, January 1958.
Curated by Francesco Arcangeli. L'Attico gallery, Rome, February 1958.

1959 Curated by Maurizio Calvesi. L'Attico gallery, Rome, May 1959.

1961 Curated by Renato Barilli. L'Attico gallery, Rome, February 1961.
Curated by Francesco Arcangeli. L'Attico gallery, Rome, April 1961.
Curated by Oreste Ferrari. Galleria Apollinaire, Milan, May 1961.

1963 Curated by Fabrizio Arcangeli. Mc. Roberts and Tunnard Gallery, London, March 1963.
Galleria del Teatro, Parma, March 1963.
L'Attico gallery, Rome, April 1963.

1964 Dedicated room, 32nd Venice Biennale. Venice, Central Pavillion, June 1964. Invited by Maurizio Calvesi.

1966 *Sentimento come storia. Opere eseguite nel 1965 della serie Sentimento come storia e Senso operante*. Curated by Giulio Carlo Argan. L'Attico gallery, Rome, March 1966.

1967 Curated by Filiberto Menna. Galleria Senior, Rome, April 1967.
Curated by Francesco Arcangeli. Studio Bentivoglio, Bologna, September 1967.

1968 Curated by Francesco Arcangeli and Maurizio Calvesi. Galleria d'Arte San Luca, Bologna, November 1968.
Bendini. Curated by Giulio Carlo Argan. Galleria Senior, INArch Palazzo Taverna, Rome, November 1968.

1971 *Vasco Bendini 1950-1953*. Curated by Flavio Caroli. Galleria Senior, Rome, December 1971.

1972 Dedicated room, 36th Venice Biennale. Venice, Central Pavillion, June 11-October 1, 1972, invited by Francesco Arcangeli and Renato Barilli.

1973 10th Quadriennale di Roma. Palazzo delle Esposizioni, Rome, April 1973. Invited by Filiberto Menna.
Curated by Pier Giovanni Castagnoli. Galleria Pietra, Milan, January 1973.
Curated by Maurizio Calvesi. Department of History of Art, University of Parma, Sala dei Contrafforti in Pilotta, Parma, June 1973.
Curated by Marisa Vescovo. Sala Comunale d'Arte Contemporanea, Alessandria, December 1973.

1975 Curated by Maurizio Calvesi. Galleria Esse Arte, Rome, April 1975.

1976 Curated by H. Landendrof. Italian Institute of Culture, Cologne, January 1976.
Carte dal 1965 al 1975. Curated by Giovanni Maria Accame. Galleria Bologna Due, Bologna, February 1976.
Curated by Maurizio Calvesi. Modern Art Museum, Saarbrücken, November 1976.

1977 Curated by Rudolf Bornschein. Modern Art Museum, Saarlouis, July 1977.
Curated by Cesare Vivaldi. Galleria Bottega d'Arte, Acqui Terme, November 1977.

1978 Curated by Marisa Vescovo. Lo Spazio galley, Naples, January 1978.
Opere su carta dal 1965 al 1968. Curated by Filiberto Menna. Galleria Spazio Alternativo, Rome, May 1978.
Il percorso di Bendini. Curated by Renato Barilli and Sandro Sproccati. Galleria Comunale d'Arte Moderna, Bologna, November 1978.

1980 *Stabilità dell'instabile, memoria del futuro, memorie*. Curated by Emilio Villa. L'Attico gallery - Esse Arte, Rome, April 1980.

1983 *Polveri d'oro*. Curated by Claudio Cerritelli. Circolo Artistico, Bologna, November 1983.

1984 Curated by Francesco Poli. Unione Culturale Antonicelli-Weber & Weber gallery, Turin, January 1984.
Curated by Alessandra Borgogelli. Studio Malossini, Bologna, February 1984.
Sette stanze, un giardino. Curated by Gino Baratta and Francesco Bartoli. Casa del Mantegna, Mantua, July 1984.

1988 Curated by Filiberto Menna. Galleria Traghetto, Venice, June 1988.
L'Astratto vissuto e i suoi maestri italiani dagli anni Cinquanta. 40th Premio Michetti, Palazzo della Mostra, Francavilla al mare, July 1988.
Curated by Vito Apuleo and Pierre Restany. Break Club gallery, Roma, October 1988.

1989 *Vasco Bendini. Opere su carta 1950-1956, 1980-1988*. Curated by Fabrizio D'Amico.

Contemporary Art Pavillion, Milan, January 1989.
Galleria Comunale d'Arte Moderna, Palazzo Rosari Spada, Spoleto, January 1989.
Vasco Bendini. Tempo come creazione. Pinacoteca Comunale, Santa Maria delle Croci, Ravenna, March 1989.
Curated by Flaminio Gualdoni. Galleria Mazzocchi, Parma, November 1989.
Raccolta del Disegno Contemporaneo – Acquisizioni 1989. Galleria Civica, Palazzo dei Musei, Modena, November 1989.
Segni come Sogni. Curated by Cesare Vivaldi. La Giarina Contemporary Art, Verona, December 1989.
Curated by Giorgio Cortenova. Palazzo Forti, Verona, December 1989.

1991 Curated by Flaminio Gualdoni. Galleria Verlato, Milan, January 1991.
Gioco come gioco. Curated by Ginestra Calzolari and Paolo Fossati. French-Italian Cultural Association, Bologna, May 1991.
La pittura si immagina. Galleria Martano, Turin, September 1991.
Vasco Bendini. Disegni 1950-1985. Curated by Paolo Fossati and Dario Trento. Galleria Mazzocchi, Parma, November 1991.

1992 *Opere storiche.* Galleria Civica, Modena, March 22-May 3, 1992; *Opere recenti.* Galleria Comunale d'Arte Moderna, Bologna, March 22-May 3, 1992; *L'opera su carta.* Centro Sevizi Culturali Santa Chiara, Trento, March 21-April 26, 1992. Curated by Walter Guadagnini, Danilo Eccher, Flaminio Gualdoni, Oscar Goldoni.
Profili. Curated by Fabrizio D'amico. 22th Quadriennale di Roma, Rome, Palazzo delle Esposizioni, July 1992.
Curated by Fabrizio D'amico. Galleria dei Greci, Rome, November 1992.

1993 *Opere storiche. Anni Cinquanta-Sessanta.* Arte 92 gallery, Milan, April 1993.

1994 *Bendini.* Curated by Fabrizio D'Amico and Flaminio Gualdoni. Galleria Forni, Bologna, February 1994.
The work *Il ciclo della natura* is acquired by the Food and Agriculture Organization of the United Nations and exposed in the Pavillion B of the Roman Headquartes.

1995 *Vasco Bendini, litografie 1961-1962.* Curated by Flaminio Gualdoni. Galleria Mazzocchi, Parma, Decembre 1995.

1996 *La Ballata dei Dieci Cieli.* Curated by Silvia Pegoraro Loggetta Lombardesca, Ravenna, March 1996.
Vasco Bendini, litografie 1961-1962. Curated by Marina Miraglia. Istituto Nazionale per la Grafica, Rome, May 1996.

1997 *Un mondo al limite (1990-1995).* Curated by Flaminio Gualdoni. Palazzo Coen, Palazzo Comunale, Salò, November 1997.
Vasco Bendini. Gli anni dell'informale: 1950-1963. Curated by Roberto Pasini. Arte 92 gallery, Milan; Galleria Mazzocchi, Parma, February-April 1997.

1998 *Vasco Bendini, opere 1950-1963, 1988-1994.* Curated by Fabrizio D'Amico. Museo Laboratorio di Arte Contemporanea, Sapienza University, Roma, May 1998.
Traiettorie 1998. Curated by Martino Traversa and Gian Paolo Minardi. Teatro Farnese, Parma, September 23-October 7, 1998.

1999 *Bendini, opere 1942.* Curated by Marco Goldin. Palazzo Sarcinelli, Conegliano Veneto, May 1999.

2001 *Vasco Bendini, Segni segreti, opere dal 1950 al 2000,* Galleria Guidi, Accademia di Belle Arti, Bologna, April 2001.
Giardino dei sensi. Vasco Bendini inedito (1999-2000). Curated by Riccardo Prina. Castello di Masnago, Varese, June-August 2001.

2003 Premio Lissone, Award for his career. Curated by Flaminio Gualdoni. Civica Galleria d'Arte Contemporanea, Lissone, January 19-February 23, 2003.
Vasco Bendini-L'Immagine Accolta. Curated by Ivo Iori. Museo Bocchi, Palazzo Sanvitale, Parma, November 2003.

2005 *Dell'Immagine e del fare Arte.* Galleria de' Foscherari, Bologna, October 15-December 15, 2005.

2006 *Vasco Bendini. L'ultima carta del castello.* Curated by Massimo Airoli. Associazione Culturale Senzatitolo, Rome, April 14-June 3, 2006.
Vasco Bendini. L'immagine Accolta. Curated by Gianluca Ciccarelli and Gabriele Simongini. Ulisse Gallery Contemporary Art, Rome, September 28-November 25, 2006.
Il respiro della Materia. Curated by Giorgio Cortenova. La Giarina Contemporary Art, Verona, October 7, 2006-January 30, 2007.

2007 *Vasco Bendini – Opere 1950-2006.* Curated by Maurizio Calvesi. Frittelli Contemporary Art Gallery, Florence, February 10-March 31, 2007.

2008 *Vasco Bendini. Malia dell'enigma.* Curated by Bruno Corà and Edoardo Piersensini. Galleria Niccoli, Parma, February 16-April 10, 2008.
Vasco bendini. luceLenta. Curated by Tommaso Trini. Frittelli Contemporary Art Gallery, Florence, October 4-6 December 6.
L'immagine dell'occhio. Curated by Massimo Airoli. Associazione culturale Senzatitolo, Rome, December 2008.

2009 *Vasco Bendini, dalla serie Oggetto come Storia, opere su carta 1966-1973*. Il Triangolo Nero gallery, Alessandria, November 2009.

2010 25th Premio Internazionale Pittura Scultura Arte Elettronica G. Marconi – Vasco Bendini. Curated by Claudio Cerritelli e Bartolomeo de Gioia. Circolo Artistico Iterarte, Bologna, April 2010.
Curated by Claudio Spadoni. Museo d'Arte della città di Ravenna MAR, Ravenna, August 2010.
Il tempo, la luce. Curated by Flaminio Gualdoni. Galleria Bianconi, Milan, October 6-November 11, 2010.

2011 61st Internation Art Exhibition/Premio G.B. Salvi. Curated by Gabriele Simongini. Palazzo della Pretura, Sassoferrato, July 29-September 4, 2011.

2012 *Vasco Bendini/Matteo Montani. Così lontani, così vicini*. Curated by Gabriele Simongini. Museo Palazzo de' Mayo, Chieti, November 30, 2012-January 20, 2013.

2013 *Vasco Bendini 1966-1967*. Curated by Gabriele Simongini, MACRO, Rome, February 28-May 5, 2013.

2015 *Vasco Bendini: anni Cinquanta*. Galleria SIX, Milan, March 7-June 13, 2015.
RH Contemporary Art, New York, March 12-June 6, 2015.
Interrogare la Materia. Curated by Luigi Meneghelli. La Giarina Contemporary Art, Verona, 10 October 10, 2015-February 27, 2016.

2016 *Vasco Bendini. Opere 2000-2013*. Curated by Fabrizio D'Amico. Accademia Nazionale di San Luca, Rome, May 30-October 1, 2016.
Ospiti di Casa Zucchelli. Vasco Bendini. Fondazione Zucchelli, Bologna, September 17-October 1, 2016.
Vasco Bendini: L'Immagine accolta. Curated by Flaminio Gualdoni. Galleria Monopoli, Milan, September 20-November 5, 2016.

2017 Arte Fiera Bologna. Galleria SIX, Milan, January 2017.
Segni del quotidiano. Galleria SIX, Milan; RCM Galerie, Paris, October-December 2017, in collaboration with the Libera Associazione-Archivio Vasco Bendini.
Vasco Bendini. Un mondo al limite. Curated by Ivo Iori and Marcella Valentini. Galleria d'Arte Moderna Ricci Oddi, Piacenza, November 11, 2017-January 7, 2018.

2018 *Bendini*. Galerie 21, Livorno, May-July 2021.

2019 *Vasco Bendini. Stabile instabilità*. Curated by the Libera Associazione-Archivio Vasco Bendini. Conceptual Gallery, Milan, December 12, 2019-February 1, 2020.

2020 *Vasco Bendini. Opere storiche*. Galleria d'Arte Maggiore, Bologna, January 16-April 15, 2020.
Vasco Bendini. Io che cammino. Frittelli Contemporary Art Gallery, Florence, February 28-April 24, 2020.

2022 *Vasco Bendini. Ombre prime*. Curated by Bruno Corà. Galleria Nazionale d'Arte Moderna e Contemporanea, Rome, March 29-June 19, 2022.
Omaggio a Vasco Bendini. Curated by Lorenzo Fiorucci. Palazzo Collicola, Spoleto, April-May, 2022.
Vasco Bendini. Curated by Valerio Dehò. La Giarina Contemporary Art, Verona, June 2022.
Io che cammino – 100. Curated by Italian Institute of Culture in cooperation with Frittelli Contemporary Art Gallery. Bratislava Castle, Slovacchia, June 23-December 4, 2022.

Works in Museums and public collections

Accademia di Belle Arti di Roma, Rome.
Accademia Nazionale di San Luca, Rome.
Centro Studi e Archivio della Comunicazione, CSAC, Università di Parma.
Cincinnati Art Museum, Ohio.
MAC – Museo d'Arte Contemporanea di Lissone.
BNL Collection. BNL BNP Paribas, Rome.
Intesa Sanpaolo Collection, Banca Intesa Sanpaolo, Milan.
Cariparma Collection. Fondazione Cariparma, Parma.
Fondazione Centro Studi sull'Arte Licia e Carlo Ludovico Ragghianti, Lucca.
Genus Bononiae. Museums in the City, Fondazione Cassa di Risparmio in Bologna.
Fondazione per l'Arte Moderna e Contemporanea CRT, Turin.
Fondazione Ramazzotti, Linate.
La Salerniana – Museo d'Arte Contemporanea e Moderna Galleria Civica "G. Perricone", Erice – Trapani.
Civica Raccolta del Disegno di Salò.
Galleria Civica di Modena, FMAV – Fondazione Modena Arti Visive, Modena.
Pinacoteca comunale di Palazzo Sarcinelli, Conegliano Veneto.
Fondazione Michetti, Francavilla al Mare (Chieti).
Galleria d'arte moderna Aroldo Bonzagni, Cento (Ferrara).
Galleria d'Arte Moderna Achille Forti, Verona.
Galleria d'Arte Moderna Ricci Oddi, Piacenza.
GAM Art – Galleria d'Arte Moderna, Salerno.
GNAM – Galleria Nazionale d'Arte Moderna e Contemporanea, Rome.
Saarlandmuseum – Moderne Galerie, Saarbruecken.
MACRO – Museum of Contemporary Art of Rome.
MAR – Museo d'Arte della città di Ravenna.
Mart – Museum of Modern and Contemporary Art of Trento and Rovereto.
Museo d'Arte Moderna e Contemporanea del Castello di Masnago, Varese.
Castello Sforzesco, Milan.
Museo della Grafica, Pisa.
MAMbo, Museo d'Arte Moderna di Bologna.
MoCA, Museum of Contemporary Art, Skopje.
FAO – Food and Agriculture Organization of the United Nations, Rome.
PAC – Padiglione d'Arte Contemporanea, Milan.
Galleria d'Arte Moderna G. Carandente, Palazzo Collicola, Spoleto.
Casa del Mantegna, Mantua.
Princeton University Art Museum, New Jersey, USA.

Monographs

1960 Andrea Emiliani, *Vasco Bendini*, Bologna: Edizioni Alfa.

1963 Francesco Arcangeli and Maurizio Calvesi, "Vasco Bendini," *Quaderni dell'Attico*, no. 4, Rome: Edizioni dell'Attico.

1965 Eugenio Riccomini, *Disegni di Vasco Bendini*, Rome: Edizioni dell'Attico.

1968 Maurizio Calvesi, *Tabù e Trasgressione / disegni di Vasco Bendini*, Bologna: Edizioni Alfa.

1979 Maurizio Calvesi, *Vasco Bendini*, Naples: edizioni Lo Spazio.

1986 *Vasco Bendini: Venti disegni erotici (1956-1984) con una dichiarazione di poetica*, Mantua: Galleria Gianluigi Arcari. Catalog of an exhibition of the same title, presented at the Gianluigi Arcari, Mantua, June 18-October 18.

1987 Giuseppe Bilotta, edited by, *Bendini: disegni 1950-1984*, Naples: Istituto Grafico Editoriale Italiano.

1991 Paolo Fossati, *Vasco Bendini: gioco come gioco*, Ravenna: Essegi. Catalog of an exhibition of the same title curated by Ginestra Calzolari, presented at the Galleria Verlato, Bologna, May 1991.
Paolo Fossati, edited by, *Vasco Bendini: disegni 1950-1985*, Parma: Galleria Mazzocchi. Catalog of an exhibition of the same title, presented at the Galleria Mazzocchi, Parma, November 9-December 31.

1993 Fabrizio D'Amico and Flaminio Gualdoni, *Vasco Bendini*, Rome: (continua) edizioni d'arte.

1995 Flaminio Gualdoni, *Vasco Bendini: litografie 1961-1962*, Parma: Galleria Mazzocchi.

2006 Edoardo Piersensini, *Vasco Bendini: fra il nulla e l'infinito*, Rome: Ulisse Editore.

2010 Gabriele Allegro, *L'attraversamento concettuale della materia: opere su carta 1964-1974*, Alessandria: Linelab edizioni.

2012 Flaminio Gualdoni, Ivo Iori, *Vasco Bendini*, Parma: Grafiche Step.

2013 Gabriele Simongini, edited by, *Vasco Bendini 1966-1967*, Macerata: Quodlibet. Catalog of an exhibition of the same title, presented at the MACRO, Rome, February 28-May 5.

Editorial project
Forma Edizioni srl
Firenze, Italia
redazione@formaedizioni.it

Editorial director
Laura Andreini

Editorial staff
Maria Giulia Caliri
Monica Giannini
Raffaele Moretti
Giulia Turini

Graphic design
Valeria Pugliese

Photolithography
Forma Edizioni

Texts
© the authors

Translation
Aelmuire Helen Cleary
Sonia Hill

Photo credits
Where not otherwise specified, photos should be understood to be courtesy of Libera Associazione-Archivio Vasco Bendini

© Giuseppe Rambelli, private collection, Parma – Courtesy Galleria d'Arte Niccoli pp. 9, 33, 67, 68, 69, 70, 71

© Roberto Bossaglia – Courtesy Collezione Santori Lettieri, Rome pp. 10, 19, 22, 84

© Agostino Osio – Courtesy Frittelli Arte contemporanea pp. 10, 35

© Nino Migliori – Courtesy Libera Associazione-Archivio Vasco Bendini pp. 118, 120, 124, 128, 129, 130, 131

© Roberto Bossaglia – Courtesy Libera Associazione-Archivio Vasco Bendini pp. 125, 129, 133

© Aurelio Amendola – Courtesy Libera Associazione-Archivio Vasco Bendini p. 130

© Luis Filipe de Oliveira do Rosario – Courtesy Libera Associazione-Archivio Vasco Bendini pp. 130, 132

Courtesy Collezione Tonelli pp. 13, 28, 29

Courtesy Galleria Nazionale d'Arte Moderna e Contemporanea, Rome pp. 14, 27

Courtesy Collezione Francescopiero Calzolari, Bologna pp. 12, 23, 59, 60, 61, 107

First edition: July 2023

VASCO BENDINI
OMBRE PRIME
29.03 – 19.06.2022

Curated by
Bruno Corà

Galleria Nazionale d'Arte
Moderna e Contemporanea

Director
Cristiana Collu

Coordination
Giovanna Coltelli

Temporary Exhibition Department
Keila Linguanti
Liselotte Corigliano
Anna de Angelis
Francesca Palmieri

Press Office and Communications Department
Elena Bastia
Isabella de Stefano

Special Projects and Digital Communication
Alessio Boi

Conservation
Paola Carnazza
Rodolfo Corrias
Maria Letizia Profiri
Silvia Puteo
Luciana Tozzi
with Roberto Possenti
and Veraldo Urbinati

Director's Secretary Office
Paola Castrignanò

Coordinated image and graphics
Designwork

Transportation
Spedart S.r.l.

Technical set-up
Demasi Restauri
Quadra Srl

Graphics set-up
Gruppofallani

Lighting
AC Impianti

Insurance
AGE Broker

Interns
Claudia Bovienzo
Chiara Anastasia Moda

Special thanks to everyone who has made this project possible, and in particular to:
Archivio Collezione Giancarlo Tonelli, Luis Do Rosario, Frittelli Arte Contemporanea, Gaetano Lettieri, Galleria d'Arte Niccoli, Irene Santori, Marcella Valentini Bendini, Museo di Arte Moderna e Contemporanea del Castello di Masnago, Francescopiero Calzolari

and all those who preferred to remain anonymous.

This volume was printed in July 2023
by Lito Terrazzi, Prato, Italy